THE EXPLORERS

THE HISTOR

THE

F SAN DIEGO *VOLUME ONE OF A PLANNED SERIES ON THE HISTORIC BIRTHPLACE OF CALIFORNIA*

EXPLORERS

Written By

RICHARD F. POURADE

EDITOR EMERITUS, THE SAN DIEGO UNION

Commissioned By

JAMES S. COPLEY

CHAIRMAN OF THE CORPORATION, THE COPLEY PRESS, INC.

Published By

The Union-Tribune Publishing Company

FIRST PRINTING NOVEMBER 1960

SECOND PRINTING MARCH 1962

CONTENTS

ILLUSTRATIONS

DEDICATED

To all who would know of the exploits of those great
leaders in history who opened the Nation's Southwest
to the grateful population of today and to the millions
who would live in this favored land tomorrow.

JAMES S. COPLEY

ACKNOWLEDGEMENTS

James S. Copley first suggested that a new and complete history of San Diego was needed and should be undertaken, in view of the wealth of material that was becoming available and not yet properly assembled, and the arrival in the Southwest of so many thousands of newcomers totally unacquainted with its past. The task did not appear at first glance to be a too formidable one. But as research progressed, it became clear that a single volume could not do justice to a story of such historical importance and interest.

As the history falls naturally into separate phases, a decision was reached to prepare and publish several volumes, each one, however, to be complete in itself. Volume I deals with the explorers who discovered the New World and finally worked their way up to California. Other volumes will deal with the Spanish and Mexican periods, and with the modern period beginning with California's admission to the Union.

We have entitled this first volume, The Explorers. Much of the material and original manuscripts and maps came from the Archives of Spain, Mexico and Guatemala. We also had the assistance of many persons and drew liberally on the invaluable work of the American Academy of Franciscan History and of such great historians as Hubert Howe Bancroft, Herbert Eugene Bolton, Henry Raup Wagner, Robert Glass Cleland and Charles E. Chapman.

Among those who assisted were Dr. Adele Kibre, a research scholar working in the Archives of the Indies, at Seville, Spain, for the University of California and the Library of Congress; José de la Peña, director of the General Archives of the Indies; Juan Ignacio Rubio Mane, director of the General Archives of Mexico, Mexico City; J. Joaquín Pardo, director of the General Archives of Guatemala, Guatemala City; J. Alfred Barrett-Reed, representative of the government of Guatemala; Father Maynard J. Geiger, Franciscan historian at The Old Mission in Santa Barbara; Dr. Abraham P. Nasatir of San Diego State College, San Diego; Dr. Carl H. Hubbs, Dr. Douglas L. Inman, Joseph L. Reid, and James R. Moriarty of the Scripps Institution of Oceanography, La Jolla; Clark Evernham, director, and the late Malcolm Rogers of the Museum of Man, San Diego; Brig. Gen. Maurice G. Holmes, USMC, Ret., PhD., a scholar in the field of Spanish nautical explorations; Gerald MacMullen, director, and the staff of the Junípero Serra Museum, San Diego; Dr. John Barr Tompkins and Robert H. Becker of the Bancroft Library of the University of California, Berkeley; Frederick Hall of The Newberry Library, Chicago; Robert O. Dougan, librarian, and Herbert C. Schulz, curator of manuscripts, at the Huntington Memorial Library, San Marino; Richard Dillon of the Sutro Branch of the California State Library, Sacramento; and Mrs. Zelma Locker and staff of the California Room of the San Diego Public Library, and Stuart Lake, the author.

Richard F. Pourade
Rancho Santa Fe, California

. . . for I trust that God will give me the strength to reach San Diego, as He has given me the strength to come so far. In case He does not, I will conform myself to His most holy will. Even though I should die on the way, I shall not turn back. They can bury me wherever they wish and I shall gladly be left among the pagans, if it be the will of God.

Fr. Junípero Serra

PROLOGUE

San Diego, the birthplace of civilization on the West Coast, was discovered in 1542. This was only fifty years after Christopher Columbus had touched land in the Western Hemisphere for the first time. These fifty years were momentous ones, a period of explorations of vast unknown lands and uncharted seas, of cruel but heroic conquests, of the final collapse of ancient civilizations whose origins are shrouded in mystery, of the bringing of Christianity by sword and cross to millions on new continents whose sizes and outlines were only dimly perceived.

When Juan Rodríguez Cabrillo, the Portuguese-born conquistador sailing under the flag of Spain, put into San Diego Bay on Sept. 28, 1542, the glory of Spain was reaching its height. Mexico and Peru had been subdued. The wealth of the Aztecs and of the Incas had begun flowing back to the mother country. The whole world caught fire, in excitement, envy and intrigue. Though the records are silent, Cabrillo himself must have been searching hopefully for new cities of gold, for the long-sought short route to

SOMEWHERE ALONG THE BEACH, where Ballast Point curves into the bluffs of Point Loma, Juan Rodríguez Cabrillo stepped ashore at San Diego and claimed it for Spain. Three Indians were witnesses to the discovery of California on the morning of Sept. 28, 1542. Other Indians fled in fright.

China and the Strait of Anián, which the explorers of all seafaring countries believed existed. This was a passage from the Atlantic to the Pacific Ocean, somewhere to the north, by which ships could sail directly from Europe to the Spice Islands of the Indies.

Cabrillo never found the gold, China, or the Strait of Anián. More than four and a half centuries later a U. S. Navy submarine slid under the northern ice pack, above Alaska in the Bering Sea, and reappeared in the Atlantic Ocean. Cabrillo lies buried on tiny San Miguel Island off the coast of Southern California. His grave has never been found. A brave man, a skillful fighter, and an able navigator, he succumbed to infection from a broken bone. His expedition got as far north as the coast of Oregon without him.

The importance of his discoveries, and of those in command of his ships after his death, was not appreciated at the time, and his original maps and log have never been found. Most of the names which he gave to the ports of California were erased from the records. Because of the discoveries of Cabrillo, San Diego remained under Spanish rule for almost three hundred years. Phases of Spanish life still linger here, in place names, in much of the architecture, in the crumbling missions, the thick walls of the adobe buildings of Old Town, and the enchanting rituals of Indians who cling to tribal memories. How could Spain, a country so poor and weak today, have conquered and held such vast lands for so long? San Diego was governed by Spanish kings for three times as long as it has lived under the American flag.

Spain was a powerful country for only a short time, as history goes. The people of the Iberian peninsula had been fighting among themselves for several thousand years, when, in the Eighth Century, the Moors crossed over from Africa and subjugated the mixed races which, when driven together by war and bloodshed, eventually became the Spanish people. For seven hundred years the Christian people of Spain fought against the Mohammedan Moors until, under Ferdinand and Isabella, Moorish power was broken in 1492, and the last of them were driven from the peninsula. The conquistadores who were to subdue the New World were the heirs of seven hundred years of barbaric struggles. Murder, betrayal, chivalry, as well as courage, had been, out of circumstance, their way of life. The Indians of the new lands were no match for their cunning and ferocity.

Spain's great years had arrived and the energy of her people exploded over the world. Columbus was the first of a long line of explorers and conquerors who set out from Spain. Newly discovered lands were settled and organized, and Spanish armies fought all over Europe and in Africa. The wealth of the New World was poured into suicidal wars in a vain effort to unify all of Europe. But there was never enough gold for all that Spain sought to do or was forced to do. And in time, the incessant conflicts took their toll of men, industry, the arts, and agriculture until finally the Spanish Armada, that was to crush the growing maritime threat of England, was destroyed in the English Channel in 1588. Spain's energy was blowing itself out. The end was in sight. It was all over in a century. But for two hundred years more Spain continued to hold tenaciously to her colonies overseas as she slowly sank back into the past out of which she has not yet fully emerged.

The history of San Diego is the drama of the Pacific. San Diego was only a vague and distant possession of the great Spanish empire. Sixty years after Cabrillo, another Spanish explorer, Sebastián Vizcaíno, arrived to give the port the name it bears today. Then 167 years were to pass before any more attention was paid to California. In Mexico, cathedrals were built and universities founded. The conquistadores and those who followed them became the landed hidalgos who fastened on the country a feudalistic system that could be broken only by revolution and civil war. Indian villages became the towns and cities of Acapulco, Loreto, La Navidad, Colima, Culiacán and Sinaloa, from which were to come the men and supplies for the founding of new colonies in California. Under the pressure of Russian probings along the coast and the menacing excursions of English and other foreign ships, Spain at last bestirred herself to establish some kind of a settlement at San Diego. Thus San Diego became the birthplace of Christianity on the West Coast.

What kind of a land was San Diego? It was a lonely place, geographically. San Diego always has been considered isolated, with deserts and mountains to the east and south, an ocean to the west, and only a narrow coastal plain opening to the north. It was isolated in the sense of being separated from the main stream of history as it unfolded across the Atlantic, to the eastern shores of America, and as it developed in Mexico and parts of South America. But in the long reach of time, San Diego has been in the path of significant movements of people and events. Anthropologists believe the Indians of the Americas came by way of a Siberian land bridge, in prehistoric times, many of them coursing down along the Pacific Coast, some to remain, others eventually to populate Mexico and South America, to build civilizations that in some aspects rivaled those of the Old World. Most certainly other peoples came as visitors by sailing across the great sea. Ancient Chinese literature tells of visits to the land of Fusang on the other side of the ocean. The description is that of California. Certainly it didn't require any great feat of navigation. A ship, no matter how clumsy, could sail from China to the California coast without ever being too far out of sight of land. The Manila galleons of Spain, loaded with the riches of Asia, sailed north from the Philippines, picking up the Japanese current and easily crossing the Pacific, making a landfall near Monterey, and then sailing downhill with the wind behind them to Acapulco. Reports of visits of Asiatics from the Fifth Century onward persisted up until the time of Portolá and Anza in the late 1700's.

One such legend describes a group of men with kinky hair and ships with golden peacocks as figureheads near the mouth of the Colorado River. They indicated that they had come from beyond the ocean sea toward Asia.

It seems strange that the Chinese, and in particular the Japanese, did not take more interest in these lands and the Pacific Ocean. Three hundred years ago, Japan was a powerful and warlike maritime country, highly advanced in science, law and mathematics, with big armies and navies, and cunningly watched the Spanish trading in the Philippines and the excursions of other Europeans in Southeast Asia. Their visitors and traders carefully scrutinized the Spanish fortifications in the Philippines. The wary Spanish, fearing the worst, expressed doubt as to Japanese motives; what was on Japanese lips did not always seem to be what was in their hearts. Then suddenly, in apparent resentment at the efforts of the Spanish to Christianize them, the Japanese turned inward, ended their conquests, and shut themselves off from the world. The Pacific, or the South Sea as they called it then, became virtually a Spanish lake. It wasn't until 1853, when Commodore Perry of the United States Navy re-opened the gates of Japan, that this aggressive and capable people came back into the Pacific.

San Diego was untouched by all these things. The Indians who settled here from time to time never got beyond an aboriginal existence. But Indians of the same linguistic stock, the Aztecs, were to take over the remnants of still earlier civilizations in the Valley of Mexico and erect the great and beautiful city of Tenochtitlán, destroyed by Hernán Cortés and his conquistadores, and now the site of Mexico City; and to the south in Yucatán and the highlands of Central America, the Mayans built a hundred temple cities and plotted the movements of the sun and the stars. By the time the Spanish arrived, most of their cities had been abandoned and overwhelmed by the jungle. The people no longer remembered much of their past.

For 250 years, the great ships of Spain known as the Manila galleons, in their yearly circle from the Philippines back to Acapulco, sailed past the harbor of San Diego and, as far as anybody knows, never stopped. Toward the last, they represented what was left of the power and glory of Spain and of her domination of the Pacific. Fernández Duro, the historian of the Spanish Navy, records that "her military reputation, her ascendancy on the seas, her famed political policies, and the riches that seemed inexhaustible, had long since disappeared. There were left, for the remembrance of so much greatness, an undisciplined army, a navy of rotting ships, an incapable government, and an empty treasury."

When, in 1769, Fr. Junípero Serra arrived to help establish the Presidio of San Diego and to found nine of the chain of twenty-one Franciscan missions, California was opened to settlement. Then, too, came a realization of the region's great value. But Spain proved to be too tired to do much about it. When Mexico declared her independence from helpless Spain in 1822, it was a long time before anybody in San Diego heard about it. When the mission systems were broken up by the Mexican government, by secularization, and their vast lands distributed, a quaint pastoral interlude began, fostered by the old factor of political and economic isolation. It was the Days of the Dons, of vast private baronial ranchos and tremendous herds of cattle, of a time when life in the Presidio of San Diego was easy and pleasant, and fiestas and sports filled the days. California became, in imagination at least, a land of romance. The handsomely equipped *vaqueros* of the ranchos became the legendary cowboys of the western plains. But all this couldn't last. Americans—traders, trappers, gold seekers and adventurers—were pressing hard upon California, by land and sea. The threat of the possible seizure of California by other European powers, particularly England or Russia, was ended when California became a part of the United States in 1848. The pastoral lull lasted but fifty years. It was all over in the early 1860's. The great ranchos were sold or divided. Old Spanish families were scattered and their rambling adobe haciendas fell into ruins. The last of direct Spanish influence was gone. San Diego itself was destined to become the home of the new force that henceforth was to dominate the Pacific, the United States Navy.

The threads of the start of this long and fascinating story strangely enough are picked up in the old city of Seville in southwest Spain. This is an island seaport, sixty miles up the navigable Guadalquivir River, which empties into the Atlantic Ocean. From here sailed most of the explorers and conquerors. And here was the seat of the Royal Council of the Indies, which governed the New World. In the Casa Lonja or the Old House of Trade, completed in 1598, are located the Archivo de Indias, with hundreds of thousands of documents and volumes of records.

Here, and in the National Archives of Mexico and Guatemala, we find many of the manuscripts which tell us much of what we know about Cabrillo, Vizcaíno, Fr. Serra, Portolá and Anza, and the others who explored and settled California. Here are the first descriptions of San Diego, the first map made of San Diego Bay, and the first records of the population and happenings of the Presidio of San Diego. And here are buried Spain's lost hopes in the Pacific.

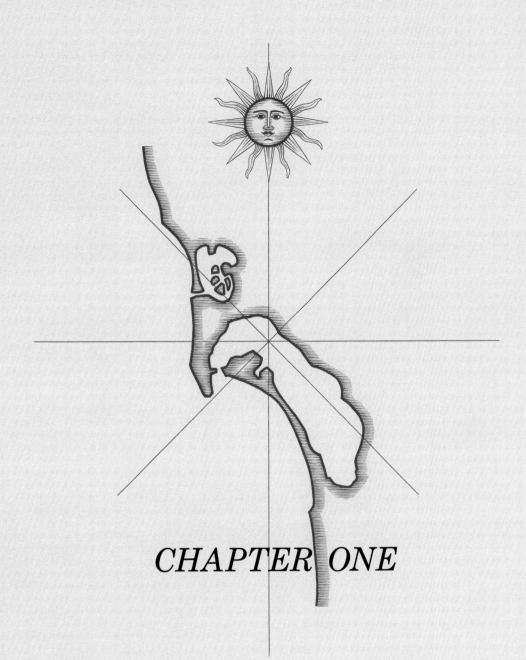

CHAPTER ONE

BEFORE THE EXPLORERS

San Diego was a well populated area before the first Spanish explorers arrived. The climate was wetter and perhaps warmer, and the land more wooded than now. The remnant of a great inland lake covered most of Imperial Valley. The San Diego River wandered back and forth over the broad delta it had formed between Point Loma and Old Town, alternately emptying into Mission Bay and San Diego Bay.

The natural food supply was so abundant that the state as a whole supported an Indian population far greater than any equal area in the United States. The native population of the southern counties alone must have been at least 10,000.

The early maps made of San Diego Bay by the Spanish explorers show the same general configuration as of today, except, of course, for the many changes in the shoreline made by dredging and filling in recent years. The maps, crudely drawn without proper surveys, vary considerably in detail. Thousands of years ago, in the late part

THE INDIANS who greeted the first Spanish explorers at San Diego were the Diegueños, and Cabrillo reported them as large and comely. The men largely went naked, though not the women. They daubed themselves with blue, black and white paint, made excellent bows and arrows and were skillful in use of the throwing stick.

Map showing how San Diego looked in the Ice Age, before Point Loma and the Coronado Strand had become attached to the mainland, or the San Diego River had cut its gorge, today's Mission Valley.

of the Ice Age, Point Loma was an island, as were Coronado and North Island. Coronado used to be known as South Island. There was no bay, as we think of it now. A slightly curving coastline was protected by the three islands, of which, of course, Point Loma was by far the largest. What we now know as Crown Point in Mission Bay was a small peninsula projecting into the ocean.

On the mainland, the San Diego and Linda Vista mesas were one continuous land mass. The San Diego River, in those days a roaring torrent, gradually cut a canyon five hundred feet deep through the mesa on its rush to the sea. The melting of the continental ice caps over thousands of years slowly raised the level of the ocean by a hundred feet, and, as it rose, the river lifted itself on the deposits of its own silt. The silt today is about one hundred feet deep in the bed of the river and forms the broad flood plain of Mission Valley.

Through all these centuries the river poured its mud and debris into the open sea, building up a delta which eventually tied Point Loma fast to the mainland. All of the low flat land between Old Town and Point Loma is a delta deposit. This closed San Diego Bay on the north to make two bays out of one, Mission Bay on one side of the delta and San Diego Bay on the other. To the south another process was at work. Silt from the Tia Juana River did not produce a delta similar to that of the San Diego River. Instead, southwest storm winds or an eddy on the lee side of Point Loma shifted the river's sediments northward, depositing them in long sandy spits connecting North Island and Coronado to each other and to the mainland. Thus San Diego Bay was landlocked south and west.

Mission Bay once was open to the sea and deep. But gradually material which was eroded from the south shore of La Jolla and cut from the embankment at Pacific Beach, along with sediments washed down from Soledad Mountain, was carried southward by waves and currents and deposited across the wide mouth of Mission Bay, creating the sandy spit of Mission Beach and leaving only a narrow tidal opening. And inside, a once usable deep-water bay was slowly choked up by deposits from the San Diego River. The expedition of Sebastián Vizcaíno in 1602 first noted Mission Bay. Ensign Sebastián Melendes, sent out with an exploring party, reported it was yet a "good port." For many years it was known as False Bay.

The shifting of the course of the San Diego River has been of considerable historical interest. Lieut. George Horatio Derby, of the United States Army Corps of Engineers, in a report to Congress in 1853 stated:

"At the time of the first establishment of the Mission of San Diego, and the 'Presidio', or the military post, this plain, and in fact the whole valley for six miles above, was covered with a dense forest of sycamore, willow, and cottonwood, with an undergrowth of various kinds of shrubbery, among which the wild grape was most abundant. At this time, the river ran through the most northerly part of the plain, skirting the hills . . . and emptied into False Bay. This course it continued until 1811, when, by continued deposit of sand, its bed was so much elevated that it altered its channel to the southwest, still however, emptying into False Bay, until 1825, when a great freshet occurring, it overflowed its banks, destroying many gardens and much property, and formed a new channel discharging into the harbor of San Diego. From the continued accumulation of sand, its course has somewhat fluctuated but has never been essentially altered since that period."

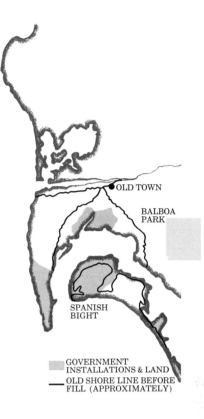

OLD TOWN

BALBOA PARK

SPANISH BIGHT

■ GOVERNMENT INSTALLATIONS & LAND
— OLD SHORE LINE BEFORE FILL (APPROXIMATELY)

In 1889, George Davidson, of the United States Coast and Geodetic Survey, set 1835 as the time when the San Diego River again began emptying into San Diego Bay. Old Spanish charts, made long before this time, also show the river emptying into San Diego Bay. Thus it shifted back and forth across its own delta. Lieut. Derby said that while Mission Bay once was sufficiently deep to admit vessels of considerable size, by 1810 it was filled with shoals and sand bars, and hardly deep enough at low tide for a sail boat. Lieut. Derby was sent to San Diego to restrain the river, to force it into a more permanent bed and prevent the threatened silting up of San Diego Harbor, as had happened with Mission or False Bay. The original Derby Dike was built of dirt in 1853-54, but had to be reconstructed in 1877. It ran from a point near the base of Presidio Hill to the inland foot of Point Loma, and successfully diverted the flow of the river back into Mission Bay, thereby saving San Diego Harbor.

The report by Lieut. Derby of a heavily wooded river valley, and particularly the comments of the early explorers about a forest on Point Loma, troubled historians down through the years. They generally concluded that the explorers must have been mistaken, or their words not properly understood or translated. Fr. Antonio de la Ascensión, who accompanied Sebastián Vizcaíno, records in his detailed report of the expedition that on the morning following their arrival at San Diego in 1602:

"The General ordered some men to go and look over a 'montesillo' which protected the port from the northwest wind. Captains Alarcón and Peguero and Father Antonio went with eight harquebusiers and found on it many live oaks, junipers, and other trees such as rockrose, heather, and one very similar to the rosemary. There were many fragrant medicinal and healthful herbs. From the top of the hill all that spacious *ensenada* (bay) could be clearly seen. It was a port very capacious, good, large and safe, as it was protected from all winds. This hill is about three leagues long and half a league wide, and to the northwest of it there is another good port."

Historian Henry R. Wagner wrote that strictly speaking the word "monte" means a forest or thicket but he concluded that, as there is no likelihood that Point Loma was covered by trees other than some scrub oak and brush, Fr. Ascensión undoubtedly used the word

Model of a Diegueño Indian's house.

Bow and arrow found in East County.

in its other variation of "little mountain." Richard Henry Dana, the author of "Two Years Before the Mast," who visited San Diego in 1835, wrote of a "large and well-wooded headland," but also commented later that wood was very scarce in the vicinity of San Diego and that the trees were small ones growing in thickets. But perhaps they weren't so mistaken. There is considerable scientific evidence that the area was much wetter at one time and that the last three hundred years have been relatively dry. Dr. Carl L. Hubbs, of the Scripps Institution of Oceanography, in climatic studies has shown that large populations of Indians lived in places where now they could not possibly find enough fresh water to live. He has also shown that a fresh-water lake, one hundred and five miles long, thirty miles broad, and three or four hundred feet deep, once filled the Salton Sea Basin. It is known as Lake LeConte, Lake Cahuilla, or Blake Sea. As the weather turned drier and the Colorado River swung to the east so as to discharge directly into the Gulf of California rather than through the Salton Sink, the great lake rapidly disappeared, evaporating probably at the rate of about five feet a year, though it was still in existence until about three hundred years ago. Recession lines left as the lake dropped were visible until the last few years, during which jeeps have messed up the evidence. The memories of this great inland sea lived in Indian legends, and Spanish explorers were sufficiently impressed to place it on maps.

Spanish explorers also reported forests of trees at Santa Barbara, to a greater extent than now, and their maps show the lower part of the Central Valleys of California covered with swamps and marshes. Much of this growth and wetness, if they did exist, have largely disappeared with declining rainfall.

Dr. Hubbs believes the desert, in the Southwest in particular, has been getting drier over long periods of geological time, and that the prospect is for continued aridity, broken by occasional wetter periods, and thus for a continued march of the desert. The drought that started in 1934 was perhaps the most severe of any which has occurred since the Ice Age or during the last 15,000 years.

The Indians who made their home in San Diego County looked with considerable suspicion and apprehension on the white explorers who came by sea. They indicated by signs that they had received word of other white men, with swords and guns, roaming deep in the interior, and the reports were not good. The Indians' first inclination was to shower the visitors with arrows. But they proved willing to listen to reason. So the tragedy of the American Indian was enacted in San Diego, as elsewhere, despite all that the missionaries sought to do. A law of nature says that the decrease of a native race is in proportion to the immediacy and fullness of contact with a superior civilization. This was true of the Indians in Northern California. The two principal San Diego Indian groups, the Diegueños and the Luiseños, fared a little better. The Diegueños in particular proved to be an independent though unorganized people, proud and arrogant, stubbornly resisting conversion, passionately clinging to old customs and beliefs, often resorting to force, and surviving in larger numbers than any other California Indians. But even those numbers were pitifully small. The argument over whether the San Diego Indians were superior, or inferior, to other American Indians has never ceased. They certainly had not attained the state of development of the Indians the Spaniards found in the Valley of Mexico, Yucatan and Peru. They were good craftsmen, though. The arrowpoints made by the men were as good or better than any in North America, and the women made pottery and baskets of excellent quality. Opinions of them held at the time must have been prejudiced somewhat by the prior experience of the Spaniards with some of the Indians of Baja California: the farther down the peninsula, the lower the Indian.

Baskets made by San Diego Indians.

A German Jesuit missionary, Fr. Johann Jakob Baegert, who spent the years from 1751 to 1768 administering to 360 Indians of the Mission San Luis Gonzaga, in the southern interior of Baja California, returned to Germany after the expulsion of the Jesuits, and in a book of his experiences described the Indians there as physically strong, but lazy and stupid, being liars and thieves, dirty in all respects, polygamous and wicked, lacking any idea of morals, admiring nothing, having no terms of relationship such as father and son, and only able to count, at best, to six. Obviously they needed attention. But the exasperated padre acknowledged that the Indian was happy. He liked his hot, barren country, had nothing to worry about, had nothing, yet all he needed, and always was in good spirits, laughing and joking. These were the lowly Pericú Indians, unrelated to the Diegueños and whose language had no connection with any of the aboriginal stock in North America.

The Indians of San Diego County, described in Cabrillo's report as comely and good-humored, were much higher in the scale of human development, but as happened elsewhere, their decline under the impact of civilization was so swift that most of their religion, their strangely moving mythology, and their tribal lore and customs were lost forever, so that a true evaluation has been difficult to reach. By the time Americans had arrived in goodly numbers, the Indians who remained in or near the settlements and towns had slipped into a state of near-degradation and were treated contemptuously as "digger Indians." Those who had retreated deeper and deeper into the hills, and those living in the mountains and deserts,

Large Indian Olla found near Rincon.

were decimated by disease, by the inevitable changes in living habits, and by neglect.

The Indian picture as a whole is a confused one, though there are reasonable grounds for believing that the cultures of all Southwestern Indian groups are related to each other and in turn to those of Mexico, though regional and area distinctions are very sharp. The Aztecs who conquered Mexico City are related, linguistically, to the Shoshoneans of San Diego County.

The Shoshoneans occupied almost a third of California, as well as vast areas of the Great Basin, and even today they are the largest group of Indians in America. The Uto-Aztecan mass of allied tribes to which they belonged stretched all the way from Panama to Northern United States. The ancestors of the Mexican Nahua, to which the Aztecs belonged, and the California Shoshoneans were associated thousands of years ago.

There were two linguistic groups of Indians, the Yuman and the Shoshonean, in Southern California and on some of the offshore islands. The Indians who later were given the designation of San Dieguños, as coming under the jurisdiction of the Mission of San Diego, were of Yuman stock; while the Luiseños, identified with the area of the San Luis Rey Mission, were of Shoshonean stock.

There were many tribes of these two linguistic groups scattered over Southern California. The Hokan family included the Northern Dieguños, the Southern Dieguños, the Kamia, and the Yuma tribes. The Uto-Aztecan, or the Southern California branch of the Shoshonean family, included the Luiseño and Cupeño, Pass Cahuilla, Mountain Cahuilla and Desert Cahuilla. Farther to the north were the Gabrielino, Nicoleño and Juaneño, who have disappeared.

The Dieguños were the most important to San Diego history. They occupied all of the territory south of a line running from south of Carlsbad eastward to just south of Escondido and then northeasterly to Warner's Ranch. The eastern boundary is vague, but it is believed they did not go below the eastern slopes of the mountains. The Indians at Mesa Grande and Santa Isabel were Dieguños. The Luiseños principally inhabited the valley and surrounding hills of the San Luis Rey River. Their territory extended northeast from Warner's Ranch to Soboba Hot Springs, about four miles northeast of Hemet, and then generally west and southwest to the coast just south of San Juan Capistrano.

The Cahuilla, who also figured in San Diego's history, were found in mountain and desert areas northeast and east of Warner's Ranch and, while of the same Shoshonean linguistic stock as the Luiseños, they differed in their tribal organization, traditions and religious beliefs. They spoke a dialect distinct from the Luiseños. A large and important group, they had little contact with early Spaniards and never came under the influence and supervision of the missions.

The Cupeños, one of the smallest Indian groups in California, were identified with Warner's Ranch and its hot springs, and while generally considered a distinct tribe, they apparently belonged to the Shoshonean linguistic stock. The territory they controlled at the headwaters of the San Luis Rey River was no larger than five by ten miles. Another little known tribe was the Kamia, sometimes called the Kamya, Cameya or the Quemaya. This was a Yuman tribe that lived between San Diego and the lower Colorado. Their identity does not seem too clear and their chief place of residence

MAP SHOWING THE DISTRIBUTION and sub-divisions of Yuman and Shoshonean tribes which populated San Diego and adjacent counties.

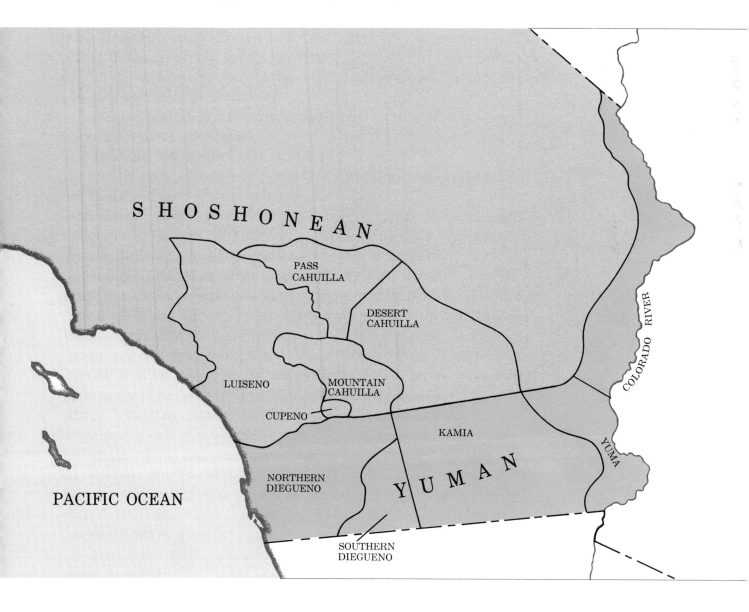

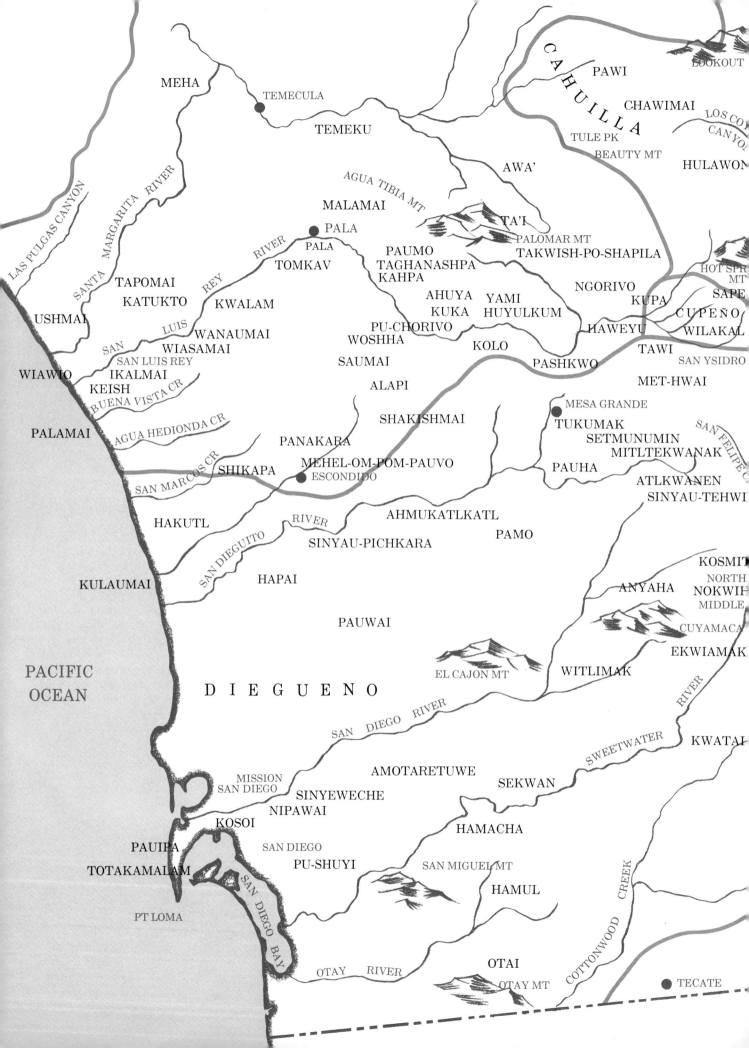

was probably across the line in Mexico. They generally are associated with the Diegueños.

The Luiseños are believed to have numbered between three thousand and four thousand at their maximum; the Cupeño, about five hundred; the Cahuilla, about twenty-five hundred; and the Diegueño-Kamia, about three thousand. This would make a total population of approximately ten thousand in a Southern California area largely made up of San Diego, and Imperial and Riverside Counties. They were not true nomads, and all tribes had some place they called home. The Diegueños knew nothing of agriculture: they didn't need to. They lived in *rancherías* in the upland valleys in the winter. They spent the summer roaming from place to place, in search of food, camping wherever they were, under the trees. Houses were used only in the winter. They were made of poles of sycamore or oak tied together at the top, then thatched with deer weed tied by strands of yucca.

Though most of the Diegueño villages were inland, there were eight permanent settlements around San Diego itself, and a number of camp sites used for fishing. The villages were located at La Jolla, just south of the present La Jolla Beach and Tennis Club; in Soledad Canyon; at the mouth of Rose Canyon, which was the largest of the group; at the foot of Presidio Hill; on the north side of the San Diego River near the entrance to Murray Canyon; on the south side of Mission Bay, along West Point Loma Boulevard; on the bay side of Point Loma; and near the foot of Market Street.

The men usually went naked. Women wore a two-piece petticoat, the back garment of willow bark and the front of the same material or of strings partly braided or netted. Sometimes they covered themselves with rabbit skins. Both men and women wore long hair, the men bunching it on their heads and the women allowing it to hang loose. Tattooing was common with the women generally wearing more designs than the men. The most common pattern was two or three vertical lines on the chin, but often they marked their head, cheeks, arms and breast.

Much has been made of their eating habits, which were often described in contempt as denoting the Indians as hopeless savages. They mainly lived on acorns, seeds, nuts, and bulbous roots, but ate about anything that moved—rabbits, hares, woodrats, ground squirrels, gophers, grasshoppers, caterpillars and ground worms. They made crude traps. Deer, antelope and mountain sheep were killed with bows and arrows, but the Indians rarely hunted bears, moun-

Map showing Indian camping sites in the San Diego Bay area, Mission Bay and La Jolla. Excavations by archaeologists show that Indians lived at these sites over long periods of time.

MAP SHOWING WHERE INDIAN RANCHERIAS or villages were once located in San Diego County. Some of these place names survive today.

11

Old Diegueño Indian wooden war club.

Throwing stick used to kill rabbits.

tain lions or wildcats. Around San Diego Bay, the Indians also ate fish and mollusks, and made tule balsas or rafts which they propelled with double-bladed paddles.

Violence was part of their life. Wars were largely feuds over trespassing, and enemies were decapitated and no prisoners taken. It is claimed that jealous women upon occasion would commit suicide. In war they would cut the entire scalp, including the ears, from their foe, and preserve it. Victories in war were celebrated in a night of dancing, and the dancers would take turns in setting the scalp of the fallen enemy on their own heads.

Among California Indians generally, death was very mysterious. They prepared for it over many years and always wanted to die where they had lived. Ashes of the dead were placed in pottery jars and secreted in the ground. An image ceremony began with a night of wailing; the images of the dead, made of mats stuffed with grass and with features of haliotis shell, were marched around a fire for six nights, and finally at daybreak were placed, along with some of the dead man's possessions, in a house of brush open to the east and burned. The dead were made content, but at the same time it was made certain that they did not return.

Even in death the Diegueños were set apart. The Yuman groups to which they belonged probably were the most irreligious Indians of North America. Mr. Malcolm Rogers, of the San Diego Museum of Man, was of the opinion that they never mentioned death, nor referred to the dead. About the time of the Spanish conquest, some of the Luiseño medicine men began to proselytize among the Northern Diegueños but without much success.

Most of what we know about them has come down from the people who tried either to civilize them or subdue them. They did have a religion and an oral literature, but much of the latter was recorded only in later years as it survived in the tribal memory of Indians still living in San Diego's back country. The Diegueños danced for the revival of the moon toward the end of its waning. Song and stories tell of a spirit world in which the little animals of their daily lives assumed human qualities; others concerned the eternal mysteries of all men — of how the world began, where man came from, and the struggle between good and evil.

The Luiseño initiation ceremonies for the coming of age of boys and girls, ceremonies so natural to native races, seemed severe, though perhaps they served the purpose of preparing them for a stoical acceptance of life and all it might bring. Girls were forced to swallow balls of tobacco. Later, they were placed on their backs in pits lined with heated stones, and then more warmed flat stones were placed on their abdomens. Here they remained for three days, men dancing around them by night and women by day, and let out once each twenty-four hours while the pit was reheated. In turn, boys in their final ceremony were laid on ant hills, or put into a hole containing ants, and then more insects were shaken over them from baskets. It was a grueling experience, and was concluded when the ants were whipped from their bodies with stinging nettles.

The Luiseños handed down to their children the age-old lessons that made and preserved family life and gave rise to civilization. Indian boys and girls were taught to respect their elders, to listen to them, to give them food freely and not to eat meals secretly, to refrain from anger and to be polite to relatives. A. L. Kroeber, of the University of California, whose study of the California Indians has been the foundation of much of what is known about them, says the Luiseños taught that if these rules were followed, then one would be stout, warm and long-haired, would grow old in good health and have children to whom to pass on counsel, be talked of when death came, and have one's spirit go to the sky to live. The disobedient and heedless would be bitten by the rattlesnake or spider.

Woman's dress of milk-weed fibres.

The fragments of their past which have been left to us do not tell much in trying to settle the argument over the place of San Diego County Indians in American history. The Luiseños seem to have been more mystical than the Diegueños, and more capable of abstract thought, as indicated in their mythology. The Diegueños were superior story tellers. One of the most intriguing bits of history is the Indian tradition of a flood which submerged all the earth except one peak. This same story is found, in some variation, among many of the primitive peoples of the world. The University of California recorded the old legend as remembered by a surviving Indian. He tells it as follows:

"There is a wonderful little knoll, near Bonsall, the Spanish name it Mora, the Indian name it Katuta, and when there was a flood that killed all the people, some stayed on this hill and were not drowned. All the high mountains were covered, but this little hill remained above the water. One can see heaps of sea-shells and seaweed upon it, and ashes where these people cooked their food, and stones set together, left as they used them for cooking, and the shells were those of shell-fish they caught to eat. They stayed there till the water went down. From the top of the hill, one can see that the high mountains are lower than it is. This hill was one of the First People."

Sisal and fibre sandals from Cuyamaca.

In the religion of the Luiseños, as recalled by Indians of modern times, is the story of the Eagle, expressive of their preoccupation with death.

"The Eagle, seeking escape from death, went north from Temecula to San Bernardino, came around by the east to the south and west through Julian, Cuyamaca, and Palomar, going towards Temecula, and died at Temecula. The Eagle sang this song at Temecula. When he got sick he talked this way. He was talking about the spirit. When they were all going along they could hear something singing far away, and the Eagle said that was the spirit, and he told the people that everywhere he had been, north, south, east and west, death was there waiting for them. It was very near. No one knew when it would come, but they would all have to die."

And die they did. Few pure Indians are left to recall the legends of the past. Tribal identifications have become indistinct as a result of marriages between tribes and mixed marriages with Spanish, Mexican and American settlers. Others have vanished into the American melting pot. By 1960 there were less than two thousand scattered on eighteen reservations in San Diego County, totaling about 120,000 acres. Some historians have been critical of the missionaries, in their treatment and concentration of the Indians, but opinion in such cases seems based more on prejudice than on truth. Civilization was advancing on the New World, and the Indian had no hope of retaining his identity. The missionaries, if anything, helped to bridge the overwhelming gap between aboriginal life and the 18th Century.

The missionaries brought the Indians to Christianity, as best they could, and tried to teach them how to live with each other in peace, how to raise food, and to learn the trades necessary for survival under completely new conditions. But the Indians never could entirely understand the importance of discipline and order. The California tribes which had the closest association with the white men are now extinct. The San Diego Indians were made of sterner stuff. When the missions had been abandoned and the padres largely gone, Indians were hunted like animals, to be shot, put to work, or herded into reservations no better than stockades. In some cases casual efforts were made to exterminate them. They endured a century of neglect.

The reservations ultimately were to save the Indians from extinction. Brought together with their own kind, and protected from abuse, they were given time to make new adjustments to life. They still speak the Indian language, along with English and Spanish, though they no longer practice their old religious ceremonies. What they remember of their songs and dances are seen and heard at the occasional fiestas held at the missions and churches on the reservations. The Catholic Church once again administers to their spiritual needs, as it did at the time of the padres. San Diego has been left a rich heritage in such Indian names as Cuyamaca, Jamacha, Jamul, Pala, Pauma and Temecula. The older Indians prefer the

Trade beads found in burial place.

Modern map shows Indian reservations in Southern California Counties.

14

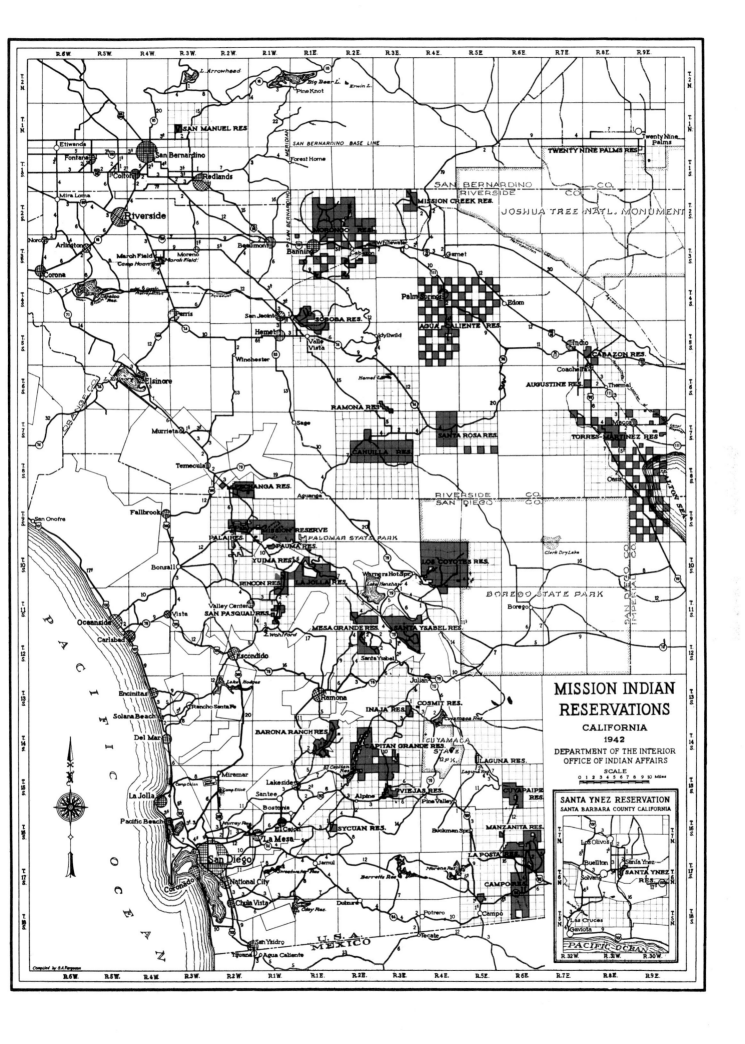

MISSION INDIAN RESERVATIONS

CALIFORNIA
1942
DEPARTMENT OF THE INTERIOR
OFFICE OF INDIAN AFFAIRS

SCALE
0 1 2 3 4 5 6 7 8 9 10 Miles

SANTA YNEZ RESERVATION
SANTA BARBARA COUNTY CALIFORNIA

Compiled by G.A.Ferguson

security of their tax-free reservations. However, many of them, and particularly the young, seek work outside. Some do not return. They have won all the privileges of other citizens of the United States, even to voting, and seem destined, at last, to be assimilated.

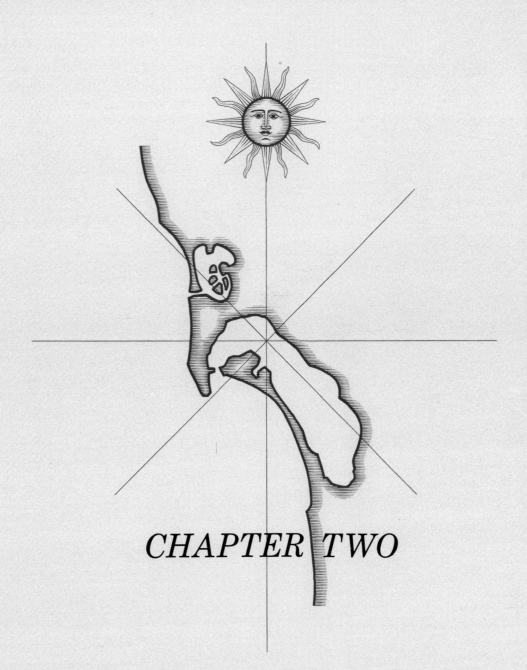

CHAPTER TWO

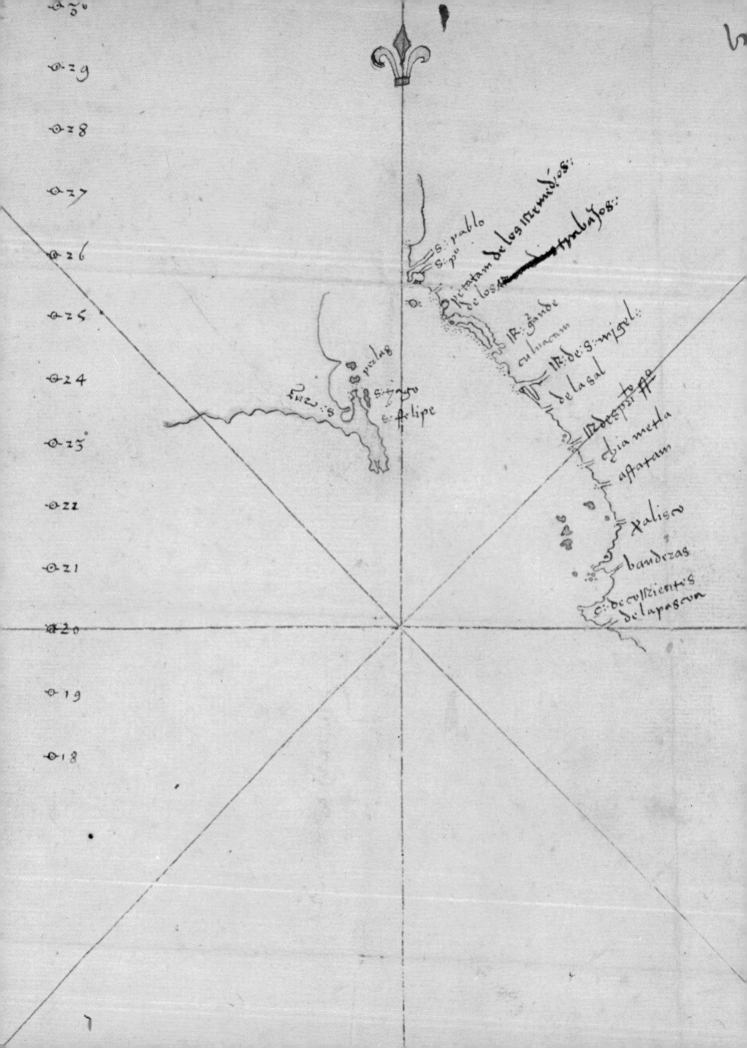

THE EARLY EXPLORERS

The historical events that led to the discovery of San Diego began with Hernán Cortés, the conqueror of Mexico. Cortés reached the Caribbean islands from Spain in 1504, when he was 18 years of age, twelve years after their discovery by Christopher Columbus. The continent of America still was a long unknown coastline just over the horizon, and for all anybody really knew, it was another island or extension of the Asiatic mainland. The tantalizing Spice Islands of the East Indies were believed to be somewhere within easy sailing distance.

Cortés, who started out to be a lawyer, became a wealthy rancher and miner in the islands of Santo Domingo and Cuba, and kept the hot fires of adventure burning by romance and intrigue. In 1518, at the age of 33, he was stirred by the reports of golden cities in the interior of the mysterious lands then being scouted by cautious but eager explorers. With the backing of Gov. Diego Velázquez of Cuba he assembled a fleet and a private army and embarked on a career of conquest.

A MAP OF LA PAZ BAY attributed to Cortés, who planted a colony there in 1535. He called the place Santa Cruz. The colony nearly starved before it was taken off in 1536. This was the first push north that eventually led to the discovery of San Diego. All that was known of Baja California at that time is shown on this map.

Hernán Cortés was an impressive figure.

Two years later the wealth of all Central Mexico and its rich cities lay at his feet, the great Aztec capital of Tenochtitlán was in ruins, and new expeditions of conquest and exploration began to fan out to the north and south. In one of the armies that conquered southern Mexico and much of Central America was Juan Rodríguez Cabrillo. Other expeditions came up against the shores of the Pacific Ocean, which they named the South Sea. In the first 20 years, after Cortés' arrival in Mexico, expeditions probing northward by land ventured far up into what is now the United States, and others, proceeding by sea along the western American coast of the South Sea, explored the Gulf of California, or the Vermilion Sea, as it was called, and surveyed much of the Baja California coast as far north as Cedros Island, about 300 miles south of San Diego. Another expedition into the upper Gulf of California left its ships and proceeded in small boats up the terrifying Colorado River, for the first glimpses of California, two years before Cabrillo arrived at San Diego.

Treasure, of course, was the great lure; after the riches of Mexico and Peru the Spaniards were ready to believe in anything. The old European story of seven rich cities in an unknown land called Cíbola was revived by a shipwrecked explorer who had wandered for eight years across much of the American interior, and averred he had seen them glistening in the sun in all their golden splendor. And there just ahead was always the fabled kingdom of the Amazons, rich in gold and pearls, and dominated by women of incomparable beauty, ruled by the virgin Queen Calafía.

Strangely, Baja California, a largely barren and uninviting peninsula of deserts and sharp mountains, 800 miles long and 30 to 145 miles wide, became linked in imagination with the mythical island known as California, which was described by a fanciful Spanish writer of the times, Garcí Ordóñez de Montalvo, as lying at the right hand of the Indies, very close to the terrestrial Paradise. Even Cortés believed the story. In a letter to the King of Spain he told of an expedition to the South Sea that brought news of pearls, of a good harbor, and an island inhabited by women without any men, and very wealthy in pearls and gold. The push to the north was on. More adventurers of all types poured into Mexico.

Cortés began to send ships to seek for rich lands. In 1532 the first two sailed but came to grief on the east side of the Gulf, where the crews either deserted or were killed by natives. Cortés' enemy and rival, the notorious Nuño de Guzmán, then the governor of Nueva Galicia, salvaged what he could of the vessels and their cargoes of provisions. In 1535 Cortés dispatched two more ships, one commanded by his relative, Diego Becerra, and the other by Hernando de Grijalva. For some reason the latter left his ship and returned to Acapulco, whereupon his men mutinied, murdered the tyrannical Becerra, and sailed on under the leadership of Fortún Jiménez, the first white man known to have reached Baja California. They approached the southern tip of Southern California, which they thought to be an island, and landed at what is now the Bay of La Paz, on the Gulf side and in protected waters. Later twenty men were killed by the natives. The attackers were not the legendary beautiful Amazons but males of probably the lowest type of Indian to be found on the American continent. The ships got away across the Gulf only to fall into the hands of the greedy Guzmán. The fate of Jiménez is uncertain. It has been thought that he was killed on Baja California, but other evidence suggests that he too escaped and was seized and imprisoned, if not killed, by Guzmán. The few men who finally returned brought wild tales of vast wealth in pearls.

Cortés, as much excited as anybody, now began preparations to establish a colony on Baja California. On May 3, 1535, with three ships he entered the Bay of La Paz, and, believing the peninsula to be an island, named it Santa Cruz, the day on the religious calendar when he arrived. The pearls were there to be sure, enough of them to stir the greed of any man. All along the shores were mounds of shells which had been discarded by Indians primarily interested in food and not in pearls. There were at least 30 pearl oyster beds, which, however, were in 150 to 300 feet of water. As the natives were anything but friendly or eager to dive at command, the Spanish had to be satisfied with shells torn loose by storms and tossed up on the beaches. The arid land was unable to support a colony, and the difficulty of supplying it by sea was increased by storms and contrary currents. On one stormy passage, crossing the Gulf from the mainland, Cortés himself had to take the wheel of his ship when his pilot was killed. Upon his return to the little colony he had left at La Paz, he found 23 of the colonists dead of starvation, and those still alive greeted him with curses. The last of the colonists was taken off in 1536. Cortés, incessantly humiliated by an ungrateful Spain, now saw the viceroy appointed by the Spanish Crown to rule Mexico become his rival in power and splendor. But just over the curve of the earth there were always more lands to discover and more riches to seize, and Cortés kept at it as long as possible. All of the explorers and mariners of that day were convinced that somewhere to the north was the passage through which ships could sail directly from the Pacific to the Atlantic. For centuries cartographers were to persist in identifying Baja California as an island, despite the evidence of many explorations to the contrary. This long-sought passage, and the lure of pearls and gold, continued to pull expeditions northward.

Early map of California as an island and the Strait of Anián.

21

Progress was slow, however, the clumsy ships struggling against the winds that blow from the north and northwest most of the year. Many vessels were lost on inhospitable coasts, others vanished, and crews of ships that managed to return to their ports of departure often were so decimated by scurvy that nobody was left to shift the sails. Still, the spirit of adventure and the excitement of an age of discovery drove them on.

There were four early expeditions important to San Diego, in 1539, 1540, 1541 and 1542, the last being that led personally by Juan Rodríguez Cabrillo. The first was that of Francisco de Ulloa, in the accounts of which there has been more confusion than light as to where he did go, and what happened to him.

Cortés sent out the expedition of Ulloa, though his instructions as to its purposes never have been found. Not until the early 1920's was a narrative of the expedition discovered in the Archives of the Indies in Seville, written in Ulloa's own hand. It is a detailed and exciting story.

Ulloa sailed from Acapulco harbor on July 8, 1539, with three ships whose tonnage was recorded in the old Italian liquid measure of boutes, or bottles. A boute was half a ton. The *Santa Agueda* was listed as 240 bottles, the *Trinidad*, 75 bottles, and the *Santo Tomás*, 60 bottles. The expedition spent some time at Manzanillo harbor and left there Aug. 27. Four days later they were caught in a terrible storm, and Ulloa soon realized that the little *Santo Tomás* was in deep trouble.

Ulloa's narrative tells of the storm and the hope that the *Santo Tomás* would get through safely to the rendezvous at La Paz:

"Wracked by the wind and waves, she began to make water so badly that those aboard could not keep it down, according to what they told me, shouting to me that they were sinking and could not keep afloat. God grant that this may not be true and they are there safe."

That was the last seen or heard of the *Santo Tomás*.

After leaving La Paz, the remaining ships veered off toward the mainland and proceeded up the Gulf. The last greenness of the tropics had given way to the flat, arid lands of northern Mexico. They stopped at Guaymas, which Ulloa named El Puerto de los Puertos, or Port of Ports, and then came to a dead end against the broad sandy delta of the then unknown Colorado River. They were puzzled over whether the strong current they experienced might be from some great river, or whether it was merely the sea pushing

This old legal deposition includes in its pages a written report by Ulloa on his explorations along the Baja California coasts.

Mexico
Año de 1540

Marques del valle

[illegible]

En la gran cibdad de temistitan mexico desta nueva españa en veynte e nueve dias del mes de mayo año del naçimiento de nuestro salvador jhesu christo de mill e quinientos e quarenta años ante el muy noble señor Juan de Burgos alcalde hordinario en esta dha cibdad de mexico por sus magestades e por ante mi alonso diaz de gibraleon escrivano de sus magestades e [illegible] vezino de la dha cibdad de mexico parescio presente francisco [illegible] de terrazas en nombre del señor marques del valle e presento [illegible] del dho señor [illegible] que es este que se sigue

muy noble señor. francisco [illegible] de terrazas mayordomo del muy yllustre señor marques del valle e en nombre del dho señor marques paresco ante vuestra merced e digo que [illegible] de [illegible] los [illegible] de [illegible] [illegible] francisco de velasco [illegible] de mi parte de la tierra [illegible] de mi parte [illegible] los [illegible] del dho señor marques [illegible] [illegible] [illegible] [illegible] [illegible] [illegible] [illegible] [illegible] [illegible] [illegible] [illegible] de mi parte [illegible]

[illegible] [illegible] del dho [illegible] [illegible] [illegible] [illegible] [illegible] [illegible] [illegible] [illegible] [illegible] [illegible] [illegible] [illegible] [illegible] [illegible] [illegible] [illegible] [illegible] [illegible] through narrow inlets in and out of lakes somewhere in the interior. They were experiencing the phenomena of the great tidal clash, when the power of the descending river drives against the ascending tide surging up the narrow Gulf. The waters can rise and drop 40 feet with terrifying effect.

Ulloa records that the violence of the tides caused "the sea to run with so great a rage into the land that it was a thing to be marveled at, and with a like fury it turned back again with the ebb."

Noting the reddish sea, Ulloa says, "We named it the Ancón de San Andrés and Mar Bermejo, because it is that color and we arrived there on Saint Andrew's day."

He is believed to have anchored his ships in a channel near the Sonora shore. To the northwest they could see the distant mountains of San Diego.

"The next day, Monday, Sept. 28, we wished to continue on, but as the day dawned, it being low tide, we saw the whole sea where we must pass, between one land and the other, closed with shoals, and in addition to this sea, saw between one land and the other, many summits of mountains, the bases of which we could not see for the earth's curvature."

It was a vast emptiness of lonely deserts and stark hills. Its very bleakness should have crushed any hopes the Spanish might have held of finding golden cities, but it didn't. Ulloa learned little, except that Baja California obviously was a peninsula — though nobody was to believe his report.

He did accomplish one thing: he undertook to claim all he could see for the King of Spain. The official notary with the expedition recorded that:

"The very Magnificent Francisco de Ulloa . . . actually and in reality took possession for the Marqués [Cortés] in the name of the Emperor, our master, King of Castile, placing his hand upon his sword and saying if any person disputed it he was ready to defend such possession, cutting trees with his sword, moving stones from one place to another and taking water out of the sea and throwing it on the land."

In like manner, did a large section of California, Arizona and Mexico pass into the possession of Spain. The Indians may have had different ideas about this but they didn't seem to figure in the schemes of conquest and royal prerogative.

Turning back, Ulloa followed the eastern coast of Baja California, landing often and skirmishing frequently with hostile Indians, and finally arrived at La Paz.

In his narrative, Ulloa again had occasion to describe the storms and variable winds so common in the Gulf in summer. Recounting another fearful experience in which his ship was caught between the mainland and an island off La Paz — which Cortés had named Santiago and which is now known as Cerralvo — he wrote:

A typical conquistador of Conquest.

"Because the wind was unstable, changing quarter every little while, night caught us between this island of Santiago and the mainland. It was so dark and fearful, with the wind and thunder, lightning and some rain, the winds at times contrary, now one way and now the other, that at times we thought we were going to be lost. Some said they saw St. Elmo. Whatever it was I did see, I saw it on the *Trinidad*, which was where it appeared. It was a shining object, on the top of the main mast. I do not assert whether it was a saint, or some other thing, but whatever it was, devout thanks did it get, and our Lord was pleased that shortly the weather improved and turned calm and clear."

Rounding Cape San Lucas Ulloa took his little fleet of two ships up the west coast of Baja California and at least got as far north as Cedros Island, or the Island of the Cedars, a little better than half way up the peninsula. Whether he actually went farther has been in dispute. As his log has never been found, we have only the final statement in his narrative, dated April 5, 1540, at Cedros Island, written as a letter to Cortés.

"I have determined, with the ship *Trinidad* and the few supplies and men to go on, if God grant me weather, as far as I can, and the wind will permit, and send this ship (the *Santa Agueda*) and these men to New Spain with this report. God grant the outcome be such as your lordship desires, whom may it please to advance your illustrious lordship in person and estate through a long period. I kiss your lordship's illustrious hand. Francisco de Ulloa."

This dramatic statement has led some historians to conclude that Ulloa sailed on, as did the Ancient Mariner, and meeting disaster was cast up and died on some shore of the Southern California coast. What actually did happen to him presents some mystery, though. None of the old Spanish records have any reference to his being lost, and these include statements from those who sailed with him.

According to Bernal Díaz del Castillo, the historian of the conquest of Mexico, Ulloa returned to the port of Jalisco, and a few days afterward, while he was ashore resting, one of the soldiers on his flagship waylaid and killed him with a sword. However, in 1543, in answering a legal interrogation in Spain as to the whereabouts of the daughter of one of his former pilots, Cortés replied that Ulloa had carried her off and could give the information better than he, thus indicating that he, Cortés, believed Ulloa was alive at the time.

Early Spanish maps indicate that explorations were made at least 100 miles north beyond Cedros Island before the time of Juan Rodríguez Cabrillo; therefore it is reasonable to suppose that the information must have been supplied to cartographers by Ulloa upon his return to Mexico.

His was the last expedition with which Cortés had any official connection. Frustrated by his enemies in New Spain, and with no new riches to send to his king, he returned to Spain in 1540 to con-

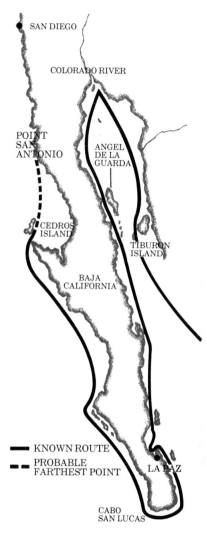

Map of the voyage of Francisco de Ulloa. He ascended the Gulf of California to the mouth of the Colorado River and proved that Baja California was a peninsula and not an island.

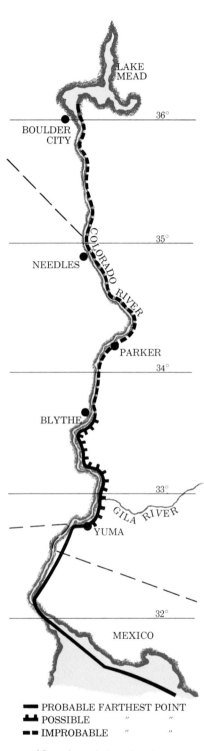

LAKE
MEAD

36°

BOULDER
CITY

COLORADO RIVER

35°

NEEDLES

PARKER

34°

BLYTHE

33°

GILA RIVER

YUMA

32°

MEXICO

━━ PROBABLE FARTHEST POINT
▲▲ POSSIBLE " "
■■ IMPROBABLE " "

Alarcón claimed that he ascended the Colorado to 36° latitude.

tinue his attempts to win the honors and titles which he believed he deserved.

With Cortés out of the way, Antonio de Mendoza, one of the great viceroys of Mexico, took over the search for the Seven Cities of Cíbola and sent out a wave of new expeditions. He, too, would find an Aztec or Inca treasure. He sent Francisco Vázquez de Coronado, governor of Nueva Galicia in Mexico, by land and Hernando de Alarcón by sea. Coronado wandered through Arizona, New Mexico, the Texas Pan-Handle, and Kansas, and finally came to the unhappy realization that the pueblos of the Zuñi Indians in New Mexico, their pale-yellow adobe deceptively gleaming in the thin air like a mirage, were the source of the twisted story of the distant cities of gold. Alarcón sailed up the Gulf of California with supplies for Coronado, but as the main body of the latter's expedition had struck inland, east and north, they never were very near each other. A patrol sent by Coronado to make contact with Alarcón missed him entirely.

Alarcón never found any rich cities either, but, besting Ulloa, he took to small boats and went up the Colorado River at least as far as the present site of Yuma, Arizona, at the point near where California, Arizona and Mexico come together; some historians are convinced he went as far north as the present Lake Mead. It was a remarkable journey by a remarkable man. Somewhere along the route he may have stepped ashore on California soil. But his report of the journey, in a letter to Mendoza, is concerned mostly with his dealings with the Indians and not with geography, so the honor of the discovery of California must remain with Cabrillo.

Alarcón outfitted two vessels at Acapulco, the *San Pedro* and the *Santa Catalina*, and then picked up the *San Gabriel* at the port of Culiacán. With them as cartographer went Domingo Castillo, who had been with Ulloa.

Alarcón sailed to the head of the Gulf of California, where his ships were caught up in the tremendous tidal bores, which are particularly severe at that time of year, just before the September equinox. There his crews wanted to turn back, as Ulloa had done, but Alarcón was made of sterner stuff. With a flourish of bravery, he reported later to the viceroy that "since your lordship has commanded me to report on the secrets of the Gulf, I was determined, even at the risk of losing the ships, not to fail, under any pretext, to reach its end."

No current or river was going to best him. Passing through the twisting shoals, he almost lost his vessels when they were grounded by the fall of the tidal bore. "We were in such danger," he wrote, "that many times the deck of the flagship was under water. And had it not been for the miraculous rise of the tide, which had raised the craft, and, as it were, given us a chance to breathe again, all of us would have been drowned."

Once over the shoals they came to the actual mouth of the mighty Colorado River, which runs with such furious power for 1700 miles. The thankful captain named it Río de Buena Guía, or the river of Good Guidance. This was on Aug. 26, 1540.

As the current was too strong to sail against, the crews took to small boats, which they rowed, sailed or towed from shore up through the country of the tall and powerful Yuma Indians. Alarcón was a swashbuckling figure, vain and proud, with a rich beard that fascinated the Indians. He always was handsomely garbed, and had a drummer and fifer along to herald his comings and goings. As the tribes were sun-worshippers, the resourceful Alarcón nominated himself as the Son of the Sun, a ruse which worked magic with the Indians. He was able to assuage his Christian conscience by distributing little wood and paper crosses to the natives.

Welcomed and honored, as befitting a gallant captain of Spain, he worked up the river for 15 days, landing here and there to meet with the friendly, curious Indians, receiving many conflicting answers to his questions about the existence of Cíbola, and hearing Indian gossip of other bearded men roaming in the interior.

Alarcón finally went back down the river for more supplies. His second trip up the Colorado, which began Sept. 14, again over the protests of his men, provides an intriguing odyssey for historians. He mentions in his account that he went as far north as 85 leagues, which would place him about 300 miles north of Yuma, or near the site of Hoover Dam, and there, he says, they "came to some very high mountains through which the river flowed in a narrow canyon, where the boats passed with difficulty because there was no one to pull them." This description, however, also fits the vicinity just above Yuma, where the Colorado runs for about a mile through a narrow channel between high cliffs. His computations on latitudes in the gulf region mean little as they were faulty and conflicted with those of Ulloa and other explorers. He also fails to mention sighting any of the rivers, such as the Gila, which empty into the Colorado on the east. The actual distance from the mouth of the Colorado River to Yuma is only about 50 miles, but all of 150 miles by way of the winding river channel.

After he had heard reports from the Indian grapevine that Coronado had reached Cíbola, Alarcón lost all hope of contact with him and decided to return home. He erected a cross, buried letters for Coronado, and placed a sign reading, "Alarcón came this far. There are letters at the foot of this tree."

Alarcón sailed downstream and returned to Colima, Mexico, where he was pressed into the continual wars with the Indians, and so dropped out of history. But the cross and the letters he left behind were to play a part in another expedition, which, in turn, provided one of the most intriguing mysteries of the Pacific Coast.

Melchior Díaz was next on the scene. He was captain of a rather small off-shoot expedition which Coronado, after reaching the grimly disappointing Cíbola, sent toward the coast in search of Alarcón and his supplies. Díaz returned to a settlement the Spaniards had founded along the Sonora River in Mexico which they had named Corazones or "Town of Hearts," and from there he trekked west with 25 mounted soldiers, a contingent of Indian allies, live sheep for food, and a greyhound dog.

Over the terrible Sonora desert they broke the path for the inland route to California, which the Spaniards later named Camino del Diablo, or the Devil's Highway, and eventually came to the Colorado River near its junction with the Gila. The same Yuma Indians who had welcomed Alarcón only a short time before now were profoundly disturbed. The magic of the Son of the Sun had died away, and the Indians became uneasy when more white men, armed and obviously covetous, arrived from a new direction.

Díaz was as much impressed with these handsome Indians as was Alarcón and noted that in traveling from place to place in the cold desert nights they carried firebrands to warm their bodies. So, the Colorado River got still another name, this time the Río del Tizón, or the River of the Firebrands.

Harassed by the Indians, they proceeded downstream to a point described as about half way between Yuma and the head of the Gulf, where they reported they found the cross and the tree carved with Alarcón's message. The spot was nowhere near that indicated by Alarcón in his message. But Díaz' own ideas of his whereabouts were not too clear either. He dug up the letters and read of Alarcón's disappointment in not finding Coronado and his report that he had determined Baja California to be a peninsula and not an island.

With the knowledge that Alarcón had gone downstream, Díaz decided to do a bit of exploring on his own initiative. He went north, crossed the river despite treacherous efforts of the Indians to kill him, and went to look for the "other coast, which in that region turned south or southeast."

In Baja California, Díaz and his men stumbled into an area of hot springs and mud volcanoes, evidently in the region near the Cocopa Mountains, where they feared to cross the rumbling earth. Escaping from this new threat to their lives, they met with a personal tragedy when Díaz was impaled on his own lance in an accident while he was chasing his dog. He lived for twenty days, doctoring himself, as his men, under frequent attack from Indians, carried him back into Mexico by litter across the lonely stretches of sand and hill. He died on January 18, 1541, and was buried somewhere between the Gulf and the Sonora Valley.

This expedition perhaps contributed little of historical value, as the actual journals or diaries about it have never been found. We have, though, a curious comment by a later Spanish narrator, Capt. Pedro Monge. He reported that a patrol from the Coronado expedition went northward along the mainland coast and near the mouth of the Colorado River they came upon men with kinky hair working metal from slag brought from somewhere in the interior, who indicated by signs that their homeland was toward the west, beyond the Ocean Sea, toward Asia or China, from which they had come in exotic vessels with carved golden pelicans as figureheads. We know no more about the incident. If Díaz had lived, perhaps he would have left us a conclusive report of an age long contact between the American and Asiatic mainlands.

There was one more expedition that reached north toward San Diego before that of Juan Rodríguez Cabrillo. Captained by Francisco de Bolaños, it was a small, advance fleet which Cabrillo dispatched sometime in late 1541 or early 1542, from the port of Navidad, where he was preparing for his own expedition. Bolaños seems not to have gone beyond the explorations of Ulloa, perhaps only 200 miles above Magdalena Bay. Cabrillo most certainly had Bolaños' maps, as well as those of Ulloa, on the journey that led to the discovery of California.

It is Cabrillo who holds the most interest for us, and to know him and to learn how he rose from the obscurity of a foot soldier with Cortés to an admiral of fleets of exploration, we must go back into the history of the conquest of Mexico.

Important points in early explorations.

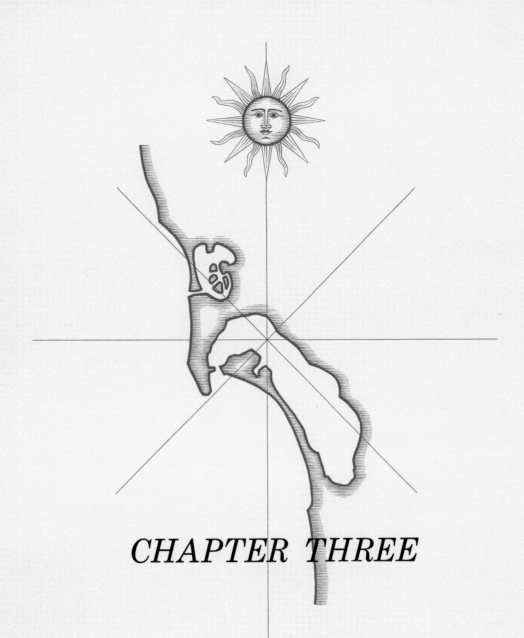

CHAPTER THREE

THE STORY OF CABRILLO

Who was Juan Rodríguez Cabrillo?

History books generally dismiss the discoverer of California as a man of mystery, who appeared on the world scene for a few brief months, and then died and was buried in an unknown grave on San Miguel Island off the coast of Southern California. But the mists of time slowly are being dissipated by research and the belated discovery of old Spanish documents in Spain and Central America.

Cabrillo's discovery of California, by the entering of San Diego bay on Sept. 28, 1542, was, historically speaking, the climax of a career of a seaman-soldier who participated in the cruel conquest of Mexico and much of Central America, helped found the first capital of Guatemala, raised a family, and then supervised the building of a fleet of ships. Some of his vessels opened the way across the Pacific Ocean to the Philippines, and others explored the long coast of both Californias.

He died a wealthy and distinguished man. But for hundreds of years history was to deprive his name of the full recognition it de-

JUAN RODRIGUEZ CABRILLO sailed into San Diego Bay in 1542. His ships were probably of the caravel type, with square stern, fairly high bulwarks, two castles and three or four masts. The sails were probably white and the lateen type, though the foremast may have been square-rigged.

Seville, Spain, the mother city of San Diego — most of the explorers sailed from here.

Casa Lonja in Seville holds the records of the discovery of San Diego and all California.

served. Even the names which he gave to his own discoveries were erased from the maps. His property was seized by jealous rivals and his family reduced to poverty. It is the familiar story of greed and neglect which so characterized Spain's control of her empires in the new world.

The historic events in which he took part, supplemented by information in the old Spanish script on long-neglected documents, produce a portrait of a man cast in the hard mold of his times, courageous, loyal and religious, but often ruthless. He was a capable administrator and organizer, who placed duty above everything. His last order at death was that his ships were to go on, as he had planned, for the glory of God and Spain.

Much of what we now know about Cabrillo comes from two documents, a summary of the journal of his explorations, and what is called the *Información* of 1560. The original journal, or log, of his explorations up the coast, and of those who continued after his death, has never been found. A summary of it was discovered in the Archives of the Indies, in Seville, Spain, and published in 1857, though its contents certainly were known to 16th Century historians and cartographers. The *Información* of 1560 contains the pleadings of his son, also known as Juan Rodríguez Cabrillo, for the return of the estates seized just before his father's death, and recites, point by point, the services of his father to the Spanish crown. The evidence presented by the son is corroborated by testimony from friends and witnesses who had knowledge of the events of the times.

The long hearings, which extended over many years, and which brought many bitter disappointments, were heard before the royal Audiencia of Guatemala, a court of last resort for the governing of Spain's New World empires, and were addressed to the King of Spain and the Royal Council of the Indies. Copies of these hearings were found in the Archives of the Indies. The originals are in Guatemala, and have been largely overlooked. With them are the royal records of the grants of vast estates, or *encomiendas*, to Cabrillo in reward for his services. These documents can still be read. More are sure to be found.

The story of Cabrillo must start at Veracruz. Before that, we know nothing. Undoubtedly he was a Portuguese navigator, either in exile from his homeland or seeking new adventures. Although in Portuguese his name would be written João Rodrigues Cabrilho, he signed himself Juan Rodríguez, or "Juan Rodz." Visconde de Lagoa, Portuguese historian, says the name Cabrillo or Cabrilho is unknown as a surname and probably indicates the town from which he came. There are many villages in Portugal called Cabril.

We do not know the age of Cabrillo at the time he arrived in

America, but he probably was in his late twenties or early thirties. It was an age of young men, of restless adventurers. And twenty-two years later he still was able to take part in a long and hazardous trip of exploration. There is reason to believe that he sailed with the Portuguese explorations of Africa and Asia, and perhaps to the coast of South America. The 16th Century Spanish historian, D. Antonio de Herrera y Tordesillas, commented on Cabrillo's fleet of exploration that the Viceroy of Mexico "appointed for their captain Juan Rodríguez Cabrillo, a Portuguese, a person very skilled in matters of the sea." If not an exile from his country, Cabrillo could have chosen to throw his lot in with the Spanish expeditions, instead of those of his own country, as the Spanish ones largely were privately financed affairs with great possibilities of personal riches.

Cabrillo stepped ashore near Veracruz, Mexico, in 1520, a soldier in the expedition of Pánfilo de Narváez, which was sent by an envious governor of Spanish Cuba to defeat and punish Hernán Cortés.

Veracruz today is Mexico's major Atlantic port. In colonial times it was the gateway for the conquest of Mexico and the funnel through which the gold and silver of the Aztecs flowed back to Spain. Little remains to recall the past except the old coral and lime fort of San Juan de Ulúa. Across the bay is the Isle of Sacrifice, where the Spaniards first noted the evidence of human sacrifices and got a glimpse of the terrors which were to lie ahead. It is a humid land, flat and sandy, smelling of the tropics.

Cortés landed on this coast in 1519, with the authority and backing of Gov. Diego Velázquez of Cuba, but soon went into business for himself. He got rid of his obligation to Velázquez by a simple maneuver. He laid out the first city of Veracruz. In the Roman tradition surviving in Spain, cities were the seats of power and authority. A *cabildo* or governing council was installed. It promptly revoked the authority which Velázquez had given to Cortés in Cuba, and then thoughtfully handed Cortés its own grant of power on behalf of the King of Spain. Cortés was on his way. He had an army of about 500 men, along with a hundred seamen. As a precaution, he burned his fleet of ships off Veracruz. Now there was no turning back. Ahead of them, somewhere up in the mountain fastness, was the feared Moctezuma and the all-powerful and rich Aztec nation; behind them, an avenging governor.

Quickly overcoming opposition along the coast, and enlisting allies among Indian tribes which resented paying tribute to the hated Aztecs, Cortés advanced toward the Valley of Mexico and the Aztec capital of Tenochtitlán. From the high cold mountains he looked down upon an amazing sight: a vast, almost flat valley with six lakes and 30 white-plastered cities shimmering in the sun like silver.

Spanish stirrups of the late 1800's.

The soldiers were frightened and said, "We are tempting God if we let ourselves into that danger, so few of us in the midst of so many."

On an island in the largest lake, Texcoco, was Tenochtitlán, the greatest and richest city of old America. It was the seat of power of Moctezuma and the Aztecs, a nation of perhaps 300,000 people. It was a kind of Venice of America, with traffic moving by canals and streets, and was connected with the mainland areas by three narrow causeways. The Aztecs originally were a small tribe which several hundred years before had drifted down from the north, some think from the American Southwest, to become the leading people of all Mexico.

The lakes have largely disappeared and Mexico City, one of the world's big capitals, now stands on the site of Tenochtitlán. The Cathedral of Mexico City is built on the very location of the temple pyramid on which 20,000 Indians were said to have been offered as sacrifices in observance of its erection.

MAP SHOWING THE TRAVELS OF CABRILLO from the time he sailed from Santiago, Cuba, with Pánfilo de Narváez until he sailed into San Diego Bay on September 28th, 1542.

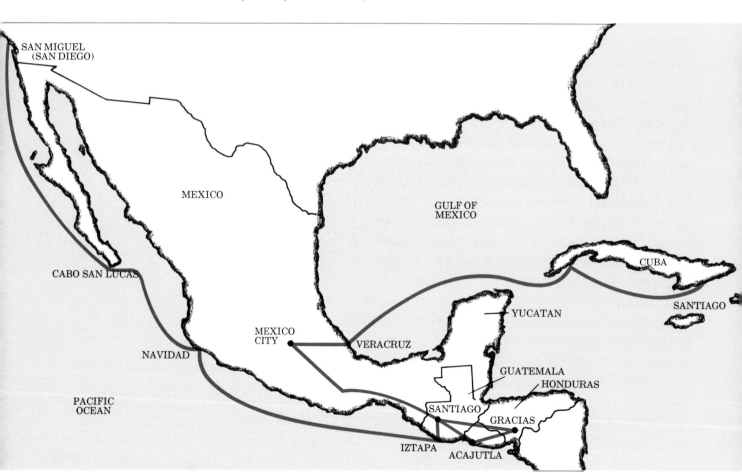

Cortés pushed into the valley. The story is well known. Moctezuma, vacillating and fearful, thought Cortés must be the legendary white-skinned god Quetzalcoatl, who had promised to return from across the sea. Cortés proclaimed the authority of Spain, banned human sacrifices, destroyed the idols, cleaned the temples of blood, and looted the Aztec treasury. He maintained an uneasy domination with a handful of Spanish soldiers in a valley with a million and a half Indians.

Pyramid of Sun near Mexico City.

It was at this moment in history that the obscure Juan Rodríguez Cabrillo landed with Narváez. He was described later in old Spanish records variously as a navigator, crossbowman and horseman. He was probably all three. Now Cortés had to make a bold move. He left the Valley of Mexico with part of his army to face Narváez on the coast. In Tenochtitlán he left one of his captains, the rash Pedro de Alvarado, who later was to become the most important person in the career of Cabrillo. Cortés surprised and easily defeated Narváez' forces, first weakening their ranks by bribery and promises of gold, land and women, then falling upon them at night. Cabrillo was swept up into Cortés' reinforced army, which turned back toward Tenochtitlán to begin an almost incredible series of military operations.

Alvarado was in trouble. No sooner had Cortés left than the Aztecs received permission to stage a ceremonial dance. Alvarado, greedy for more loot and claiming he feared they were going to attack, fell on them and slaughtered hundreds of victims. Upon his return, Cortés realized that the uneasy peace was at an end and that he would have to withdraw his forces in a hurry. They were isolated on a small island, surrounded by superior forces, with the only avenues of retreat three narrow causeways to the mainland.

Drawing of typical Aztec warrior.

Cortés saw that the key to the domination of Tenochtitlán, and the destruction of Aztec power, lay in gaining control of the lakes of the Valley of Mexico. It was a question, strangely enough, of sea power — sea power in a valley of 2,000 square miles, 7,800 feet above sea level, and completely enclosed by mountain ranges. The necessity of gaining military control of the lakes, for the amphibious warfare that must be fought, was to bring the first historic recording of the name of Juan Rodríguez Cabrillo.

One night will live long in Spanish memory. It is called the Sad Night, or Noche Triste. At midnight of June 30, 1520, Hernán Cortés began the withdrawal of his small force of about 1200 Spaniards and 4,000 Indian allies from the Aztec capital.

Cortés chose to retreat over the Tacuba causeway, a two-mile stretch breached at several places and only eight-horses wide. It was to take them four hours to go the two miles. Cortés sent as

Drawing of a High Aztec Priest.

much of the Aztec treasure ahead as possible, and then called in his men and told them to help themselves to the rest. Bernal Díaz del Castillo, who accompanied the conquistadores and later was to write the long and exciting narrative of the great adventure, remarked that it was Narváez' men who couldn't resist the appeal of the riches and loaded themselves down with the treasure that was to carry most of them to their deaths.

The retreat began on a dark, cloudy and rainy night. Cortés and a large body of men went first. In the middle were the former soldiers of Narváez. One of them was Juan Rodríguez Cabrillo. Bringing up the rear was Pedro de Alvarado. A portable bridge was carried to close the breaches, but it was difficult to handle under the relentless attacks of thousands of Indians in canoes and crowded onto the narrow causeway. Cortés later was to write that "as there was water on both sides they could assail us with impunity, and fearlessly."

Most of the Narváez men never got over the first bridge. Weighted down by gold, they stumbled before their attackers, piling up in the breach so deeply that Alvarado's men virtually crossed over their bodies. Bewildered and panicky, some Spaniards tried to turn back and were seized by the Indians and dragged off to the sacrificial altars. Those still on the causeway imagined they could hear the screams of their companions as they were stretched and cut open in horrible sacrificial deaths.

Historic tree where Cortés wept.

The survivors reached the city of Tacuba, on the mainland shore. Cortés is supposed to have leaned against a tree at the end of the causeway and wept for the loss of so many of his men. The old tree, now only a shell and said to be a thousand years old, still stands, guarded by a little iron fence, in the Mexican district of Tacuba. Nearer the center of the capital is a short stretch of boulevard named Puente de Alvarado, the bridge of Alvarado, on the site where so many men died.

In those four hours, and in the scattered attacks that followed their retreat around the lakes and back up through the mountains to friendly territory, Cortés lost 65 per cent of his Spanish soldiers, perhaps 800 men, in battle and on the sacrificial altars.

Protected and comforted by the Tlaxcalan Indians, and reinforced from Cuba and Jamaica, Cortés and his men nursed their wounds and gathered strength for the conquest ahead. First he must have a navy. He ordered the construction of thirteen thick-planked brigantines, each about 40 feet long, mounting cannons and carrying sail and a double row of oarsmen. Bernal Díaz was to write that a crew of men was sent to gather pitch to caulk the ships.

"I remember the man who had charge of and went as captain was one Juan Rodríguez Cabrillo, who was a good soldier in the Mexican campaign, who later, as a resident of Guatemala, was a very honorable person, and was captain and admiral of thirteen ships in Pedro Alvarado's behalf, and he served his majesty well in everything which presented itself to him, and died in the royal service."

Juan Rodríguez Cabrillo had entered written history for the first time. Curiously, the sentence in the original narrative, now in the National Archives of Guatemala, later was penciled out, but it can still be read.

The brigantines were tested, then taken apart and carried section by section, under the protection of 40,000 Indians, to the Valley of Mexico. The ships were reassembled and the 40,000 men dug a canal along a small stream leading into Lake Texcoco. Cortés, meanwhile, gathered up an additional 50,000 Texcocoan Indians, and the great battle was ready to be joined.

It was amphibious warfare of the kind employed 400 years later by the United States Marines in the great Pacific islands landings. The battle for the city started on the last day of May, 1521. The 13 brigantines led waves of perhaps 16,000 native canoes. They mopped up along the shores, cut off the water approaches, gained control of the lakes, blockaded the city, and landed assault troops along the causeways. The cannons slowly battered down the walls of the city, its temples and palaces.

The battle lasted for 10 weeks. How many died nobody will ever know. Some authorities estimate at least 100,000 defenders died in the siege, 50,000 by starvation. On the day of Saint Hippolytus, August 13, 1521, the last of the city was destroyed. Bernal Díaz was to write of the once beautiful city that, "Of all these wonders that I beheld, today all is overthrown and lost, and nothing is left standing."

What were Cabrillo's thoughts as he stood in the ruins of the great empire? We do not know. There were to be no great prizes for him here. Being one of Narváez' men, he still had several years of warfare ahead before he could claim the full reward for his ordeals from the crown of Spain.

Cabrillo threw in his lot with the new expeditions of Pedro de Alvarado and Francisco de Orozco, which were to conquer southern Mexico and parts of Central America. These and other campaigns in that area were epics of hardships, cruelty and treachery. Rain forests, swamps, mountains, disease, and bitterly resisting natives sometimes were not as much to be feared as the intrigue and treachery of the rapacious Spaniards themselves. The captains often turned on each other as callously as they tore the golden rings from the noses of the natives and burned their chiefs at the stake.

Cabrillo was wounded again in southern Mexico, according to the

The manuscript of Bernal Díaz' Historia Verdadera de la Conquista de Nueva España, open to show on the right-hand page a reference to Cabrillo's part in the conquest of Mexico. The passage was lined out by a later hand.

records of his descendants, but recovered to fight his way through the waves of thousands of natives which beat against the advancing Spaniards.

Alvarado's army of 120 horsemen, 300 infantrymen and 20,000 picked Indian allies climbed to the highlands of Guatemala, and found a country dotted with many towns, fields of maize and orchards, and cool streams. To the Spanish, it looked like a paradise. Between them and the final conquest of this rich land were the Quiché Indians, of Mayan linguistic stock, on whom Alvarado fell with treachery and cruelty until the waters of the Olintepec ran crimson and became known as Xequiqel, the River of Blood.

The main Quiché stronghold was the fortified city of Utatlán, which had been ruled by the same dynasty for 20 generations and was comparable to Aztec and Mayan cities in beauty and magnificence.

Historian Hubert Howe Bancroft describes it thus:

"In its center stood the royal palace, surrounded by the imposing residences of the nobles, and beyond, the humbler dwellings of the common people. The palace was one of the most magnificent structures of Central America. It was built of hewn stone of various colors, mosaic in appearance, and its colossal dimensions, and elegant and stately architectural form, excited mingled awe and admiration. Within the lofty portals, the quarters of the household guards, surrounding a spacious barrack yard, were first presented to view. Dusky warriors, lancers, and archers, clad in wildly picturesque garbs of dappled tiger-skins or sombre bear-hides, in brilliant plumes and polished arms, with silent tread measured the well paved court. In the principal apartments near at hand the various arms and paraphernalia of battle lay ready for immediate use, while on the walls hung hard-won trophies of war. Next lay the residence of the unmarried princes, and beyond this the palace proper, containing besides the apartments of the monarch the council-chamber, with the gorgeous throne canopied with costly tapestry of feather work of rare designs and wrought with cunning skill; also the royal treasury, the hall of justice, and the armory. Three separate suites of rooms, for morning, afternoon, and night, were each day occupied by the monarch, and all these more private apartments looked out upon delightful gardens, with trees, and flowers, and fruits, and in their midst menageries and aviaries, with rare and curious collections. Beyond lay the separate palaces of the monarch's queens and concubines, with their baths, and gardens, and miniature lakes; and lastly the maidens' college, in which were reared and educated the female offspring of royal blood. And all this was but one pile of buildings, the largest, it is true; but there were others of no mean pretensions, the residences of the nobles and of the wealthy trading class. Of a truth, Utatlán was a fine city, and a strong and noble one."

But all this was coming to an end. The desperate Quiché Indians sought to lure Alvarado and his men into the city, to set it afire and burn them to death. As the Spanish entered, they noticed the weakened bridges, the piles of firewood and the strange absence of all women and children. They withdrew in time, and in turn lured the

Ancient, ruined Guatemalan city.

Book recording the founding of Santiago de Guatemala in 1524, and signed by the first 100 citizens, all conquistadores, among whose signatures appears that of Cabrillo.

40

Quiché King, Oxib Quich, and his leaders to the Spanish camp to talk of a truce, seized them and forced the stripping of the city of all its wealth. Then Alvarado hanged or burned his captives.

Aroused to a final stand, the Indians suffered a fearful defeat, and the vengeful Alvarado finally burned the city, destroyed all the crops, and branded and enslaved the captives. The campaign was of such brutality that Alvarado eventually was summoned to Spain for explanation and censure. But he returned to become captain general of a new Spanish colonial empire that stretched from southern Mexico to the northern border of present Panama. Not far from his right hand stood Juan Rodríguez Cabrillo, now a captain of crossbowmen, and one-time navigator. The King of Spain at last was ready to recognize the services of a Portuguese adventurer. Cabrillo settled in Guatemala to collect his rewards.

In an old safe in a basement storeroom of the Municipal Building in Guatemala City is a faded record book, its pages frayed by centuries of handling or eaten by insects. It tells of the founding, in an Indian cornfield, of the first capital of Guatemala, Santiago de Guatemala, named in honor of the Apostle Santiago. The date was July 25, 1524.

Cabrillo's signature, "Juan Rodz" — in the customary form of the time — as it appears in the book recording the founding of Santiago de Guatemala in 1524. His is the eleventh from the top in the left-hand column.

Each of the 101 founders signed his name in this book. The first to sign was "El Sr. Captain General," who was Pedro de Alvarado. The 11th to sign was Juan Rodríguez Cabrillo. His scrawled personal signature, "Juan Rodz.," can be read to this day. On the following May 6th, his signature appeared again as one of about fifty conquistadores formally applying for recognition as first citizens and residents of Guatemala.

In 1527, the capital was shifted to a new site, in a beautiful cool valley with plenty of wood and water, on the sloping arm of a dramatically perfect conical mountain towering 15,000 feet into the clouds. It was a beautiful but deadly spot. On the maps this site is now identified as Ciudad Vieja. It is about three miles from the present Antigua, the picturesque ruined colonial city, and about thirty miles from Guatemala City. It was laid out in the traditional Spanish manner, around a central plaza, with provisions for all necessary public buildings; the remainder of the land was to be divided among the citizens, present or future.

Cabrillo established a home, went to Spain and married Doña Beatriz Sánchez de Ortega, sister of a fellow conquistador, evidently a pre-arranged marriage customary in that time, and returned to settle down and become a man of property and considerable influence. He had a number of children, who, ironically, were to live to see their father's estates stripped away from them and to experience the cynical neglect of an ungrateful Spain.

With his brother-in-law, Cabrillo engaged in mining operations along two rivers, and built up wealth and income from the possession of *encomiendas* granted to him by Alvarado. The locations of these are identifiable on today's maps of Guatemala. Probably the most important was at Cobán, in central Guatemala, now the site of one of the country's largest towns, which he held in partnership with his brother-in-law. The other *encomiendas*, as listed in the long legal hearings that followed his death, are designated as Tacuba, Jumaytepec and Jocatenango. He also was given the governorship of Xicalpa and Comitlán.

The *encomiendas* carried with them the "protection and use" of the Indians who were unfortunate enough to live in the villages or on the farms included in the grants. This generally amounted to virtual slavery. Many of the Indian tribes proved so uncooperative that the new life of the landed gentry occasionally had to be interrupted by calls to suppress rebellions. The Spanish crown frowned on slavery and the harsh treatment of the Indians, and missionaries began to appear in the colonies in large numbers, attempting to alleviate their condition and to bring them to Christianity. These missionaries also began to erect the magnificent churches which have withstood the ravages of war and earthquake.

As time went on, Alvarado more and more called on the ability and loyalty of Cabrillo. Cabrillo engaged in shipbuilding activities as well as farming and mining, in his own behalf and that of Alvarado. At one time he planned to sell horses and mules in Peru, but his vessel, the *San Antonio*, was requisitioned by Alvarado for some venture of his own and returned in a rotted condition.

Alvarado began to see himself as a great explorer by land and sea, perhaps to rival or excel the great Cortés himself. The events that were to lead to the discovery of California and the untimely death of Cabrillo began to shape up.

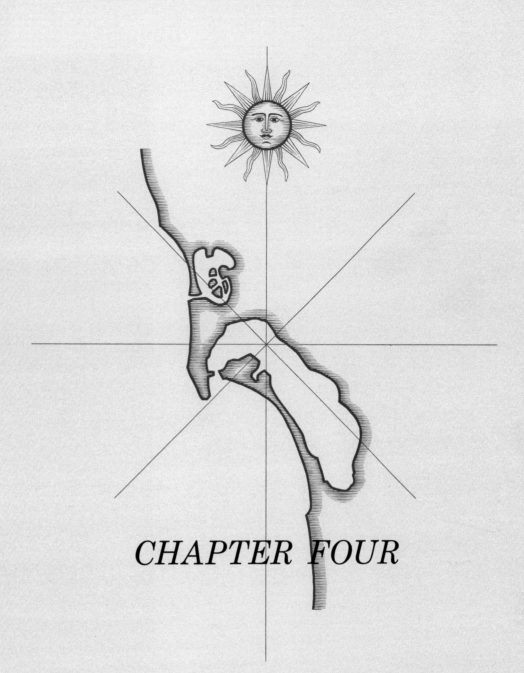

CHAPTER FOUR

✝

Relación del desembarque y hijo
Juan Rodrigues pagando por
y majestad [...]
la contra esta de la flota

N.º 145

producidor
[...]

THE FIRST TO ARRIVE

Near one entrance of a long lagoon running along the southern Guatemalan coast and almost the entire coast of El Salvador is the little village of Iztapa. It abounds with parrots and monkeys. In the summer the heat is so intense that even the natives are able to work only from about midnight to mid-morning.

Juan Rodríguez Cabrillo had been along this hot coast in the Spanish expeditions which conquered Central America, and as a one-time navigator had taken note of the abundance of strange hard woods which grew thickly along the coast, and of the big cedar and mahogany trees in the mountains. Here was to be the starting point of the course of discovery that led to San Diego. In 1536 Pedro de Alvarado, governor of Guatemala, reached a decision to build a large fleet of ships which would be capable of exploring the vast remoteness of the South Sea, as the Pacific was known at that time. Cabrillo was given the assignment, and he selected a shipyard site on the spit of land across the narrow bay from Iztapa, where the

TITLE PAGE OF THE DIARY or Log of the Cabrillo expedition. Not the original diary, which has never been found, but a summary, this document is known as the Summary Journal. Its authorship is uncertain, but it was probably written either by the pilot Ferrelo or by another member of the expedition, Juan de Páez, whose name appears at the top on the left.

A view of Iztapa, Guatemala, the little port where Cabrillo built ships for Pedro de Alvarado, whose fleet afterwards was split, one part sailing to the Philippines and the other to San Diego.

river María Linda empties into the bay and sweetens the water. Cabrillo invested in the expedition himself, owning the *San Salvador* which he was to take into San Diego Bay. Alvarado also paid him for his services with new grants in Honduras, including two towns with all Indians and chiefs.

The construction of the fleet was a long, hard and complicated task. Cabrillo moved his headquarters to what is now Gracias, in Honduras, becoming a citizen there, in order to command the supply routes which crossed Central America from the Atlantic to the Pacific. He was made *justicia mayor* of Iztapa. Under his jurisdiction, on both sides of the isthmus, went thousands of Indians, who were to pack and drag the anchors, metalwork and other equipment which had to be brought over from Spain and hauled over swamps and mountains. Death stalked every step. The Spaniards were to estimate that eighty ships could have been built at Seville, Spain, for the cost of the thirteen built at Iztapa.

The work proceeded intermittently over a number of years. But, at last the fleet was ready. Evidently, the outfitting of the ships was completed at Acajutla, farther down the coast in El Salvador. Cabrillo had built well, as history was to record. The fleet was made up of three galleons of 200 tons, seven ships of 100 tons, and three smaller vessels; it carried 1000 men and a force of cavalry. Alvarado was listed as captain-general and Cabrillo as admiral. Alvarado was to die in less than a year and Cabrillo in less than two.

The destination was the port of Navidad, Mexico, where they arrived on Christmas Day, 1540. Navidad was at one time the main Pacific coast port for Colima and is situated about twenty miles north of the present Manzanillo. History, however, has long since passed it by, and it is only a spot on the map today. The fleet's arrival brought a quick offer from Don Antonio Mendoza, the Spanish viceroy of Mexico, to cut in for a larger share of the expedition, but he and Alvarado were unable to reach a final agreement. Here death intervened. Alvarado, in 1541, answered a call to help put down an Indian insurrection in Jalisco and was crushed to death by a falling horse.

Troubles piled up for Cabrillo, and his men began to desert. The expedition almost fell apart. Back in Guatemala, Francisco de la Cueva, the acting governor and Alvarado's son-in-law, moved in and began taking possession of Cabrillo's *encomiendas* at Tacuba and Jumaytepec. Alvarado had handed out grants with such abandon that often ownership was in question. Cabrillo's son also noted in his legal pleadings that the Dominican friars moved onto the *encomienda* of Cobán, and wouldn't leave. As best he could, under the circumstances, Cabrillo began to fight back, suing for return of the revenues of the property and also suing the Alvarado estate for the expenses he had incurred in building the fleet.

The Viceroy of Mexico stepped in to take possession of Alvarado's fleet, and showed his confidence in Cabrillo by leaving him in command. Ruy López de Villalobos was assigned to sail the larger number of ships across the Pacific to the Philippines, though nobody knew for sure how far away they were. From the testimony of Cabrillo's son, after his father's death, we know that the explorer also was the one, it will be recalled, who dispatched the small fleet under Francisco de Bolaños to explore tentatively the coast of Baja California. Bolaños got as far north as 200 miles above Magdalena Bay before returning in time to go with Villalobos to the Philippines.

Still another witness claimed, though without substantiation, that it was also Cabrillo who in 1540 dispatched the ships which took Francisco de Alarcón up the Gulf of California, whence he proceeded by small boat up the Colorado River and saw California two years before Cabrillo did.

Cabrillo, with two ships, the *San Salvador* and the *Victoria*, sailed north from Puerto de Navidad on June 27, 1542. He was never to return. Cabrillo's ships probably were of the caravel type, of the round ship family. Such a vessel had a square stern, fairly high bulwarks, was narrow at the poop and wide at the bow, and undecked between two castles, one fore and one aft, the latter being the higher. Three or four masts carried lateen sails, although by this time the foremast may have been square-rigged.

A caravel. Cabrillo's ships were of this type as were those of Columbus, but Cabrillo's probably were more crude.

Two of the primary goals were the same in all these voyages: finding the promised northwest passage from the Atlantic to the Pacific and the shortest way to the rich islands of the East. It was believed that the unknown lands to the north probably were an extension of the mainland of China or, at least, were in proximity to the tantalizing Moluccas. There also is some indication that Cabrillo was looking for the mouth of a large river, which may have been identified in some way with the Rio Grande.

The Spanish summary of the journal of Cabrillo's expedition, found 300 years later in Seville, Spain, begins as follows:

"Relation of the Diary of the Voyage made by Juan Rodríguez Cabrillo with two ships, for the Discovery of the Passage from the South Sea at the North, from the twenty-seventh of June, 1542, when he left the Port of Navidad, to the fourteenth of April of the following year, when he returned to it, having gone as far as the Latitude of forty-four degrees; with the Description of the Coast, Ports, Bays, and Islands which he Examined, and their Distances, in the Whole Extent of that Coast."

But Cabrillo, of course, did not return. His ships did.

The *San Salvador* and *Victoria* went up the coast of Mexico,

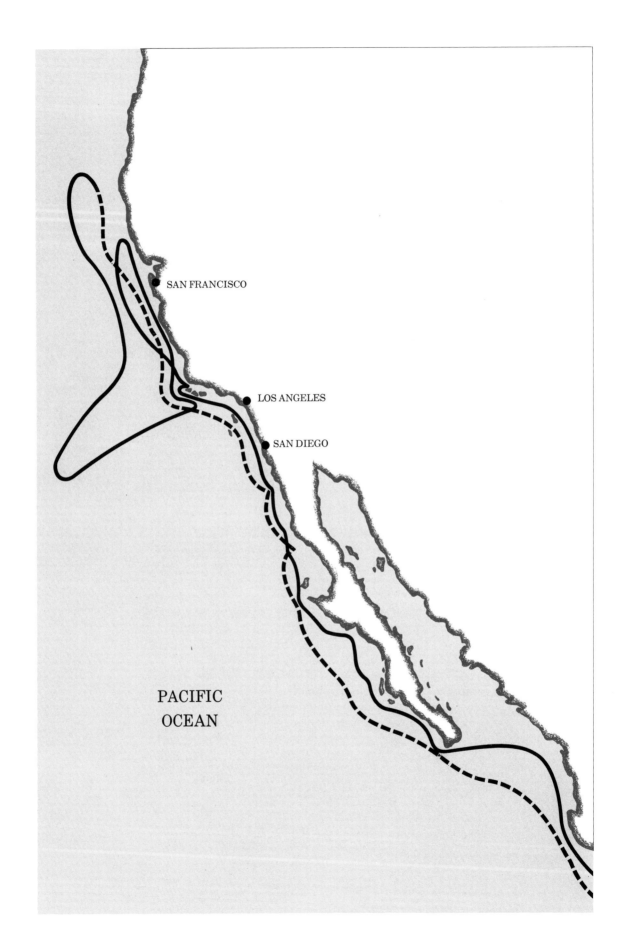

LOS ANGELES

SAN DIEGO

PACIFIC
OCEAN

48

crossed the Gulf of California and proceeded up the west coast of Baja California, sailing fifteen to twenty miles a day and anchoring at night, and evidently using maps and other information from the earlier expeditions. Cabrillo didn't begin carrying out acts of formal possession in the name of the king and viceroy until reaching San Quintín Bay. They reached Ensenada on Sunday, Sept. 17, where they remained five days, the country reminding them of Spain, and then drew near the unexplored coast of upper California and sighted the Coronado Islands.

"On the following Tuesday and Wednesday they sailed along the coast about eight leagues, passing by some three islands completely denuded of soil. One of them is larger than the others. It is about two leagues in circumference and affords shelter from the west winds. They are three leagues from the mainland, and are in thirty-four degrees. They called them Islas Desiertas (Desert Islands). This day great smokes were seen on land. The country appears to be good and has large valleys, and in the interior there are high mountains."

The next morning, Sept. 28, 1542, Cabrillo sailed along the lee side of Point Loma, anchored in the bay, and stepped ashore on California soil. Most of the latitudes which he assigned to ports he discovered were in error, and often the descriptions left doubt as to exact locations. But as to San Diego, there could be no doubt. The port that he named San Miguel is San Diego Bay, though he listed it as in 34° 20' instead of 32° 40' N. Latitude. The journal tells of the discovery as follows:

"On the following Thursday they went about six leagues along a coast running north-northwest, and discovered a port, closed and very good, which they named San Miguel. It is in thirty-four and one-third degrees. Having cast anchor in it, they went ashore where there were people. Three of them waited, but all the rest fled. To these three they gave some presents and they said by signs that in the interior men like the Spaniards had passed. They gave signs of great fear. On the night of this day they went ashore from the ships to fish with a net, and it appears that here there were some Indians, and they began to shoot at them with arrows and wounded three men.

"Next day in the morning they went with the boat farther into the port, which is large, and brought two boys, who understood nothing by signs. They gave them both shirts and sent them away immediately.

"Next day in the morning three adult Indians came to the ships and said by signs that in the interior men like us were travelling about, bearded, clothed, and armed like those of the ships. They made signs that they carried cross-bows and swords; and they made gestures with the right arm as if they were throwing lances, and ran around as if they were on horseback. They made signs that they were killing many native Indians, and that for this reason they were afraid. These people are comely and large. They go about covered with skins of animals. While they were in this port a heavy storm occurred, but

This page of the Cabrillo Log describes how his ships sailed past the Coronado Islands and came into a good port which they named San Miguel, the original name of San Diego.

MAP SHOWING THE ROUTE TAKEN BY CABRILLO, and after his death, the pilot Ferrelo, in 1542-1543. The ships started at Navidad in Mexico and got as far north as 41° 30' N. Lat., near the Rogue River in Oregon.

49

Ballast Point, West's Plymouth Rock.

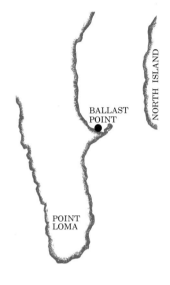

This page of Cabrillo's Log describes how the ships were forced south from Drake's Bay by severe gales, and took shelter at the Island of La Posesión (San Miguel Island), where Cabrillo died.

since the port is good they did not feel it at all. It was a violent storm from the west-southwest and the south-southwest. This is the first storm which they have experienced. They remained in this port until the following Tuesday. The people here called the Christians *Guacamal.*"

The white men which the Indians reported as roaming in the interior undoubtedly were members of the part of the Coronado expedition which was near the Colorado River.

We do not know exactly where Cabrillo first stepped ashore in San Diego Bay, though it is assumed his ships dropped anchor behind the protection of Ballast Point. The details of his stay have been lost with the journal of the expedition. The summary quoted above tells all that is known. Ballast Point was to be named by the Spanish La Punta de los Guijarros, or Cobblestone Point. It is a finger of land extending into the bay from the base of Point Loma, about a mile inside the tip. Covered with cobblestones, the spit of land curves slightly to form a safe, natural, deep-water anchorage from which the beach may be reached easily by launch.

The expedition sailed from San Diego Bay, or San Miguel as Cabrillo named it in honor of Saint Michael the Archangel, on the 7th day, Tuesday, October 3, and continued exploring and mapping the coast. While landing on San Miguel Island, or La Posesión as it was first named, Cabrillo fell on the rocky shore and broke an arm. Some members of the expedition were to argue later that it was a leg and that he fell while going ashore to help repel an Indian attack. Nevertheless, the expedition went on and got as far north as the general area above San Francisco Bay. With winter setting in, and battered by storms, they turned south in mid-November to seek a haven off the Channel Islands of Southern California. Cabrillo's life was running out; evidently gangrene had set in to complicate his injury.

Here, the journal takes up:

"Passing the Winter on the Island of La Posesión, on the 3rd of the month of January, 1543, Juan Rodríguez Cabrillo, captain of the said ships, departed from this life, as the result of a fall which he suffered on said island when they were there before, from which he broke an arm near the shoulder. He left as captain the chief pilot, who was one Bartolomé Ferrelo, a native of the Levant. At the time of his death he emphatically charged them not to leave off exploring as much as possible of all that coast. They named the island the Isle of Juan Rodríguez."

This island of San Miguel, where Cabrillo died, is about 23 miles from Point Conception, a barren, treeless, windswept mesa beset by some of the roughest currents of the California coast. Formerly there was a fresh water spring near Cuyler Harbor on the western shore, the nearest approach to a harbor. Cabrillo's grave is believed to be in this vicinity. Now there is only sand and grass, and the harsh winds that blow the year 'round have hidden all traces of the past.

The ships sailed north again, as far as Oregon. On the return voyage they became separated in a storm, and the *San Salvador* put into San Miguel on March 11 for six days, but they were re-united at Cedros Island and finally reached Navidad.

No northwest passage had been found, no short way to the Spice Islands discovered, and no gold or pearls from the fabled land of the Amazon brought back to enrich the viceroy. So nobody seemed to care very much about the seemingless endless land to the north, and Cabrillo's name began to slip into obscurity.

The news of his death off the coast of California was slow in reaching Santiago de Guatemala, but when it did a state funeral

SAN MIGUEL ISLAND, one of the Channel Islands of California, is the lonely spot where Cabrillo died on January 3, 1543. His grave has never been found.

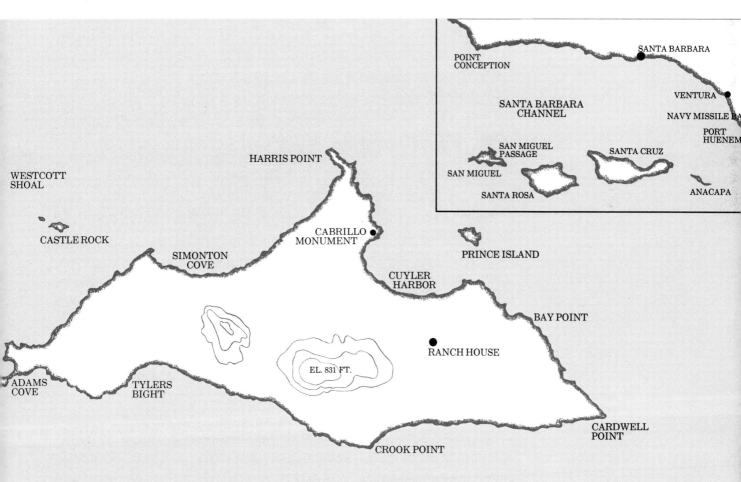

51

Ruins of Antigua in Guatemala.

The first page of the Información of 1560 in which Cabrillo's eldest son testified to the achievements of his famous father in an effort to regain estates illegally taken away from the family.

was conducted in tribute to the conquistador who had played such an important part in the pacification of Guatemala, as the Spaniards referred to the conquest, and in the founding of its capital city. Old documents record that even before his death, his enemies had begun parcelling out his property or seizing its revenues.

The forces of nature seemed to combine with the avarice of man to erase much of the life work of a courageous explorer and to keep his exploits from the recognition in history they deserved. In 1541, while he prepared the ships which eventually discovered California, disaster struck the city which he had helped found and in which he had been a leading citizen for most of twenty years.

Soon after dark, on the night of Sept. 10, the city was overwhelmed and buried under a tide of water and mud. The city had been built in a valley on the sloping arm of a great volcano which apparently had not been considered active, but over the centuries its giant crater had been filled with water, either an eruption or an earthquake shattered the basin, and a whole lake poured 10,000 feet down the mountain, picking up mud, trees, rocks and hurling them through the adobe structures of the capital city. Scores of persons died that night, including the widow of Pedro de Alvarado. Not much was left standing the next morning, and the site had to be abandoned. A new capital was erected at what is now known as Antigua. A small village, Ciudad Vieja, has been built on top of the mud that destroyed the original capital. Its large, faded blue-and-white cathedral stands on the site of the original church in which Cabrillo and his family worshipped. The church bears the date of 1531, the date of the original structure. The site of Cabrillo's home was lost forever.

Some time after Cabrillo's death, his widow remarried, and pressed her actions against those who had seized the family property. The suits were carried on by Cabrillo's son and then his grandson, over a period of many years. The widow first was required to establish proof of Cabrillo's death, the legitimacy of their marriage and that of their two minor sons, Juan and Diego. He evidently also had a daughter. Unfortunately, the questioning did not include the exact place of marriage in Spain, from which the facts on Cabrillo's nationality, place of birth, and age might have been obtained and the story of his life completed.

On Feb. 8, 1560, the son, Juan Rodríguez, submitted an *Información*, which, in answer to an official interrogation, cited 35 points pertaining to the services of his father in the conquest of Mexico and Guatemala and as admiral of a fleet of discovery; to it was attached the testimony of witnesses who had known Cabrillo or had participated in the events.

One of the witnesses was Bernal Díaz del Castillo, who testified for the Royal Audiencia of Guatemala as follows:

"It is about 23 or 24 years since I came to this city from Spain. I found living here then Juan de Aguilar, and have known him ever since. To the second question I answer that I have seen him as the husband of Beatriz de Ortega, the widow of Juan Rodríguez Cabrillo, now dead and who left children. I knew the latter in New Spain and I declare that he came with Narváez and served in the conquest and capture of the City of Mexico and vicinity. I saw him serve always with the diligence such conquests demand."

Old Antigua home of Cabrillo's friend, Bernal Díaz del Castillo.

Francisco de Vargas, who had been with Cabrillo on his expedition and witnessed his death, testified that:

"They discovered the island named 'Capitana' and, according to the latitude which the pilot calculated, they were very near the Moluccas and the spice country and in the neighborhood of China . . . If Cabrillo had not died he would have discovered the great country of spices and the Moluccas, which they were on their way to find, and perhaps would have gone even farther if there was promise of anything to discover, as he had that intention and the willingness to outdo all previous captains and discoverers and was provided with food for more than three years . . . The wife and children of Cabrillo were left in poverty. He had seen their needy condition."

The hearings principally involved the *encomiendas* of Tacuba and Jumaytepec, which had been seized by Francisco de la Cueva on the claim they had been promised to him before being granted to Cabrillo. The suits, begun by Cabrillo himself in 1542, dragged on until 1617.

At one point, the son, Juan Rodríguez Cabrillo, seems to have lost out altogether, for he was sentenced to "perpetual silence." This sentence apparently did not apply to the grandson, Jerónimo Cabrillo Aldana, who, in a petition to the Council of the Indies in 1617, again described his grandfather's services and asked for appropriate rewards for himself and his three children.

In the end, some measure of justice came to the descendants. A final decision awarded the family a stipulated revenue from the first *encomienda* in Guatemala which should become vacant. Down through the years that followed, the great-grandchildren and great-great-grandchildren reasserted their claims to the revenues of this *encomienda*, citing again their relation to the great conquistador and the important incidents of his life. These old manuscripts have come to light in the National Archives of Guatemala.

The Spanish kept much of the detail of their explorations secret, in fear of the English, Portuguese and Dutch, and in jealousy of each other. If Cabrillo's explorations were officially charted, the maps were kept secret; his actual journal or log has never been found. Sixty years after his death, Sebastián Vizcaíno followed Cabrillo's path up the coast, and, in disregard of the instructions given to him, renamed the places discovered and identified by Cabrillo. Thus Cabrillo's name and explorations virtually were erased from the records for 400 years.

An era was drawing to a close. The old conquistadores who had braved so much were disappearing from the scene. Alvarado, Cabrillo, Alarcón, Ulloa, Díaz, and many others, were dead — by the hazards and tragedies of adventure or in the endless struggles with the Indians. Cortés, who started it all, was back in Spain, almost forgotten but still trying to win the honors that meant so much to him.

There is an apocryphal story in Spain that Cortés, after waiting for years for a chance to see the king, finally managed to approach his carriage, and placing one foot on the step asked to be heard. The king demanded to know who he was. Cortés replied:

"I am the man who gave you more riches and kingdoms than have come down to you from all the kings of Spain."

He died on Dec. 2, 1547, bitter but certain in his own mind that history, if not his own age, would recognize his achievements and his greatness. A long time was to pass before the coast of California again would see the white sails of the "houses on the sea" which had disturbed the age-long existence of the Indians.

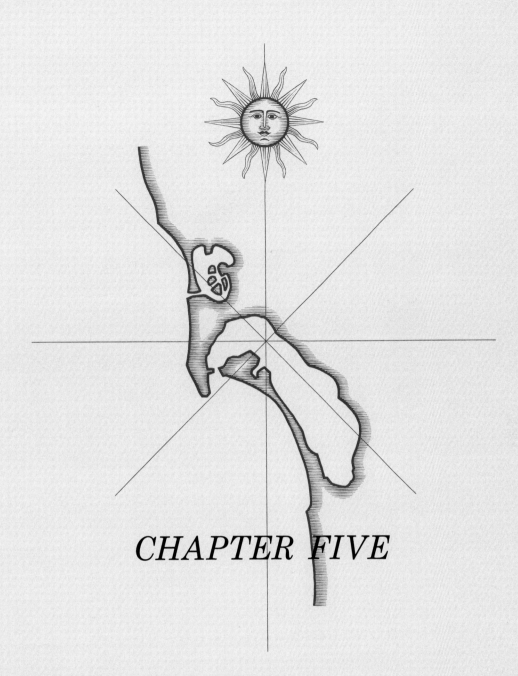

CHAPTER FIVE

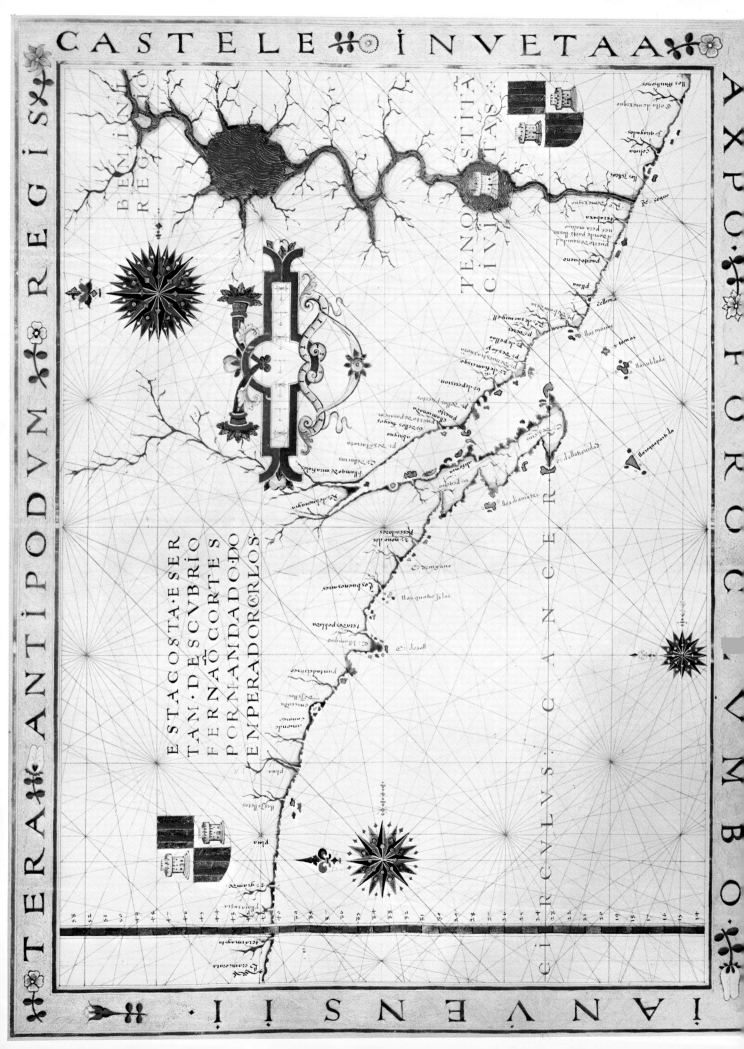

SEBASTIAN VIZCAINO

Preoccupied with consolidating her empire and extending her sway over the South Sea, and engaged in European wars financed with the wealth of the Americas, Spain for a time had little interest in further explorations along the upper Pacific Coast of North America. Interest was renewed after the appearance of English and Dutch pirates eager to pounce on Spanish treasure ships, and the resulting necessity of finding a port of refuge, as well as supply, for the fabulous Manila or China galleons, which were beginning their annual trips from Acapulco.

These events brought to the forefront one Sebastián Vizcaíno, who was to give San Diego the name it bears today.

Back in 1529, Charles V of Spain had promised Portugal to keep away from the Moluccas and to respect a boundary line well to the east of them and the Philippines, a line which in effect barred Spain from the Orient. But distances were great and memories short. In 1542, the same year that Cabrillo came to California, Ruy

THE DOURADO MAP OF 1570, showing the Pacific coast from San Blas, Mexico, to Cape Mendocino, California. The cartographer probably used information brought back by Cabrillo's pilot, Ferrelo. The map may well have been consulted by Sebastián Vizcaíno, when he charted the California coast in 1602-1603.

57

López de Villalobos crossed the Pacific to the Philippine Islands with part of the fleet built by Cabrillo in Guatemala, and with instructions to open a trade route to the riches of the East. He cruised among the Philippines and the Spice Islands, seeking information about their products, and finally lost his ships and men to mutiny and capture by the Portuguese. After two heart-breaking attempts to return to Mexico in a small ship, he died of malarial fever on Mindanao, frustrated and forgotten. Later, as a result of this incident, in part at least, Portugal and Spain agreed to a new boundary line which gave the Philippines to Spain, while Portugal retained the far richer Moluccas or Spice Islands to the south. Now it was possible for Spain to establish a trade route.

The first successful trip to Acapulco was made in 1559, on direct orders of Philip II of Spain. The outward-bound trip from Mexico was a relatively easy one; the galleons slipped a little south out of Acapulco and then, with the northeast trade winds filling the sails, slid across the South Pacific, passing the Marshall and Caroline Islands, avoiding the monsoons, and threading their way through the Philippines to Manila on the South China Sea. Coming back was a different matter and involved many more dangers. An expedition, of which Fr. Andrés de Urdaneta — a chaplain and an experienced navigator — was the most outstanding member, pioneered a practical route and crossed in 129 days, though at the cost of sixteen lives. This was a northern or "Great Circle" route, which was based in part on Cabrillo's observations of the prevailing winds in the northern Pacific. But it wasn't until after 1565 that Spanish galleons began regular annual sailings between Acapulco and Manila, maintaining a trade that lasted for 250 years.

Leaving Manila, the galleons had to clear the straits known as Paso de Acapulco, a difficult passage through the archipelago, and one which sometimes required a month of maneuvering before the open seas could be reached. There was always the threat of typhoons. The galleons picked up favorable winds to take them northeast toward Japan — which was to be avoided, as ships driven ashore were sure to be plundered — and then turned east along the 41st or 42nd parallel, and with the favorable westerlies made the long run across the Pacific. After a landfall in the vicinity of Cape Mendocino, they turned south along the California coast, and, with the wind at their stern, sailed downhill to Acapulco.

It was a grueling voyage, usually taking up to seven months as compared to three going out. By the time the galleons reached the California coast nearly all hands would be suffering from scurvy. A port for fresh supplies was considered vital if the crews, as well as the passengers, were to get to Acapulco alive.

Drawing of the explorer who gave San Diego the name it has today.

58

The establishment of the easterly and more difficult route was the work of many navigators. In 1584, the Manila galleon commander, Francisco de Gali, made the voyage and left a record of his observations. He claimed to have seen signs of the Northwest Passage, and casually mentioned passing Cape Mendocino, the first mention of it by name, though it had in all probability been sighted and named previously. Gali was ordered to further reconnoiter the California coast on his next voyage, but he died first and the work was delegated to Pedro de Unamuno, who left Manila on July 21, 1587, in a small ship, the Portuguese having seized his two larger ones. Unamuno arrived in Acapulco on November 22, after a fast trip, and has left a record of his observations of California's coast and natives.

In 1696 an Italian merchant named Gemelli made a trip in the Manila galleon and wrote about "the terrible tempests that happen there, one upon the back of another, and for the desperate

MAP SHOWING THE ROUTE OF THE MANILA GALLEONS during their round trip from Acapulco, Mexico, to Manila in the Philippines. This line of rich cargo ships ran for 250 years (1565-1815) and earned millions of pesos for investors.

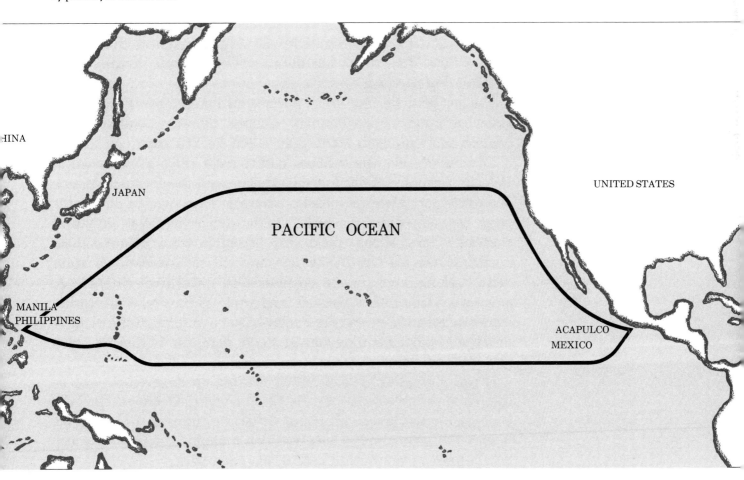

The galleon was primarily a war vessel, but the Manila galleons were built in the Philippines as cargo vessels.

Sir Francis Drake, pirate and explorer.

diseases that seize people, in seven or eight months, lying at sea, sometimes near the Line, sometimes cold, sometimes temperate and sometimes hot, which is enough to destroy a man of steel, much more flesh and blood . . ."

The galleons roughly followed the track of the sturdy junks of the Chinese, who surely knew of the winds and the currents and had been along the American coast upon occasion over the centuries, sometimes driven by storms and at other times for trade or exchange of native culture.

The situation in the Pacific was ready-made for pirates. The English and Dutch considered anything Spanish fair game, in view of Spain's attempts to conquer Western Europe, and they early began plundering her ships in the Caribbean. There were two prizes in the Pacific: the silver ships from Peru carrying the treasures of the Incas north to the Isthmus for shipment to Spain, and the Manila galleons with the luxuries of the East for the new landed aristocracy of Mexico.

The Manila galleons were wonderful ships. They were loaded with all the riches collected throughout Indonesia, China, Japan, India and even the Middle East, and traded through Manila. They creaked and heaved under the weight of tons of ivory, Persian rugs, silks of all kinds, jade and jewels, spices and exotic foods, china and porcelain, camphor and sandalwood, cottons and women's combs. The temptation offered by these lonely treasure ships of the Pacific was irresistible.

The first of the pirates to invade the South Sea was that dashing figure of romantic history, Sir Francis Drake — known to the Spanish as El Dragón, the dragon — who set out from England in 1577. He held religious services aboard the *Golden Hind* at noon, and harassed the Spanish by land and by sea along the South American and Mexican coasts. One Peruvian vessel, the *Cacafuego*, yielded more than eight million dollars in silver, gold and precious stones, as well as highly-prized Spanish charts of the Pacific. When his heavily laden ship, ballasted with silver bars, could take no more, Drake proceeded up into the Pacific, as far as or beyond the point reached by Ferrelo of the Cabrillo expedition, in his search for a short-cut passage back to the Atlantic and England, which, in common with all mariners of his day, he

MAP SHOWING SAN DIEGO BAY, made in Spain in 1603, from charts drawn by Vizcaíno's cartographer. At this time, Vizcaíno changed the name of the port from San Miguel (Cabrillo's name) to San Diego, in disregard of orders. This map was photographed in color in the Archives of the Indies in Seville, Spain.

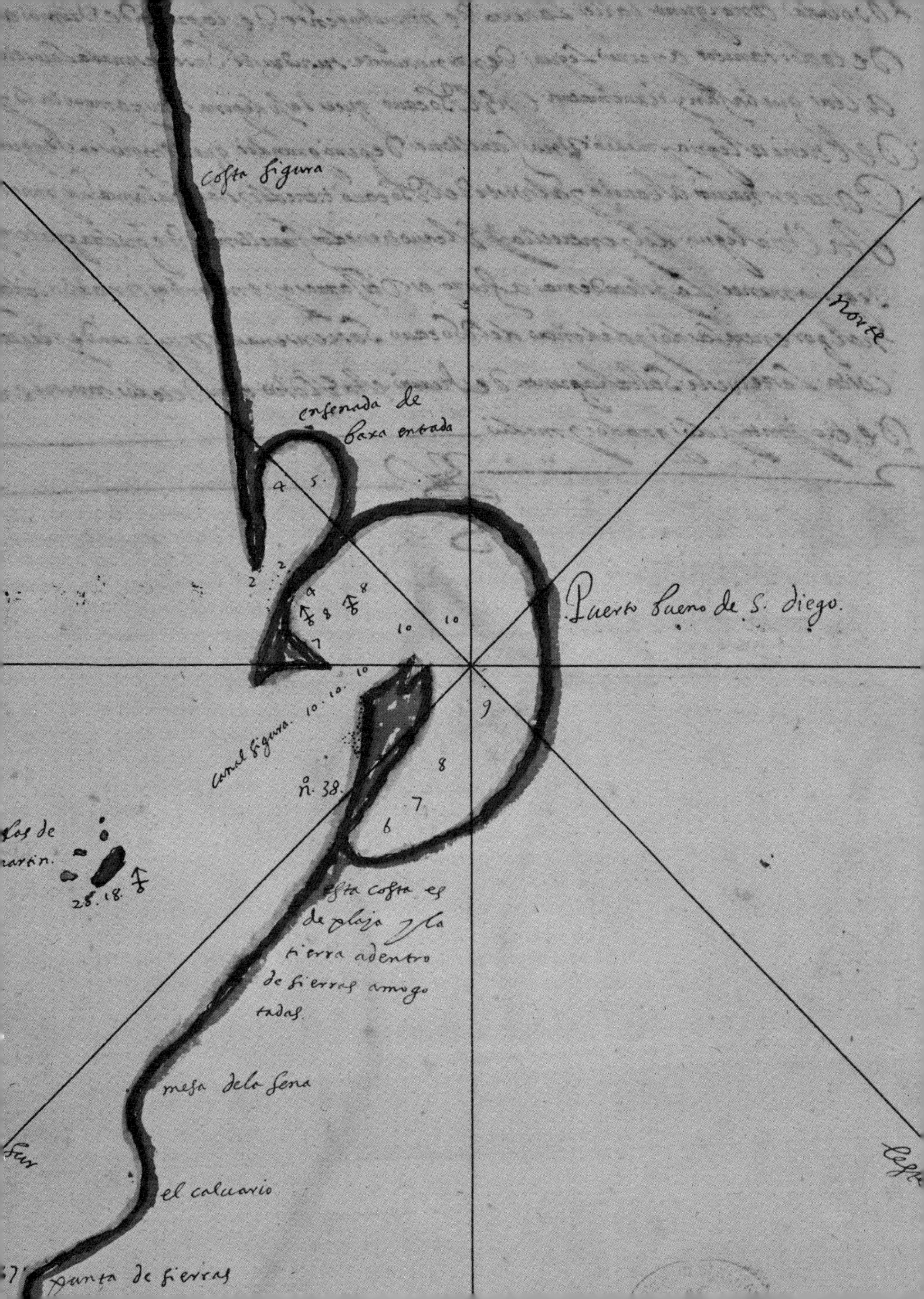

costa figura

ensenada de
baxa entrada

4 5.

2 2

a
8 8 8

7

10 10

Puerto bueno de S. diego.

canal figura. 10. 10. 10

9

n. 38.

8

7

6

las de
...arin.

25. 18.

esta costa es
de playa y la
tierra adentro
de sierras amogo
tadas.

Norte

Leste

mesa de la pena

Sur

el calvario

punta de sierras

believed existed. But finding nothing but endless sea and running into storms, he turned back toward the California coast and on June 17, 1579, came to what he described as a "conveynient harborough," which was Drake's Bay, some thirty miles north of San Francisco. Here he built a fort to store his loot while the leaky *Golden Hind* was careened and repaired. The Indians were awed by the handsome and richly garbed Drake, eagerly proclaimed him a chief, and happily, though uncomprehendingly, looked on while he formally took possession of all of California for England in the name of Queen Elizabeth. He named it New Albion.

For the Spanish, when they learned about it, this was adding insult to injury, and, alarmed at last, they began to think they had better find that Northwest Passage before somebody else did, and perhaps establish some settlements and ports of refuge along the little known coastal frontier. Captains of the Manila galleons were under instructions to keep an eye out for the passage as adventurers seeking the fabulous pearls of La Paz were to need help and protection.

Then into the Pacific came the evil and ruthless pirate, Thomas Cavendish. He not only looted but pillaged and slaughtered his way through Spanish settlements in the New World, and then, hearing a report about a Manila galleon headed toward Baja California, lay in wait in Bernabé Bay, some 20 miles east of Cape San Lucas, for the unwary galleon then on its return trip from the Philippines. This bay was to become a regular lair for buccaneers and was known to them as *Aguada Segura,* safe watering place, or *Puerto Seguro,* safe port.

The galleon *Santa Ana,* which had the misfortune to cross his path, had considerable significance for the history of California, as aboard her was Sebastián Vizcaíno, a Basque soldier of unusual talents. Vizcaíno fought with the Spanish armies in Flanders and then showed up in Mexico, where he developed an eye for business as well as intrigue. He invested heavily in merchandise in Manila and was taking it back aboard the *Santa Ana,* expecting to reap a tremendous profit, when Cavendish's pirate ships appeared from around the tip of Baja California, overhauled the *Santa Ana,* and shot her full of holes.

Vizcaíno and the other passengers and crew were put ashore near San José del Cabo, well inside the tip of the peninsula, with provisions and wood for huts, and the *Santa Ana* was looted and set afire. The burning hulk drifted ashore in a storm, and Vizcaíno was credited with organizing a boarding party which extinguished the flames and boarded up the leaky hull. After rigging up some kind of sails they managed to sail her across the Gulf to the mainland.

The pilot of the *Santa Ana*, who shared Vizcaíno's adventures, was one Sebastián Rodríguez Cermeño, who, after returning to service with the Manila galleons, may have been the second white man to see San Diego Bay. The need for a more complete knowledge of the northern coast, if only for possible ports of refuge, had been recognized and Cermeño was instructed that on his return trip with the galleon *San Agustín* he was to make surveys along the coast. In 1595 he put into Drake's Bay, which he named Bay of San Francisco. As the galleon was too large and unwieldy for coastal operations, he had aboard a knockdown launch, which they began to assemble. A sudden storm drove the *San Agustín* ashore, and it was wrecked, with the loss of several lives.

The survivors took to the launch, and Cermeño, ignoring the pleas of his crew, who, in view of the disaster, wanted to return home without delay, made surveys all the way down the coast, taking notes of points of prominence, and obtaining food and water from the Indians.

When they returned to Mexico, Cermeño was censured for the loss of the valuable galleon and received little credit for his surveys, it being decided he had merely noted points without adequately exploring bays and shores. However, as a result of the seizure of the *Santa Ana* and of Cermeño's experiences, a decision was reached that an official expedition, with relatively small vessels, should be sent to look into the possibilities of the northern coast.

At this point Vizcaíno entered the history of California. His actions with the *Santa Ana* had brought praise from the king of Spain as well as from the viceroy of Mexico. The fable of California's riches hadn't died out, and Vizcaíno obtained a license to fish for pearls off California, as well as authority for a private expedition to seize and settle lands to the north, at his own expense. At one point, Vizcaíno offered to put his seven-year-old son in pawn for 2000 pesos, and said the boy's mother would be willing to pay it off.

He had plenty of trouble getting under way, a change of viceroys complicating matters. And, as usual, Spain had a short memory. The new viceroy, Conde de Monterrey, didn't look with much enthusiasm on the Basque merchant as the person to establish settlements and colonies for Spain, and reported in a letter to the king that it "seemed to me, with regard to the person, his quality and capital are not sufficient in connection with an enterprise which may come to be of such vast importance." He felt that the king would be risking royal prestige if the expedition "were entrusted to a man as leader and chief whose position is obscure and who has not even in less degree, the resolution and capacity necessary for so great an enterprise."

Monterrey finally and with great reluctance let the Vizcaíno expedition proceed; events were to prove his fears somewhat justified.

"I have done all that lay in my power to show him honor while here and to clothe him with authority in view of the greater danger I foresee and fear on his account," the viceroy wrote, complaining of the overbold bearing of the soldiers Vizcaíno was taking with him and predicting that they would come to disobey orders, "all this giving rise to great disorder."

Vizcaíno sailed in March of 1596, with three ships, four Franciscan fathers to convert the natives, and a force of soldiers with some wives and horses. Fifty men deserted in mainland ports before the expedition reached La Paz, where Vizcaíno began setting up a colony on the same site abandoned so long before by Cortés. Vizcaíno gave it its present name of La Paz, because he had found the natives so peaceful, and then departed with two of the ships for explorations northward. Storms and troubles lay ahead. At one point, a soldier jabbed a native with his arquebus and started a fight in which a number of natives were killed, and Vizcaíno and his men had to flee in small boats. An Indian arrow struck one of the men on the nose, in the excitement the boat overturned, and 19 men were drowned.

Back in La Paz, the natives were getting unruly, despite the efforts of the padres whom they respected and liked; the undisciplined soldiers were molesting their women. Storms prevented any real attempts at pearl fishing. With supplies running low, everybody became discouraged, and Vizcaíno had to admit a temporary defeat. On October 28, two ships returned the would-be colonists to Mexico while Vizcaíno made a final effort to explore the Gulf. Storms and a broken rudder forced his small ship back, and he also returned to Mexico, where he found himself in bad repute. But, undaunted, he regaled the country anew with the old stories of pearls as plentiful as fish, of rich salt deposits, of natives begging for Christianity, wearing gold and silver ornaments and clad in cotton cloaks of luxury. This propaganda was all calculated to give him another chance, and it worked.

The viceroy went along with the scheme, writing to the king that the new expedition should be "for the purpose merely of ascertaining definitely what there is there, in order that complete assurance be had concerning the value of pearl fishing, and that greater light may be thrown on what related to the defense and security of these realms and the ships which make the China voyage."

He also wisely recommended that there be more control over the expedition, that the members be carefully screened to avoid repetition of the Indian troubles, that it be at least partly financed by the Crown, and its scope widened. This plan was approved by the

Council of the Indies, but the start was delayed by the appearance in the Pacific of the Dutch pirate Oliver Van Noort, who was reported lying in wait for the Manila galleon off Cape San Lucas. A Spanish force failed to run him down and the Vizcaíno expedition, which was to mean so much to San Diego and California, finally got under way. Vizcaíno had definite instructions as follows: he was to explore carefully from Cape San Lucas to Cape Mendocino, and could proceed as far north as Cape Blanco, but, if the coast line turned west, he was to proceed only 100 miles; he was not to survey large bays but merely to note their entrances and possibilities for shelter from storms; under no circumstances was he to change names of landmarks already on the maps; he was to establish no settlements; he was to keep out of trouble with the natives; and he was not to enter the Gulf going north, but perhaps could on the return trip.

He had four small ships: the flagship *San Diego*; the *Santo Tomás*; the launch *Tres Reyes*, and a small boat which apparently did not have a name. The *San Diego* was a ship of about 200 tons. There is no description of the *Santo Tomás* except that she was a Peruvian coasting vessel, old and unmaneuverable. The *San Diego* came from Guatemala and probably was of the caravel type, but by 1602 some or all of her masts could have been square-rigged. The *Tres Reyes* was a small frigate, built at Acapulco, with three masts and no deck — an open boat used for shallow waters but presumably very seaworthy. Aboard were a mapmaker, Gerónimo Martínez de Palacios, and three Carmelite friars, one of whom was Fr. Antonio de la Ascensión. Two reports were made on this expedition: the official journal, which bears the name of Vizcaíno, but was written by a member of his party; and a summary which Fr. Ascensión wrote in 1620 from the notes of his personal diary, and which contains graphic descriptions of the San Diego Bay area. As Vizcaíno proceeded up the coast, he renamed everything in sight in defiance of his instructions, and his names have survived to this day. His excuse was that since the Cabrillo observations were so inaccurate that he could not find the localities Cabrillo had mentioned, he had had to start all over again. Vizcaíno had an eye for history as well as for business.

Following the coast northward, the expedition noted the "many smokes," or fires, in the interior, as had Cabrillo and his men, and commented that there were so many of them that at night from afar they looked like a procession and in daytime the sky was overcast. The Indians burned vast open lands to drive game into areas where it could be hunted down and killed.

Approaching San Diego, Fr. Ascensión wrote that "they reached

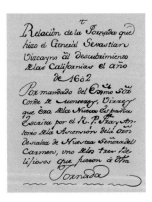

Title page of Father Antonio de la Ascensión's Account of the Voyage of Sebastián Vizcaíno.

some four small islands, two shaped like sugar loafs and the other two somewhat larger. These were named the Cuatro Coronados." Fr. Ascensión's report does not agree with Vizcaíno's, which records that they named them Islas de San Martín. Cabrillo called them the Desert Islands. But the name "Coronado" survives.

Vizcaíno's journal of the expedition reports on their arrival and stay in San Diego, in November, 1602, as follows:

"The next day, Sunday, the 10th of the month, we arrived at a port which must be the best to be found in all the South Sea, for, besides being protected on all sides and having good anchorage, it is in latitude $33\frac{1}{2}°$. It has very good wood and water, many fish of all kinds, many of which we caught with seine and hooks. On the land there is much game, such as rabbits, hares, deer, very large quail, royal ducks, thrushes, and many other birds.

"On the 12th of the said month, which was the day of the glorious San Diego, the general, admiral, religious, captains, ensigns, and almost all the men went ashore. A hut was built and mass was said in celebration of the feast of Señor San Diego. When it was over the general called a council to consider what was to be done in this port, in order to get through quickly. It was decided that the admiral, with the chief pilot, the pilots, the masters, calkers, and seamen should scour the ships, giving them a good cleaning, which they greatly needed, and that Captain Peguero, Ensign Alarcón, and Ensign Martín de Aguilar should each attend to getting water for his ship, while Ensign Juan Francisco, and Sergeant Miguel de Lagar, with the carpenters, should provide wood.

"When this had all been agreed upon, a hundred Indians appeared on a hill with bows and arrows and with many feathers on their heads, yelling noisily at us. The general ordered Ensign Juan Francisco to go to them with four arquebusiers, Father Fray Antonio following him in order to win their friendship. The ensign was instructed that if the Indians fled he should let them go, but if they waited he should regale them. The Indians waited, albeit with some fear. The ensigns and soldiers returned, and the general, his son, and the admiral went toward the Indians. The Indians seeing this, two men and two women came down from a hill. They having reached the general, and the Indian women weeping, he cajoled and embraced them, giving them some things. Reassuring the others by signs, they descended peacefully, whereupon they were given presents. The net was cast and fish were given them. Whereupon the Indians became more confident and went to their *rancherías* and we to our ships to attend to our affairs.

"Friday, the 15th of the month, the general went aboard the frigate, taking with him his son, Father Fray Antonio, the chief pilot, and fifteen arquebusiers, to go and take the soundings of a large bay which entered the land. He did not take the cosmographer with him, as he was ill and occupied with the papers of the voyage. That night, rowing with the flood tide, he got under way and at dawn he was six leagues within the bay, which he found to be the best, large enough for all kinds of vessels, more secure than at the anchorage, and better for careening the ships, for they could be placed high and dry during the flood tide and taken down at ebb tide, even if they were of a thousand tons.

"I do not place in this report the sailing directions, descriptions of the land, or soundings, because the cosmographer and pilots are keeping an itinerary in conformity with the art of navigation.

"In this bay the general, with his men, went ashore. After they had gone

San Diego de Alcalá, O.F.M., Saint Didacus, for whom San Diego was named in 1602.

66

more than three leagues along it a number of Indians appeared with their bows and arrows, and although signs of peace were made to them, they did not dare to approach, excepting a very old Indian woman who appeared to be more than one hundred and fifty years old and who approached weeping. The general cajoled her and gave her some beads and something to eat. This Indian woman, from extreme age, had wrinkles on her belly which looked like a blacksmith's bellows, and the navel protruded bigger than a gourd. Seeing this kind treatment the Indians came peaceably and took us to their *rancherías*, where they were gathering their crops and where they made their *paresos* of seeds like flax. They had pots in which they cooked their food, and the women were dressed in skins of animals. The general would not allow any soldier to enter their *rancherías;* and, it being already late, he returned to the frigate, many Indians accompanying him to the beach. Saturday night he reached the captain's ship, which was ready; wood, water, and fish were brought on board, and on Wednesday, the 20th of said month, we set sail. I do not state, lest I should be tiresome, how many times the Indians came to our camps with skins of martens and other things. Until the next day, when we set sail, they remained on the beach shouting. This port was given the name of San Diego."

It seems certain that Vizcaíno's ships first were anchored in the lee of Point Loma, behind Ballast Point, which appears prominently on the expedition's maps of the bay, but later were moved farther into the harbor for beaching and cleaning. Just where is not known. The narrative says they explored the bay for six leagues, or about 18 miles. Vizcaíno's latitude of 33° 30′ N. Latitude at San Diego was in error, as had been Cabrillo's calculation of 34° 20′ N. Latitude.

The diary of Fr. Ascensión gives us some additional information. The morning after their arrival, Fr. Ascensión and a party climbed to the crest of Point Loma, which they described as wooded, and to the north they saw "another good port." This was Mission Bay.

Fresh water evidently was obtained from springs in the general area of North Island, springs that existed into modern times. Fr. Ascensión reports:

Father Ascensión's Account of the Voyage of Sebastián Vizcaíno. This page describes how Vizcaíno sailed into a fine port on November 10th, 1602, and named it San Diego.

"Water was taken on the large sand bar in the middle of the bay. This was all surrounded by sea so that it appears to be a sand island. Some large holes like graves were dug, and when the tide was high the water which trickled into them was sweet and good, and when the tide ebbed it was brackish and bad (a secret of nature and the work of the hand of God).

"The country surrounding the port was very fertile and near the beach there are very fine meadows. The general and Father Antonio with other soldiers made a turn around all the *ensenada* and looked over the country. They were pleased to see its fertility and good character, but what gives them the greatest pleasure was the extensiveness, capacity and security of the port, its good depth and its many fish."

Fr. Ascensión reports finding a great quantity of sparkling golden pyrites: "I mean that they sparkle like spangles, a sure sign that there must be gold mines in the mountains." He thought the Indians knew something about silver, though they didn't have any.

On the sand-bar where water was found he saw a reddish material which he thought might be amber.

But most fascinating to him were the Indians and the paint they used on their bodies.

"The black paint, or rather blue paint, appeared to be silvered, and on being asked by signs of what it was made, they displayed some stones of metal of London blue from which they made it. They explained by signs that it was made from those stones by people inland who were bearded and wore clothes and ornaments like the Spaniards, pointing out some ornamental braid such as some of the Spanish wore on their jackets, and saying they were like those. They also pointed out some mulberry-colored velvet breeches well adorned with fringes which the general was wearing, and said that those people wore ornaments and clothes like our Spaniards, and that they looked like them and treated them similarly."

Fr. Ascensión wanted to do something about this.

"The people of whom the Indians told us might have been foreigners, Hollanders or English, who had made the voyage by the Strait of Anián and might be settled on the other coast of this island, facing the Mediterranean Sea of California. Since the realm is narrow, as has been said, it may be that the other sea is near that place; for the Indians offered to guide and take us to the place where they say the people are settled. If this is so, it is probable that they have large interests and profits there, since their voyage is so long and difficult. Still, it is true that by passing through the Strait of Anián and reaching their land by that latitude, their voyage is only half as long as that from the Port San Juan de Ulúa (Veracruz) to Spain. This will be clearly seen from evidence furnished by the globe. In this case it will be to His Majesty's interest to endeavor to assure himself of the fact: first, in order to know the route, and secondly, in order to expel from there such dangerous enemies, lest they contaminate the Indians with their sects and liberty of conscience, by which great harm to their souls will follow, whereby instructing them and leading them in the paths of the true law of God will be made very difficult."

His concern, however, apparently failed to alert the king. Who were the bearded strangers? Perhaps they were only members of the Spanish Oñate expedition which secretly had entered New Mexico, but probably we shall never know for sure.

When the expedition put out to sea and again headed north, the general sent Ensign Sebastián Melendes ahead with a frigate, "to examine a bay (Mission Bay) which was to windward some four leagues, and directed the pilot should sound it, map it, and find out what was there. He did so, and the next day ordered the return to the captain's ship. He reported to the general that he had entered the said bay, that it was a good port, although it had at its entrance a bar of little more than two fathoms depth, and that there was a very large grove at the estuary which extended into the land, and many Indians: and that he had not gone ashore. Thereupon we continued our voyage..."

The Diary of Sebastián Vizcaíno. This page describes how he left San Diego, sending Sebastián Meléndez ahead with a ship to survey False (Mission) Bay.

On Santa Catalina an Indian woman brought Vizcaíno two pieces of figured China silk, in fragments, "telling him that they had got them from people like ourselves, who had Negroes; that they had come on a ship which was driven by a strong wind to the coast and wrecked, and that it was farther on." Unfavorable winds prevented them from reaching the place on the coast where the Indians reported that the ship had been wrecked, and the expedition continued its voyage. Vizcaíno named Monterey Bay in honor of the viceroy and reported that it was a wonderful harbor of refuge, when actually it was only an open roadstead. This report was to cause a lot of trouble for later explorers who came by land and couldn't find Monterey Bay.

After getting as far north as Cape Blanco, and finding the coast bearing westward, he turned for home, according to instructions, and arriving in Mexico was complimented for his surveys. The journey was considered a success, despite the loss of more than forty men by accident and sickness.

Preparations were begun to occupy Monterey, and Vizcaíno was given command of a Manila galleon. But the arrival of a new viceroy again upset plans. The Marqués de Montesclaros countermanded the order making Vizcaíno a galleon commander and instead made him mayor of Tehuantepec. Later he accused Vizcaíno of trying to bribe him, and hanged the cartographer Martínez on a similar charge.

The King of Spain was somewhat displeased with all this, and insisted that Vizcaíno be given command of a galleon, that he resurvey Monterey on a return trip, and later establish a colony there. The viceroy, however, wasn't going to lose the argument entirely. He intrigued the King with some tales of mysterious islands of solid gold and silver somewhere off Japan, and as a result the planned settlement of California was abandoned.

Vizcaíno, however, bounced up as the viceroy's ambassador to Japan, with authority to look for the islands of gold and silver, which of course were never found, and to survey the Japanese coast for possible harbors of refuge for the Spanish galleons. He spent three years in and out of Japan, until 1614, and accomplished little except to antagonize the Japanese by his contempt for their royalty and customs, and to arouse their suspicions as to Spain's real intentions.

In those days Japan was a highly civilized, open country with large military forces and merchant fleets trading throughout the vast eastern Pacific. Dutch and Spanish traders and diplomats were followed by missionaries seeking to Christianize the Japanese. The activities of such men as Vizcaíno, and in particular the increasing arrival of missionaries, were in large measure responsible for a sudden and drastic decision which shut Japan off from the modern world. It remained, withdrawn and sullen, behind its own bamboo curtain until the arrival of Commodore Perry in 1853.

Vizcaíno died in Mexico in about 1628. The Manila galleon continued her lonely course across the Pacific, and, as it turned out, once in sight of the American mainland, all hands were too anxious to reach Acapulco and home to worry about stopping at Monterey or San Diego. So, as far as we know, no ship entered San Diego Bay for more than a century and a half. California, for all practical purposes, was all but forgotten, until the day came when Spain was confronted with a new threat — Russia.

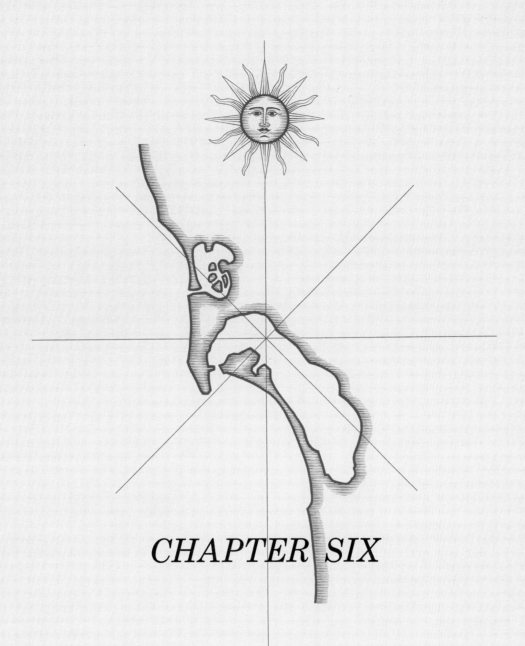

CHAPTER SIX

Sierra de S. Juan Gualberto

Los 3 Reyes

Rio Colorado

Marismas

Pantanos

S. Ignacio

S. Buenaventura

Aguaje o

S. Phelipe de IHS

Esta Costa esta de lineada se

S. Clara

SENO DE
CALIFORNIAS
Y su Costa Oriental
nuevamente descubierta, y registrada
Desde el Cabo de las Virgines
hasta su Termino
que es
EL RIO COLORADO
Por el
P. Fernando Consag
de la Comp de Iesus
Missionero
de Californias

PIMERIA

Aguaje o S. Firmin

Aguaje o S. Isabel

La Visitacion

B. de S. Luis Gonzaga

MAR DE

Caborca

S. Estanislao

S. Ju. y S. Pablo

Aguaje

I. del Angel de Guarda

CANAL DE BALLENA

Pagaju

Baya de los Angeles Agua

Los Remedios

Las Animas

ISLAS DE SALSIPUEDES

I. de S. Pedro

TEPOCA

Baya de S. Juan Bautista

I. de S. Augustin

SONORA

S. Raphael

I. de S. Estevan

S. Gabriel

I. de S. Lorenzo

Rio de Sonora

Mapas

Aguaje

PARTE SEPTEN. al

NACION

Aguaje o

S. Miguel

P. de Guaimas

Antiguos

COCHI

MI.

S. Juan

DE CALIFORNIAS

R. Hiaqui

S. Bernabe

La Trinidad

S. Carlos

Aguajes

S. Ana

C. de las Virgines

Volcanes de fuego descu.se bierra
Virgines año de 1746

Miss. de N.P.
S. Ignacio
Frontera del Norte

S. Agueda

I. de la Tortuga

MAR

DEL SUR

ESCALA
5   10   15
Leguas Españolas
5   10   15   20
Leguas Francesas

C. de S. Marcos

Petrus Mª Nascimben Soc. Iesu delineavit

33   33
32   32
31   31
30   30
29   29
28   28
27

PADRES LEAD THE WAY

In the more than a century and a half that passed between the visit to San Diego of Sebastián Vizcaíno and the arrival of Fr. Junípero Serra in 1769, only the missionaries kept alive the dream of settling California. The Roman Catholic Church came to New Spain with the conquerors, and, when the fever of discovery died away, it remained for the missionaries to push the frontier farther and farther north. For all that has been said against Spain and the cruelty of the conquest, the Crown had the most noble of intentions. New Spain would be a utopia in which new cities could be laid out and rise free of the walled confines and decay of the Old World, and where the Indians could be brought toward civilization as wards of the government. Of course, Spain had an eye to the practical side. There weren't enough Spaniards to colonize such vast territories, and Indian labor was necessary for the production of raw materials in the economy planned by Spain. And, incidentally, by keeping the Indians as wards or vassals of the Crown, the King hoped to prevent the rise of a new and always jealous feudal nobility like that which it had cost so much to destroy at home.

MAP MADE BY THE JESUIT FATHER FERNANDO CONSAG in 1746, proving California to be a peninsula. Consag ascended the Gulf of California to Montague Island in the mouth of the Colorado River.

The *encomienda* system, by which the conquistadores such as Cabrillo bound Indians to the land, was abolished. After 1549, trusteeships of land no longer included the right to Indian labor and, in 1561, the Royal Audiencia of Mexico heard the last cases of slaves to be set free. The Indians of New Spain were to form a society of peasants. They were to pay tribute; were not to wear Spanish clothes but their native costumes; were not to own or use horses and saddles, or bear arms; and though they had legal rights that could be exercised through special Indian courts, they were not to have any real political representation.

The Indians were to be forced to live in small towns built around a square, as most of them do to this day, and the square was to be dominated by the Church and the City Hall as symbols of religious and secular power. Their daily life was to be regulated by the tolling of the church bells and the orders of Spanish officials.

Noble intentions were not enough, as it proved, and the dream of a utopia slowly faded under the pressure of harsh realities and the decline of Spanish authority and prestige throughout the world. All that was accomplished was to destroy the fabric of Indian life. Thus Mexico developed along two lines: the small, poor isolated Indian communities; and the commercial establishments represented by the sprawling haciendas of landed proprietors who, for all practical purposes, became self-made nobles, aristocrats on horseback, commanding thousands of laborers and large private armies.

The Indians who went into their service, to exchange work for goods, were bound to the hacienda through debt as effectively as under the old *encomienda* system. The result was catastrophic. Between 1519 and 1650, the majority of the Indian populations of Southern Mexico and Central America were wiped out, largely by disease, which the natives had as little hope of resisting as they had of improving their way of living.

In all this immense tragedy, the Indian had only one thing to which he could cling — religion. The Catholic Church did try to bridge the overwhelming gap between the Old World and the New; the missionaries who were in the forefront of the settlement of New Spain were just as interested in the present as the hereafter. The Church has been criticized for the magnificent and costly cathedrals built over so much of Mexico, in view of the poverty and degradation of their subjects, but the spirit of the Renaissance in Europe prevailed: the more beautiful the church, the greater its glory to God — and the Church was all the Indian had.

In what Spain hoped to accomplish, the missionaries were to be the shock troops, the spearheads for the advance of civilization and Christianity, and from the first they concerned themselves with the conditions of the Indians. As a result of the Catholic Reformation in Europe, the missionary orders were spreading around the world. Men from many countries were leaving safe and often luxurious existences to don the robes of humility and to dedicate their lives to service and poverty.

The missionary work in the outer frontiers of New Spain was conducted primarily by the Franciscans, Jesuits and Dominicans,

MAP MADE BY HENRY BRIGGS IN 1625 showing California as an island. Despite the later findings of Fathers Kino, Salvatierra, Ugarte and Consag, whose expeditions proved it to be a peninsula, the Spanish government continued to map California this way for more than a hundred years.

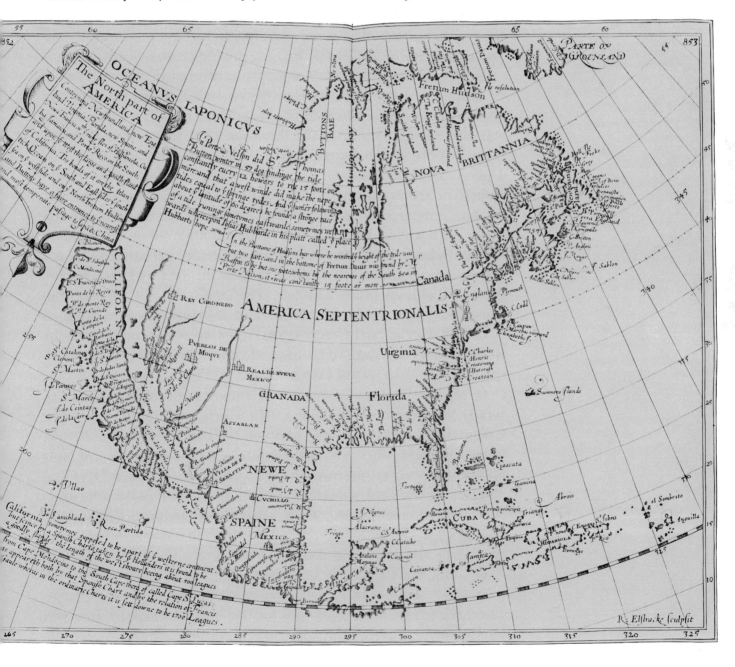

These three sketches show how the Padres differed in dress.

Dominican

Franciscan

though there also were the Carmelites and Augustinians. Fr. Ascensión, who accompanied Vizcaíno, was a Carmelite. They served as agents of both the Church and the State, and as explorers and diplomats. The Franciscans were the most important to California. The first group of them arrived in Mexico in 1522. A papal bull gave them extraordinary powers to administer sacraments, to give absolution for excommunication, to confirm, to consecrate churches, and to provide ministers. They were to have no interference.

The order was founded in Italy in the 13th Century by Francis of Assisi and was called the "Order of Little Brothers," or Friars Minor (O.F.M.), grey friars, or brown robes. They were recruited mostly from the humble classes and uncloistered mendicant labor, and gradually spread over all of Europe, Palestine, North Africa, Persia, India, and parts of eastern Russia.

The Dominicans or Black Friars, called the Order of Preachers of the Preaching Brothers, had a part in the last phases of mission building in Baja California. This order was founded in the 13th Century and, while dedicated to scholarship as well as to preaching, was similar in many ways to the Franciscan: each had begging friars, a second order for women, and a third for the laity.

While the Franciscans sought conversion by the practice of untutored simplicity and a life of absolute poverty, the Dominicans sought to overcome ignorance and error through the training of minds. While the Dominicans concerned themselves more with humanitarian legislation for protection of the Indians, the Franciscans, armed with nothing more than faith, good will and energy, proved to be more practical workers in the Christian vineyard, and won the respect and love of the Indians wherever they went.

The Jesuits were the settlers of Baja California and for a time were so powerful that they became victims of jealous rivals and royal intrigue, and were expelled from all of New Spain. The Society of Jesus — Jesuits or Black Robes — was founded by Ignatius Loyola, a Basque of noble birth, who lived from 1491 to 1556. Unlike the Franciscans and Dominicans, which were mendicant orders, the first followers were university men of some of the best families of Europe and were required to be well grounded in philosophy and theology. They were organized along military lines and, as Soldiers of God, carried on the Catholic fight against Protestantism over a great part of the world. More than a thousand of them were to be sacrificed or tortured.

The first Jesuits arrived in Mexico in 1572 and soon established a college in Mexico City. This was followed by five more in other cities. Eventually the Jesuits were to establish colleges exclusively for Indians.

Some shining figures of western history emerge from the mission period. From the very beginning the fathers championed the cause of the natives and protested against their inhumane treatment.

A Dominican, Antonio de Montesinos, who was in the first group of Dominicans to reach the Spanish possessions in the Caribbean in 1511, preached to the settlers in no uncertain terms: "You are in mortal sin . . . for the cruelty and tyranny you use in dealing with these innocent people . . . Tell me by what right or justice do you keep these Indians in such cruel or horrible servitude? . . . Are these not men? . . . Have they not rational souls? . . . Be certain that, in such a state as this, you can no more be saved than the Moors or Turks." Unfortunately, for this and other like outbursts, he was recalled to Spain. One of the colonists he denounced was Bartolomé de Las Casas, the historian, who later himself became a Dominican, and fought the cause of the Indians for the rest of his life, earning the title of "Protector of the Indians."

One of the earliest of the Franciscans in Mexico, Toribio de Motolinía, a friend of Hernán Cortés, wrote bitterly of the conditions he found at the mines in which the Indians were forced to work: "It is hardly possible to walk except over dead men or bones, and so great were the numbers of birds and buzzards that came to eat the bodies of the dead that they cast a huge shadow over the sun."

Jesuit

The first Franciscan Bishop of Mexico, Juan de Zumárraga, who arrived in 1528 at the age of sixty, was repelled by the abuses of the *encomienda* system and the distress rising from disputes among the leaders of New Spain. Fearing that he could not get a message openly to the Crown, he concealed a letter in a ball of wax which a sailor placed in a barrel of oil and later delivered to the king. The Bishop wrote to the King: "If it is true that your Majesty gave such a license, for the reverence of God, do very great penance for it.

The letter had the desired result: Nuño de Guzmán, president of the ruling Audiencia, was banished and a new Audiencia established.

All of the missionaries were not strong men, of course, and many of them at times were unnecessarily harsh in their handling of the Indians, but they were willing to die for their work and their belief, and many did. It is also true that the first missionaries to arrive in the New World, through religious zeal to wipe out heathen practices and false idols, destroyed much of the literature that could have told us more about the pre-conquest civilizations. When the mistakes were realized, the Church tried to atone for the wrongs of their "soldiers," and the friars were in the forefront of efforts to preserve the art, literature and folklore of the Indian nations.

In the march northward the Franciscans proceeded up north-eastern Mexico, and into New Mexico, Texas and Florida, while the Jesuits went up through northwestern Mexico, into Sinaloa, Sonora, Chihuahua, Arizona and finally into Baja California. Though partially financed from the royal treasury, the missions were expected to become self-sufficient and many of them actually became rich establishments through stock raising and farming. Ideally, after ten years, the missions were supposed to be turned over to the parish clergy and the mission lands distributed among the Indians. This was not practical, especially in the north, where the Indians were less developed and not readily adaptable to a settled life of cultivation and discipline. Besides, the land grabbers were always waiting to seize the best lands whenever the mission hold was relaxed. The missionaries at first hoped to teach the Indians in their own native tongues, but, as there was such a bewildering variety of languages and dialects, they resorted to the teaching of Spanish, and thus it became the spoken word of a vast area from Southern United States to the tip of South America.

The necessity of settling Baja California long had been recognized, as the finding of suitable ports of refuge for the Manila gal-

MAP SHOWING THE MISSION FIELDS of the Jesuits and the Franciscans in Mexico and Baja California between 1590 and 1769. The Cross and Flag together pushed ever northward into the U.S. Southwest.

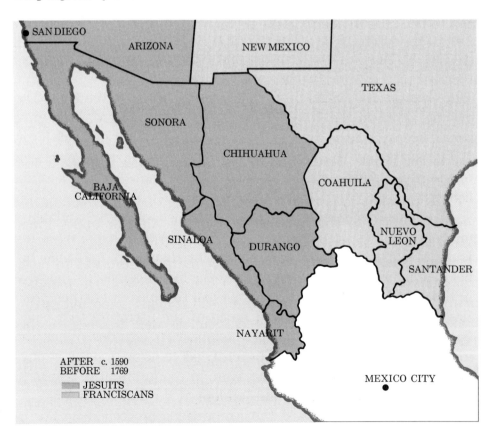

leons was a continuing problem. It was a forbidding challenge. The Jesuit Johann Jakob Baegert wrote that California "from top to bottom and from coast to coast is nothing else than a thorny heap of stones or a pathless, waterless rock arising between two oceans."

The Jesuits advancing up the Pacific Coast failed in their first attempts to colonize Baja California. Prominent in this effort was Fr. Eusebio Francisco Kino, one of the most brilliant and courageous figures of a harsh and forbidding frontier where only absolute faith in God and self could sustain men in their hardships. Fr. Kino, a distinguished mathematician, was born in Segno in the Italian Tyrol about 1645, and trained in Germany. Although he had hoped to go to the China mission field, he was assigned to Baja California along with Don Isidro Atondo y Antillón, with the official appointment of royal cosmographer. He was only to remain a year. After a colony was established at La Paz in 1683, the Spaniards had considerable trouble with the Indians and were forced to withdraw to Sinaloa. They tried again the same year with another settlement at San Bruno, just north of Loreto, among Indians of higher type, and met with some temporary success, Fr. Kino reporting he had baptized four hundred Indians. Ever restless and with an inquiring mind, Fr. Kino was the first white man to cross from the Gulf side to the Pacific. When he returned to San Bruno he found many persons ill, for the location was an unhealthy one. In 1685, a decision had to be made to abandon the mission.

His plea for continuing the founding of missions on Baja was rejected, and he sorrowfully wrote of the Indians they were leaving behind without the possibility of salvation:

"Everybody was very much grieved to see such gentle, affable, peaceful, extremely friendly, loving and lovable natives left deserted. Already many of them were begging for holy baptism . . . and they confessed that it was not easy to find another heathendom so free as these people from the ugliest vices, such as drunkenness and homicide."

Fr. Kino went to northern Sonora and southern Arizona, to the country known to the Spanish as Pimería Alta, or upper Pima Land, as an explorer, colonizer and rancher. In the next 24 years this lone, zealous, resourceful and imaginative figure was to push the frontier back to the Gila and Colorado Rivers. He founded many missions, personally baptized 5,000 Indians, imported cattle, horses and sheep, and distributed them, as well as seeds, to the Indians, and founded cattle ranches that exist to this day.

He made more than fifty long journeys by horseback, often with no soldiers and accompanied only by Indians, and in 1701 and 1702 made two explorations down the Colorado River, the second one to the head of the Gulf. His telescope provided the final proof that

Baja California was indeed a peninsula and not an island. His maps of Pimería Alta remained the basis for maps of the region until the 19th Century.

On one of the explorations that eventually proved Baja California to be a peninsula, Fr. Kino was accompanied by Fr. Juan María Salvatierra, born in Milan of a noble family, but half Spanish. Kino and Salvatierra started from the Mission Dolores on the Altar River in Sonora, crossing the heart of the desert to the shores of the Gulf, one of the toughest explorations in American history, in their continuing search for a land route to Baja California. Salvatierra describes it as follows:

FRS. KINO AND SALVATIERRA made lonely treks which took them near San Diego County years before Fr. Serra arrived.

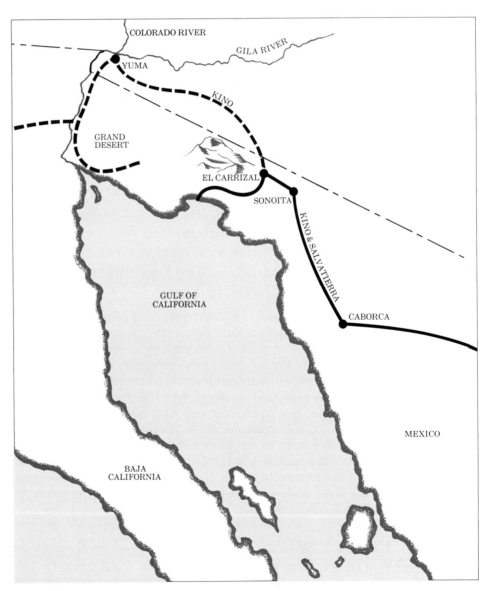

"It was horrible country, which looked more like ashes than earth, peppered with boulders and . . . entirely black, all of which formed figures, because the lava which flows down, solidifies, stops and assumes shapes . . . Indeed, I do not know that there can be any place which better represents the condition of the world in the general conflagration. And it caused still greater horror to discover that eight leagues from here stretches a great cordillera, a range of mountains, which seemed likewise of volcanic ash."

Arriving at the Gulf, they saw that there was no waterway leading west to separate California from the mainland. Salvatierra says: "We distinctly and with great clarity saw California and the cordilleras." They could see that the mountains on either side of the Gulf curved towards each other, but nearer hills closed the view to the northwest, so that their conclusion that the two masses joined could not be certain from where they stood, though it appeared that the land was closed. Turning back, they ascended a small peak, and Kino noted: "The sun set and from the peak we saw with all clarity the sea below, toward the south, and the place on the beach to which we descended. We saw the half arch of California whose end had been concealed from us by the spur of the mountains kept getting constantly closer together and joining the other hills and peaks of New Spain." The next year Kino confirmed these findings with his expedition to the Gila junction of the Colorado River and down the Colorado.

Fr. Kino died in 1711. He had gone to Mission Santa Magdalena, about twelve miles west of his headquarters at Mission Dolores, to participate in ceremonies dedicating a new chapel to his patron saint, San Francisco Xavier. During the ceremonies he was taken ill and died shortly. The bed on which he died was the same as he used in his lifetime: two calfskins for a mattress, two Indian blankets, and a pack saddle for a pillow. The final tribute to him was fitting though full of inaccuracies, and read:

"Padre Eusebius Franco. Kino — On the fifteenth of March, a little after midnight, Father Eusebio Francisco Kino died with great peace and edification in this house and pueblo of Santa Magdalena at the age of seventy years, having been for nearly twenty-four years missionary of Nuestra Señora de los Dolores, which he himself founded. He worked tirelessly in continuous peregrinations and in the reduction (conversion) of all this Pimería. He discovered the Casa Grande, the rivers Jila and Colorado, the Cocomaricopa and Suma nations, and the Quicimaspa of the Island. And now, resting in the Lord, he is buried in a coffin in this chapel of San Francisco Xavier on the Gospel side where fall the second and third choir seats. He was German by nationality and of the province to which Bavaria belongs, before he entered the Pimería having been missionary and cosmographer in California, in the time of Admiral Don Ysidro de Atonda."

(signed) Agustín de Campos

Fathers Kino and Salvatierra had never lagged in their intensive promotion of the plan to Christianize Baja California. In 1697 their labors were rewarded when the Spanish government turned over that missionary field to the Jesuits. Because of the long history of failure to colonize there, Spain expected the Jesuits to be self-supporting. With the aid of Father Juan de Ugarte, who became its treasurer, the famous Pious Fund was raised from the gifts of devoted Christians in both Old and New Spain. The fathers were given complete authority; even the military must bow to their decisions. Father Salvatierra was appointed superior, and arrived at Loreto in October, 1697, with three Christian Indians, a handful of soldiers and sailors, and the leader of the military, Captain Romero. Shortly Father Pícolo joined them. The march northward along the Pacific coast by friars and soldiers had begun.

A look at the map shows a chain of seventeen Jesuit missions, beginning near Cape San Lucas and stretching north almost to 30° N. Latitude. It was the achievement of seventy-two years. In the beginning the Jesuits' main purpose was to Christianize the Indians. Then the Spanish government asked them to locate suitable ports of refuge for the Manila galleon. Consequently the Jesuits were not only religious pioneers but explorers as well. They were to open the way to San Diego.

The mother mission at Loreto was founded in the first year and remained the capitol and base of the only presidio until 1736, when a second was established at La Paz, later to become the capital of the peninsula. To Loreto came the supply ships, battling the dreaded Gulf storms. Many of them were lost in the early years, and the Jesuits came close to starvation. But somehow they hung on. Loreto was their base, and its church their spiritual center. The original mission endured until 1830. The present church structure dates from the year 1752.

To Loreto came more and more fathers from many countries of Europe, as the work expanded west over the steep ridges of La Giganta. The usual procedure in founding a mission was to find a suitable site with water and pasturage. Trails had to be hacked out for mule trains bringing supplies from the mother mission. Then Indians were gathered and with their help buildings erected and crops sown. Ingenious systems of irrigation were devised. But on Baja California there was always a struggle with the elements. Drought caused springs to dry up and crops to wither; because of it many a mission had to move its site. Torrential rains brought

MAP SHOWING THE MISSIONS of Baja California established by the Jesuits, Franciscans and Dominicans between 1697 and 1834. Spain's plan was to have a chain from San José del Cabo all the way to San Francisco Bay.

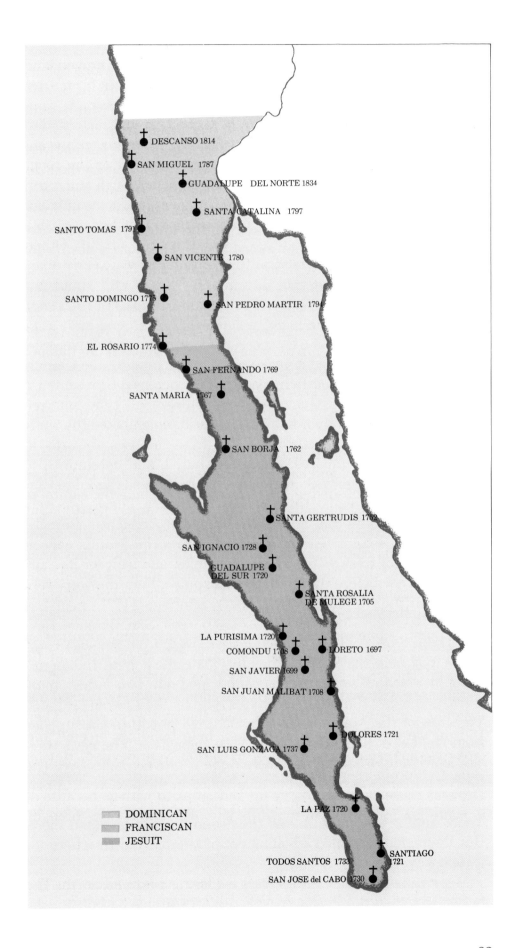

DESCANSO 1814

SAN MIGUEL 1787

GUADALUPE DEL NORTE 1834

SANTA CATALINA 1797

SANTO TOMAS 1791

SAN VICENTE 1780

SANTO DOMINGO 1775

SAN PEDRO MARTIR 1794

EL ROSARIO 1774

SAN FERNANDO 1769

SANTA MARIA 1767

SAN BORJA 1762

SANTA GERTRUDIS 1752

SAN IGNACIO 1728

GUADALUPE
DEL SUR 1720

SANTA ROSALIA
DE MULEGE 1705

LA PURISIMA 1720

COMONDU 1708

LORETO 1697

SAN JAVIER 1699

SAN JUAN MALIBAT 1708

DOLORES 1721

SAN LUIS GONZAGA 1737

LA PAZ 1720

DOMINICAN
FRANCISCAN
JESUIT

SANTIAGO
1721

TODOS SANTOS 1733

SAN JOSE del CABO 1730

83

floods to wash away the hard-won fields; winds of hurricane force knocked down the first crude buildings. If the weather proved kind, along came swarms of locusts to strip the green leaves from every growing thing. After years of struggle, however, the fathers could point proudly to orchards, patches of vegetables and melons, date palms — some of which still survive — fields of grain, sugar-cane and cotton, flocks of cattle, sheep, horses and mules. Over the rough trails the fathers went forth to found new missions north and south.

First they established a group of central missions, some of which were to endure the longest. This group included San Javier (1699), Mulegé (1705), Comondú (1708), and Purísima (1720). Others founded early proved impractical to maintain and were early abandoned. The churches at San Javier and Mulegé still stand and are used by worshippers today. The Cochimí Indians of the region still remembered Father Kino, welcomed the fathers, and, aside from a few malcontents who occasionally stirred up trouble, were on the whole friendly and amenable to the teachings of the Church.

The tribes in the southern part of the peninsula presented a tougher problem. The Guaicures were a degraded type, quarrelsome and revolting in their habits. They still remembered the white men who had tried to settle at La Paz, from the time of Cortés to Atondo. They remembered, distrusted, hated, and determined to resist. Their numbers were augmented by half-breeds and deserters from the crews of free-booting vessels and galleons. The Jesuits were determined to get a foot-hold here. They discovered San Bernabé Bay, the long-sought harbor of refuge, where the Manila galleon could put in for fresh water, green vegetables, and fruit for its scurvy-ridden crew before the last lap to Acapulco. Four missions were founded in the region: La Paz (1720), Santiago (1721) near Las Palmas Bay, San José del Cabo (1730) near San Bernabé Bay, and Todos Santos (1733), which later moved, from the east coast to the west near the Pacific. Then in 1735 came a great Indian uprising in which all four missions were wiped out, two fathers murdered, and many Christian neophytes slain by their pagan brothers. The crew of the Manila galleon, which had put in to get supplies from Del Cabo, narrowly escaped with their lives. The news traveled slowly and when military help came it proved ineffective. The La Paz mission was rebuilt, but abandoned in the next year. A permanent garrison was stationed there. Later Missions Santiago and Todos Santos were rebuilt, and the neophytes concentrated there. But the region remained a boiling pot of trouble and treachery for many years.

Meanwhile the missionaries were exploring west and north. The fathers searched the Pacific coast south for suitable harbors for the galleons, since after the uprising San Bernabé was no longer a safe haven, and fresh supplies were cut off by the destruction of Mission Del Cabo. Nothing was found suitable, for there was no water in that arid waste to supply a mission. Little by little the fathers pressed to the north. Father Taraval, a Jesuit from Lombardy, visited Sebastián Vizcaíno Bay, Scammon's Lagoon, and even paddled a canoe to Cedros Island.

Perhaps the greatest of the pioneers was Father Juan de Ugarte. Little is known of his early life, but he did become a professor of philosophy at the Jesuit Colegio Máximo in Mexico City, where he met Father Salvatierra. As treasurer of the Pious Fund, he helped raise funds for the first mission at Loreto and went there himself in 1701. Eventually he went to the mission of San Javier. It was a difficult and troublesome assignment, the Indians trying his patience and charity with their ridicule of his language mistakes and their reluctance to adapt themselves to a more domesticated life. But he won their confidence slowly and surely by administering punishment as he felt it necessary, and by his physical prowess. He was a giant of a man and awed the Indians by slaying mountain lions, an act forbidden them by their superstition.

A contemporary wrote of him:

"I cannot think of this without being moved to compassion and without recognizing the power of God, the sight of a gentleman, raised amid comforts of a wealthy home, now reduced to a tedious and burdensome life, and buried in obscure and remote solitude, a man of letters and highly esteemed in the schools and pulpits of Mexico, a man of sublime genius, voluntarily condemned to associate for thirty years with stupid savages."

Father Ugarte became the superior of the missions in Baja California after Father Salvatierra's death and founded the first school for Indian boys and girls, and a hospital for the sick. All this was in addition to the regular work of preaching, teaching, baptizing, and hearing confessions. His work really marked the beginning of the mission system to be developed so much in future years in both Lower and Upper California.

He found time to do much exploration in the Gulf, even building a ship with his own hands and the help of the natives. His boundless energy gave him no rest, although he was constantly suffering from an asthmatic cough and fever in the last years of his life. When urged to retire, he said: "Rest and quiet make me suffer more, and from this you may judge that travel and labor is for me a relief."

He literally wore himself out in his intense devotion to his missions, and was the actual savior of the whole Baja California project when the discouraged Father Salvatierra had wanted to give up. No man was ever more loved and respected by the Indians of Cali-

SAN DIEGO

MONTAGUE
ISLAND

CONSAG
ROCK

ALTAR
RIVER

ANGEL
DELA
GUARDA

SALSI PUEDES
ISLANDS

TIBURON
ISLAND

PUNTA
SAN CARLOS

SANTA
ROSALIE

MULEGE

LORETO

▬ ▬ CONSAG 1746
▬▬ UGARTE 1721

LA PAZ

Map showing the explorations of the Jesuit Fathers Ugarte and Consag, who sailed from Loreto and ascended the Gulf of California to the mouth of the Colorado River in 1721 and 1726 respectively.

fornia. He died at San Javier in 1730, at the age of 69.

In 1737, a mission was founded between the central and southern groups, San Luis Gonzagá, located in an oasis forty miles east of Magdalena Bay. To it as missionary came that remarkable Alsatian, Father Baegert, who labored there in solitude for fifteen years. He has left a valuable record of his life on Baja California in a book which is today still popular in translation, and which gives a careful description of the terrain and natives.

As the missionaries pushed their way north, they found great Indian populations to Christianize. Already the older foundations were in a decline because of the inroads of diseases brought by white men. Against them the Indian had little resistance. Mission Guadalupe del Sur was founded in 1720, northwest of Mulegé. Then came San Gertrudis in 1752, which was founded by a Croatian Jesuit, Father Consag, another ardent explorer. He too ascended the Gulf, confirming the findings of Alarcón, Fathers Kino and Ugarte that California was a peninsula and not an island. He left a map to prove it. On this expedition, to the north of the Salsipuedes Islands so dreaded by mariners, he discovered Los Angeles Bay, which he recommended as a base for supply ships from Sonora.

Father Consag ascended the Pacific coast by land beyond the point reached by Father Taraval. On a sandy point he found the shore littered with Chinese tiles and porcelain from a wrecked galleon. In his diary he speaks of the cold fog there as "the sad mantle of the sea."

Time was running out for the Jesuits, but still they moved north. In 1762, Mission San Francisco de Borja was founded with funds donated by a member of the famous Borja family. It was located twenty miles east of Sebastián Vizcaíno Bay. There labored the last great exploring Jesuit, Father Link. His most important expedition was to the northeast in an effort to find a mission site near the Colorado River, which was thought to be much closer than it actually was. The plan was to connect the Baja California missions with those of Sonora and Arizona. But Link's progress was barred by the Sierra San Pedro Mártir, and he had to turn back. It was he who discovered the site of San Fernando Mission, to be founded later by Father Serra. No Jesuit got farther north than Father Link.

Only one more mission was founded by the Jesuits: Santa María (1766), to the south of Sierra San Pedro Mártir. Originally situated at Calamajue, where ruins still remain, it was moved because of bad water to a point fifteen miles from San Luis Gonzaga Bay.

Suddenly came the end with the expulsion of the Jesuits, which was to set the stage for the settlement of San Diego and the opening of Alta California after all these years. The decision for the expulsion from New Spain was reached in secrecy. Sealed instructions opened by the Viceroy of Mexico on June 24, 1767, called for the arrest of all Jesuits in colleges and missions and for their removal to Veracruz for deportation. The job of expelling them from Baja was given to Don Gaspar de Portolá, the newly appointed governor of California.

The expulsion from Baja California was a time of deep sadness. The Jesuits — five Spaniards, five Germans, three Austrians, two Mexicans, and one Bohemian — gathered at Loreto for their departure on February 3, 1768. Behind them they left their life work and twenty of their fellow Jesuits who had died and been buried in the hard land.

Father Baegert, who described Baja California so grimly, wrote that at San Javier, on the last journey to Loreto,

> "After we had celebrated High Mass on the Day of the Purification of St. Mary, such general crying and pitiful lamenting arose among all the natives present that I, too, was moved to tears and could not restrain myself from weeping all the way to Loreto. Even now, while I am writing this, tears enter my eyes."

As the Fathers were carried to the waiting ship by Indians chanting the Litany of Loreto, even Portolá wept.

The Jesuits were also expelled by Portugal and her colonies in 1759, and by France in 1764. The Society of Jesus was dissolved in 1773 and restored in 1814. While there was great opposition to its members, no open accusations were made, and no trials held. Many resented the name of their society and its appropriation of the name of Jesus, the individualism and independence of its members, who, they claimed, meddled in politics and concealed vast wealth in the distant Baja California missions. Obviously their critics had never visited that barren land, which boasted but one small mine at Santa Ana in the south, with very little take. The Jesuit fathers had toiled for seventy-two years to convert ignorant natives, battling against heat, disease, discouragement, and loneliness. Any treasure they had was of heaven, not earth.

Today little physical evidence of their work remains: a few orchards, a few stone churches, and widely scattered ruins.

The mission fields of Sonora, Arizona, and Baja California were to be turned over to the Franciscans. In 1768, they took over fourteen Jesuit missions in Baja California, of which they were to transfer all but one to the Dominicans in 1774. Later the Dominicans were to extend the Baja California mission chain to La Frontera, the territory north of San Fernando. They founded seven missions between 1774 and 1797, and two more in the 19th Century. This chain stretched to within fifty-five miles of San Diego. All but

Map showing the Jesuit explorations in Baja California in the 18th Century.

two were near the coast on the best route to San Diego, which had been laid out by the Franciscans, and was known as the Pacific Trail.

Each of the Dominican missions lasted roughly for fifty years, unless first destroyed by the natives. Their importance diminished as the number of natives dwindled under the impact of disease and a changed way of life. By 1830 the old Jesuit missions were discontinued by decree, until only San Fernando and six to the north were in operation. The last padre in La Frontera missions quit in 1849, after which time all mission sites were sold or granted to individuals.

But at the time of the expulsion of the Jesuits, the missions were the only signs of civilization in an inhospitable land. The Franciscans from San Fernando College in Mexico City, sent to take them over, were to carry out a plan still unrevealed to them but already set in motion: to establish the first missions in Alta California at San Diego and Monterey. Father Junípero Serra was selected as their leader.

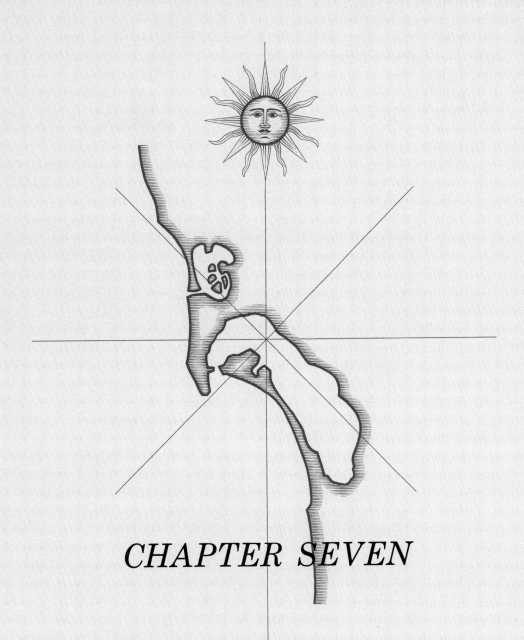

CHAPTER SEVEN

FRAY JUNIPERO SERRA

Four decades of prayer and service prepared Fr. Junípero Serra for the historic tasks that were yet to lie ahead. He was born on November 24, 1713, in Petra, a small inland village on the island of Mallorca, the largest of the Spanish Balearic Islands in the Mediterranean. Life there today has changed little from what it was in Fr. Serra's time. It has a soft climate, a lush greenness, with fishing villages, vineyards, and fruit orchards. The people, who still wear their distinctive costumes, are deeply religious, and there are many beautiful old churches.

His parents were humble and devout farmers; the whitewashed stone house in which he was born has been preserved and stands in what is now known as Calle Junípero Serra. As in any village of the old world, the cobbled street is hardly wide enough for an automobile. There is a bedroom on the main floor known as the borning room, though as a boy Fr. Serra slept in a cubbyhole. As among peasant people everywhere, the animals of the farm lived near him in close relationship. The farmer's day was from dawn to dusk; after

FATHER FRAY JUNIPERO SERRA, O.F.M., the founder of nine of the missions of Upper California, of which San Diego was the first. A native of Mallorca, he traveled thousands of miles to bring the Gospel to the Indians of the New World.

dark the principal light was from an open fireplace in which the family meals were prepared in pots hung from hooks.

Fr. Serra was baptized in the parish on the day of his birth, named Miquel Joseph, and confirmed when he was one and a half years old. As a little boy he was encouraged by his parents to visit the Franciscan church and the Friary of San Bernardine. There at the boys' school he studied Latin and came under the influence of the friars, and there he developed the desire to become a Franciscan himself. At the age of sixteen he was taken by his parents to Palma to study for entrance to the priesthood. When he applied for the novitiate, he was rejected because of his youthful appearance — he had always been undersized and apparently often ill in early childhood. But when his actual age was finally learned, he was accepted and received a habit on September 14, 1730, at the age of 16 years and 9 months.

He himself later wrote that "in the novitiate, I was almost always ill and so small of stature I was unable to reach the lectern, nor could I help my fellow novices in the necessary chores of the novitiate." But he was undaunted.

Many years afterward, he remarked rather wistfully: "However, with my profession I gained health and strength and grew to medium size." But when he was in Mexico in the Sierra Gorda, it was noticed that he had to insert his mantle between his shoulder and the large beam — which he was helping a group of Indians to carry — to make himself taller. In 1943 at the Carmel Mission in California, Fr.

THE EXTERIOR AND INTERIOR of the birthplace of Fr. Junípero Serra in the little town of Petra, on the Spanish island of Mallorca. A monument marks the building and the narrow cobblestone street is named in his memory.

Serra's remains were exhumed and measured by two anthropologists, who found him to have been 5 feet, 2 or 3 inches in height.

After the novitiate came the ceremony of the profession, when the provincial sat before the kneeling novices and queried: " 'My sons and most beloved brothers, what do you ask?' They answered in unison: 'I desire to profess the Rule of Our Most Beloved Father Francis, confirmed by the law of Pope Honorius III, by living in obedience without property and in chastity, in order to serve God better and to save my soul.' " Each novice then became a Franciscan for life. Fr. Serra took the name of Junípero after Brother Junípero, one of the lay brothers of Saint Francis, sometimes known as "The Jester of the Lord." This man was simple and unassuming; Serra longed to be his equal in humility.

Fr. Serra was now living at the friary of San Francisco, studying philosophy and theology at the Lullian University at Palma, which was run by the Franciscans and called "The Pontifical, Imperial, Royal and Literary University of Mallorca." We know that he was ordained by February of 1739, and taught philosophy at San Francisco from 1740 to 1743. In his class were Juan Crespí and Francisco Palóu, who had known each other since early boyhood days, and were destined to go with Fr. Serra to far-off California. It was Fr. Palóu who was to write the life of the leader he so admired.

According to Fr. Palóu's history, Fr. Serra received the degree of Doctor of Sacred Theology in 1742 and was listed in university records as Dr. Junípero or Dr. Serra. He was the holder of the chair of Prince of the Subtle Master from 1744 to 1749, when he was selected to preach the sermon at the most solemn of the university feasts, the Feast of Blessed Raymond Lull, in honor of that great lay Franciscan, the patron saint of Mallorca, who was stoned to death trying to convert Moslems in North Africa. Of that sermon one of the professors said, "This sermon is worthy of being printed in letters of gold."

Already an honored and respected teacher, student, and librarian of the monastery, he suddenly felt a call to leave his career behind him and to go, as had so many others before him, to teach the heathen and recapture the fervor felt during his novitiate. For a long time he kept his real feelings to himself — though rumors circulated that one of the fathers desired to enter the mission field — and he prayed that a companion to go with him would be forthcoming. It was at this time, apparently, that he became intimate with his former students, Frs. Crespí and Palóu, and Rafael Verger. Fr. Palóu says the same feeling arose in him at about the same time.

"I did not want to decide the matter without first consulting my beloved father, master and lecturer, Fray Junípero Serra. One day when he came to my cell, and when I was alone, I seized the occasion and unburdened the feeling of my heart, asking him to give me his opinion. When he learned of my intention, he began to shed tears, not of affliction as I first thought, but of joy. Then he said to me: 'I am the one who intends to make this long journey and I have been sorrowful because I would have no companion for so long a journey, but I would not on that account turn back from my purpose . . . and just now I resolved to speak to you and invite you to go along on the journey.' "

Fr. Serra then wrote to the administrator for Franciscan affairs in the Indies for permission to go to America. The request was refused, as the quotas from their jurisdiction already had been filled, but it was suggested that they join one of the colleges in Spain, and as members of that college go to the Indies. Fortunately, of 33 Franciscans who had been chosen for the College of San Fernando, five had reconsidered their step for fear of the sea. As a result, there was an opening for both Fr. Serra and Fr. Palóu.

After preaching a last sermon from the parish church in Petra, where he had been baptized, Fr. Serra began his farewells, though without disclosing to his aged parents where he was going. He begged forgiveness of the friars, received the blessing of the superior, and was so touched that his speech failed him and he could hardly utter a word. He went about kissing the feet of all the friars, and with Fr. Palóu immediately went to the wharf and embarked on an English packet boat for Málaga.

Apparently Fr. Serra had some difficulties on the boat as the captain, an English Protestant, engaged him in theological arguments and threatened to throw the two friars overboard. According to Fr. Palóu, the captain at one point held a knife at Fr. Serra's throat. From Málaga they went to Cádiz where they were joined by Frs. Crespí, Verger and Vicens and sailed from there in August. On board the overcrowded boat were 21 Franciscans and 7 Dominicans. It was a hard voyage across the Atlantic, and 99 days before they reached Veracruz. Fr. Palóu wrote that Fr. Serra constantly wore suspended from a chain around his neck a crucifix a Spanish foot in length. Apparently he never took it off during the rest of his life, even while sleeping.

The date of arrival at Veracruz was December 6, 1749. Fr. Serra was now 36 years old, and was to serve in Mexico nineteen years, from 1750 to 1768.

Old Spanish immigration records of the time describe him as swarthy, of medium height, with black eyes and hair. The weakness of his childhood must have long since disappeared, because he engaged with deep fervor in the self-inflicted physical penances that were so common in those days. He endured chest pains all his life as a result of striking himself with stones at the end of his sermons, putting a burning torch to his chest, or scourging himself until the blood ran. He kept long vigils with very little sleep. He never complained of things that came his way and seemed to invite suffering. He was very abstentious, living on herbs, fish, fruit and tortillas, disliking meat but fond of drinking chocolate.

The government had the responsibility of transporting the Franciscan fathers from Veracruz, 270 miles to Mexico City, on mule or horseback, over the same route used by the conquistadores. Because the fathers were weak from their voyage across the sea, the prohibition against riding was not applicable in such conditions. But Fr. Serra received permission to walk with one companion and, though this was not the rainy season, they ran into rains. It was on this long walk that Serra's feet began to swell with fatigue and mosquito bites, and he received the leg affliction that remained with him to the last day of his life.

At San Fernando College in Mexico City, he was assigned to the directorship of the Novice Master. Delighted, he asked, but was denied, the right to be considered a novice again and to live in a small cell. He was eager then to get into the field, and after five months was allowed to leave for the missions in the Sierra Gorda, several hundred miles north of Mexico City, with Fr. Palóu as his companion. It is believed that Fr. Crespí probably went with them. Fr. Serra walked the long route to Jalpan (or Xalpan) despite the fact that his foot was giving him trouble again.

Eventually Fr. Serra was made President of five Sierra Gorda missions. He built the Church of Santiago de Jalpan, which is still in use, and supervised the founding of the four other churches.

He lived the simple life of a dedicated servant of God, ministering to the Indians, and learning their language in order to preach to them in their native tongue and to teach them to act out religious dramas. He helped improve their agriculture and stock farming. Under his guidance the missions became so firmly established that when they were handed over to the secular clergy in 1770, they were considered models of excellence.

After he had been in that region for eight years, leaving only twice to go to Mexico City, he was recalled to San Fernando in 1758, and chosen to go to the San Sabá River missions in Texas, which had been opened in 1756. Two of the missionaries had been martyred by Apaches, and Fr. Serra, willing to accept martyrdom like most of the friars, was eager to go, but again he was to be denied his wish as the government said that no more missionaries would be sent until the region had been pacified.

Fr. Serra remained at San Fernando for ten more years, available at all times to be sent to any part of New Spain. An episode that occurred while he was preaching at San Fernando and described by Fr. Palóu indicates the method of preaching by Fr. Serra and others of his time.

"During one of his sermons, in imitation of Saint Francis Solanus, to whom he was devoted, he took out a chain and after lowering his habit so as to uncover his back, having exhorted his hearers to penance, he began to scourge himself so violently that the entire congregation broke into tears. Thereupon, a man from the congregation arose and hurriedly went to the pulpit, took the chain from the penitential father, descended from the pulpit and went and stood in the highest part of the sanctuary. Imitating the venerable preacher, he uncovered himself to the waist and began to perform public penance . . . So violent and merciless were the strokes that, before the whole congregation, he fell to the floor, they judging him dead. After he received the last Sacraments where he fell, he died."

It was customary when the natives resisted the friars' appeals, that the missionaries were allowed to scourge themselves in an effort to break hard hearts, though they were cautioned to be extremely prudent to avoid too dramatic methods, and warned that the temperament and psychology of the people, the conditions of the moment, environment and time, all had to be kept in mind in the choice of the means used to bring about repentance.

Fr. Serra's missionary activity during these years was mostly in south and central Mexico, in what is modern Oaxaca, Morelia, Puebla, and Guadalajara; the region east of Sierra Gorda; and in the province of Mesquital, part of Mazatlán. The work was very exhausting, and the only rest he had was during the time required to go from one town to another or the return to the college after a mission. One time he was poisoned, someone putting rattlesnake venom in the chalice. He refused an antidote but recovered just the same.

Just how much Fr. Serra walked instead of riding is not known, but, as he was an inspired missionary with a sensitive conscience, he probably walked as much as his sore leg would allow. Whatever the method, the travels were long, difficult and painful.

In all this he never lost his humility. He continually strove to encourage his helpers in their troubles and loneliness, was full of energy and drive, and though impatient with routine, took the time to learn to sew and to cut out shirts, pants and blouses for the Indians so that he could instruct them to do things for themselves.

Fr. Serra was away from Mexico City when he was selected as president or superior of the Baja Missions, but when recalled he accepted, and with fifteen others said farewell to the College of San Fernando. When he arrived at Loreto on April 1, 1768, he was fifty-five years of age. What was the situation faced by Spain in which he was to play such an important part?

In this period the glory of the Spanish empire was fading fast. The spirit of conquest and adventure was almost dead. The long struggle of Spain, England and France for eastern North America, which saw five European wars, largely was over. Westward, Spain had managed to save Texas, and she occupied half of Louisiana as a buffer to hold back the English, and later the Americans; but Alta California was becoming a new scene of international struggle. On the east coast great waves of migrations of English, German, Swiss, Scotch and Irish had given the British colonies a population of more than a million and a half, and they were beginning to get restless and talk of independence. The Spanish colonies in most of the New World were sinking into stagnation, the missionary zeal had abated somewhat, the mystery of a northern Atlantic-Pacific passage had lost its allure, and no new fleets had been fitted out and sent up the coast for more than a century and a half. The fear that some day the English might appear from the northeast to seize California and harass the entire Pacific coast were not strong enough to arouse the Spanish from their apathy. However, Spain suddenly was to experience a partial awakening of the old fervor. This was brought about by the threat of Russia.

The Russian threat was not a new one. The explorations of the Russians along the Alaskan coast from 1741 to 1765 were fairly well known to the Spanish. The Russians for many years had coasted along the shores of the Sea of Okhotsk, until Peter I became fired with a desire to know what was beyond the sea and whether Asia and America were connected, or separated by water. It wasn't until after his death, however, that on February 5, 1725, Capt. Vitus Bering left on the first of two expeditions sponsored by Catherine I. By the end of five years he had located and charted the eastern Siberian shore, located and named St. Lawrence Island and the Diomede Islands in the Bering Strait between Siberia and Alaska, and entered the Arctic Ocean, establishing the fact that Asia and America were separate continents. After that, he sailed to Alaska and discovered the Aleutian Islands. While the expedition ended in tragedy and Bering was killed, the sea otter skins brought back by the survivors started a rush to the Aleutian Islands.

The Russians were to develop a profitable trade in furs, mostly with China. In the reign of Catherine II, 1729 to 1796, the first permanent Russian settlement in Alaska was established on Kodiak Island, and Sitka was founded as the capital in 1799. Eventually, the great Russian fur monopoly was to be ruled by Aleksandre Baranov, who gradually extended it down the coast and founded a settlement at Fort Ross in Alta California in 1812.

Long before the Russians had gone as far south as the region of

Where the Russians crossed the Bering Sea.

San Francisco, the danger was beginning to be recognized by Spain, and on top of that more ships of Great Britain and the American colonies were venturing into the North Pacific.

In the more than 160 years that had passed since Sebastián Vizcaíno mapped the California coast, Spain, as we have seen, had failed to heed the pleadings of the missionaries to colonize Alta California, and had failed to possess and use any of the California ports for the relief of the Manila Galleons, though always intending to do so at some future date. Nothing was done until the reign of Carlos III, who, at last, was aroused to some kind of belated action.

The official record or *diario* of the expedition ordered to colonize California reads: "The High Government of Spain being informed of the repeated attempts of a foreign nation upon the northern coasts of California with aims by no means favorable to the Monarchy and its interests, the King gave orders to the Marqués de Croix, his Viceroy and Captain General in Nueva España, that he should take effective measures to guard that part of his dominions from all invasion and insult."

Spain, well aware of her neglect and failures, was looking back now. In some measure the recognition and honor which Hernán Cortés had so sought in life was beginning to come to him in death. The plan for the establishment of a government for Baja California and parts of northern Mexico recalled that "if since the glorious conquests which the great Hernán Cortés made . . . effort had been made by his successors . . . to carry out the lofty designs of that hero, the light of the Gospel and the supremacy of the August Kings of Spain would have reached even to the farthest limits, not yet known, of this immense continent. But as the spirit of activity and of conquest was extinguished with the life of that inimitable man, with his death came to an end the rapid advances which he made in this New World . . ."

José de Gálvez, the Spanish inspector general already in Mexico to inspect and reform the administration of New Spain, was given the job of planning an expedition to occupy and hold Monterey, which was known through Vizcaíno's report; San Diego was to be an intermediate base between it and Loreto. A combination of soldiers and settlers was to hold the country, with missionaries to convert the Indians.

Gálvez was to be assisted by Don Gaspar de Portolá, Capt. Fernando Rivera y Moncada, commander of the leatherjackets at Loreto, and Fathers Serra and Palóu. The instructions were clear and explicit. Portolá was to be titular head of the expedition. Fr. Serra was to head the missionaries. Lt. Pedro Fages was to be chief of the military expedition going by sea and was to retain command

Title page of the contemporary copy made by Figueroa of the Noticias or Historical Memoirs of New California by Father Francisco Palóu.

of the soldiers on land until the arrival of Portolá. The ships *San Carlos* and *San Antonio* were to take the supplies, 25 Catalonian soldiers who had embarked from Cádiz, Spain, and part of the colonists by sea to San Diego. Portolá and Rivera were to lead a land expedition in two sections. A third ship was to follow with additional supplies. Saint Joseph was designated the official patron saint of the expedition. Fr. Serra would go on to Monterey while Fr. Parrón remained at San Diego to establish a mission there.

At a *junta* held at San Blas on May 16th, 1768, a plan of action was adopted and signed by participants: "In consequence of all this, the Illustrious Señor Don Joseph de Gálvez, with the approval of all, agreed and resolved that there be made ready at once all the necessary supplies of provision, rigging, sails and whatever else is thought useful and indispensable to be put aboard the two afore-mentioned new brigantines which are to undertake the voyage to the harbor of Monterrey by leaving the coast and the chain of islands behind and undertaking the voyage on the high seas, thus to reach the proper latitude as far as the winds of the season will permit so as not to experience the delays, misfortunes and sick-nesses which were suffered by the expeditions of Don Sebastián Vizcaíno, & others made during the last two centuries."

Both skippers had the reports of Vizcaíno as to the latitude in which the port of San Diego was to be found, but they proved to be in error, and, despite all the precautions, the experiences of those going on the *San Antonio* and *San Carlos* were to turn out far worse than those of the earlier explorers.

There were many things to do in the months that preceded the start of the expeditions. The task of taking over the Jesuit missions had to be completed, and the question of authority over them be-tween the Franciscans and the military caused some friction. Though no hidden gold or sacks of pearls had been found, stories of riches buried in some forgotten mission were to persist into the 20th Century. What little wealth the missions had was to be in part confiscated to help the supplying of the expeditions and the estab-lishing of the new missions in Alta California.

Portolá had volunteered to lead the expeditions, and well he might; the governorship of Baja California had little to hold a man of his ability, tact and courage. He had the task of removing the Jesuits, and from this we learn much about his character. Fr. Baegert wrote that "gratitude as well as respect for his good name compels me to state here that Governor Don Gaspar Portolá . . . treated the Jesuits, considering the circumstances, with respect, honor, polite-ness, and friendliness. He never caused the least annoyance, sin-cerely assuring us how painful it was to him to have to execute such

The first page of Father Francisco Palóu's Fore-word to his Noticias or Historical Memoirs of New California, a work in four volumes.

99

a commission. On several occasions tears came to his eyes, and he was surprised to find Europeans willing to live and die in such a country."

Portolá obviously had no intention of living and dying in Baja California. He was an unmarried soldier of noble rank, born in Catalonia, and had seen service with the Spanish army in Italy and Portugal. His appointment as governor of Baja California was supposed to have been a promotion, but in the view of Fr. Baegert it amounted to exile: "His punishment . . . could not have been more severe (except death, the gallows, or prison for life) had he sworn a false oath to the king or proved a traitor to his country . . . His field chaplain, Don Fernández, a secular priest, wanted to leave the country as soon as he saw that there was no one to speak to all day long and nothing to do but sit in his hermitage, to gaze at the blue sky and the green sea, or to play a piece on his guitar."

An active and devout man, Portolá proved to be an able organizer and a good leader, preferring democratic procedure to arbitrary direction, and got along well with all the missionaries. He expressed continual concern over the health of Fr. Serra and doubt whether he could stand such a long and hazardous journey; he worried lest Fr. Serra's infected leg might cause delays and difficulties.

But he could not prevail against Fr. Serra's sense of dedication. "Despite the fact that I remonstrated with him," commented Portolá to Fr. Palóu, "and pointed out the delay it would cause to the expedition if he should become incapacitated along the road, I was unable to convince him to remain and have you go in his place. When I spoke to him of the matter, his consistent answer was that he trusted in God to give him the strength to enable him to reach San Diego and Monterey."

The year was 1769. The expedition was divided into four sections. The *San Carlos* sailed from La Paz on January 9th and the *San Antonio* on February 15th. The land expeditions started from a gathering place named Velicatá, near the present site of El Rosario, in northern Baja California, where a new mission was to be established. Capt. Rivera and Fr. Crespí left on March 24th, and Capt. Portolá and Fr. Serra followed on May 15th.

CHAPTER EIGHT

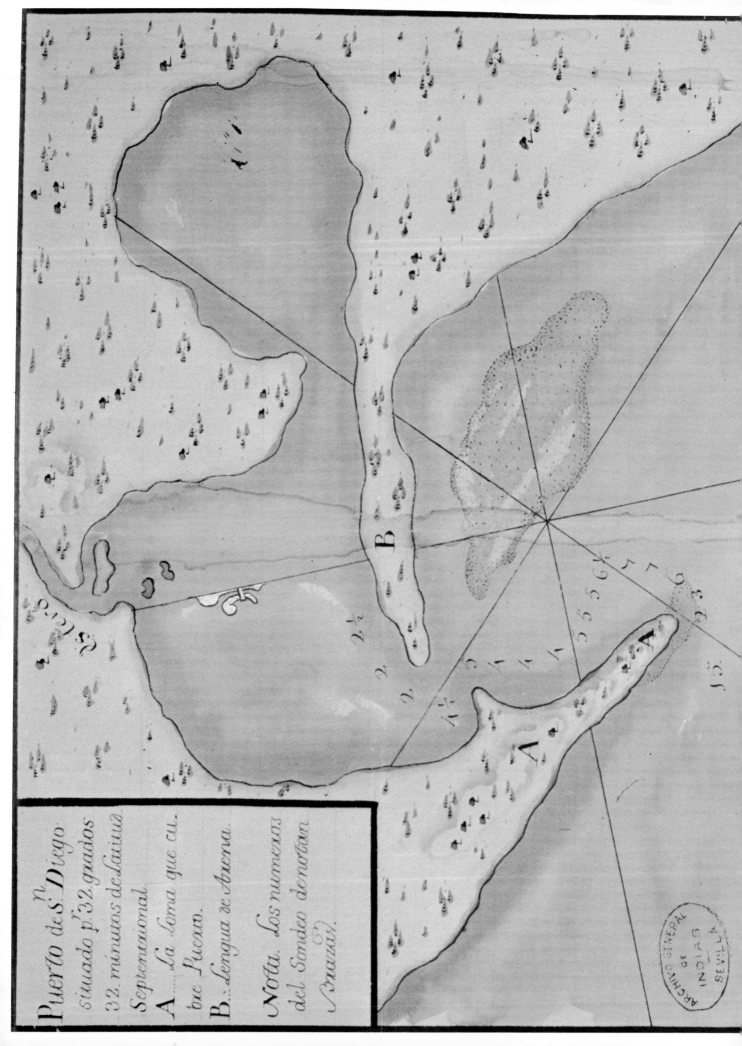

Puerto de S.ⁿ Diego
situado p.ᵉ 32.grados
32.minutos de latitud
Septentrional.
A.....La Loma que cu...
bre Puexto.
B...Lengua de Arena.

Nota. Los numexos
del Sondeo denotan
Braxias.

B

A
A

2¼
2
3
4
4
4
5
5
6
7
8
9
10
15

2½
3½
4½

EXPEDITIONS BY SEA

Tragedy was to sail with the *San Carlos*, as it did with the *San Antonio*. She arrived at La Paz from Guaymas in a leaky condition and had to be careened and repaired, but in less than two weeks the work was done, the vessel loaded, and the troops taken aboard. Among those on the *San Carlos* were Vicente Vila, the captain and a lieutenant in the Royal Navy and an experienced mariner, who kept a diary or log of the voyage; Miguel Costansó, a cartographer who was to map the ports and lay out the royal presidio at Monterey; Fray Fernando Parrón, chaplain from San Fernando College; Pedro Prat, army surgeon; Don Pedro Fages and his 25 Catalán soldiers; Don Jorge Estorace, mate; and 23 sailors, cabin boys, cooks, and blacksmiths — a total of 62 persons. San Diego is indebted to Vila and Costansó for a detailed story of the experiences and sufferings at the first little settlement to be founded here.

Fr. Palóu describes the ceremonies before leaving for San Diego:

"Everything being ready for the voyage of this packet, which was going as flagship, his Illustrious Lordship (Gálvez) set January 9th, 1769, for the

MAP OF SAN DIEGO BAY made by Vicente Vila, captain of the San Carlos. Bringing men and supplies for the Portolá expedition, Vila anchored in the bay on May Day, 1769, and remained in the port until August, 1770, during which period he made this chart.

103

departure. On that day all prepared themselves with the holy sacraments of confession and communion. After the conclusion of the Mass, all of those who were to sail being assembled, his Lordship made them a wise and tender speech, charging them with the affair in the name of God and the King and of their viceroy in New Spain. He said that he was sending them to raise among the heathen of San Diego and Monterey the standard of the Holy Cross, and that in order to facilitate and secure the desired end, he charged them to observe peace and harmony among themselves and obedience and respect to their superiors, especially the missionary father, Fray Fernando Parrón, who was going for the consolation of everybody, and that they should heed him, love him, and respect him. This tender exhortation finished, they made their fare-wells, and the missionary father received the blessing of the reverend father president (Serra), who was present and pronounced a benediction on the ship and banners."

Evidently it had been intended that the *San Carlos* and the *San Antonio* sail together. Storms interfered with their plans to rendezvous at San Bernabé Bay, and Gálvez finally ordered the *San Carlos* to proceed by herself.

The voyage to San Diego took 110 days. They met with adverse winds, and because of leaking casks had to go to the coast to seek out water, and another time, buffeted by winds, were blown 200 leagues off their course. The haul up the coast always is difficult enough without extra troubles, as Costansó noted, "on account of the prevalence of north and northwest winds, which, with little interruption continue throughout the year and are directly contrary to the voyage, as the coast bears northwest to southeast."

The ship's log tells of the troubles that dogged her meandering course, and the effects of the spread of scurvy, that terrible enemy of seamen. Over a long period of time a diet deficient in ascorbic acid, or Vitamin C, which is found in fruit, green vegetables and fresh milk, will cause scurvy. The diet of sailors in those days consisted of biscuits and salt or dried meat. The effects of scurvy are bleeding gums, loosening and loss of teeth, ulcers of the limbs, anemia, and general debility increasing until death.

On January 22-23, it was noted that

"at four o'clock in the morning, Agustín Medina, a seaman, had his leg broken by the tiller. At seven in the morning, the caulker informed me that he had found in the pump the same three and a half inches of water that had been bailed out on the day before. It was found to be fresh water from the casks, as the staves were spreading with the violence of the constant pitching . . . On April 18-19: At one o'clock in the afternoon, Fernando Alvarez, the boat-swain's second mate and coxswain of the launch, died . . . On April 23-24: On this day the sick and those who had not yet fulfilled their religious duties confessed and received the sacrament. At six o'clock in the evening the pilot, Manuel Reyes, died . . . at eight in the morning, the body of Reyes was cast overboard."

One of the difficulties accounting for the long time it took to reach San Diego was in finding the port, as the latitudes given by the explorers so many years before were far from exact. The ships made landfalls near San Pedro instead of San Diego, as Vizcaíno had placed San Diego at 33° 30′ N. Latitude, while the entrance to the bay is at 32° 40′ N. Latitude.

The *San Antonio*, a smaller ship than the *San Carlos*, was loaded at San Blas and sailed from San Bernabé Bay near the end of January, placed under the protection of St. Anthony of Padua. Aboard were Capt. Don Juan Pérez, former master of the Manila Galleon;

MAP SHOWING THE COURSE of the San Antonio before she reached San Diego in April, 1769. Owing to incorrect information as to the latitude of San Diego Bay, she overshot the mark and wandered among the Channel Islands before discovering the error. The crew became ridden with scurvy.

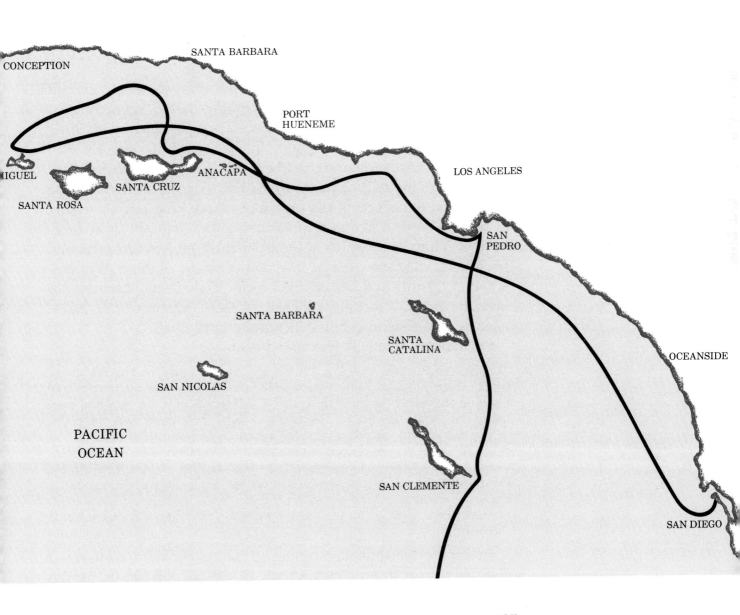

Miguel del Pino, mate; Frs. Juan Vizcaíno and Francisco Gómez; subaltern officers, carpenters and blacksmiths for the settlements, and sailors, the total numbering possibly twenty-eight. No log of this journey has ever been found, though the diary of Fr. Vizcaíno has been privately published.

The crew and passengers of the *San Antonio* also suffered from scurvy on the winter journey that took 54 days, and they also were unable at first to locate the harbor of San Diego, which Vizcaíno had described as surely the best in all of the South Sea. The ship wandered among the Channel Islands for a time and then put back south and finally entered the port on April 11, 1769, the first ship known to visit here in 167 years. The *San Carlos*, which had left long before her, was nowhere to be seen.

Despair was beginning to overtake those on board the *San Carlos* when, on April 28, a fog lifted and to the south of them they sighted the Coronado Islands, which they recognized from the descriptions of the Vizcaíno expedition. In his log, Vila reported with obvious relief that they "are the best and surest marks for making the port of San Diego which is situated about five and a half or six leagues due north of these islands."

That afternoon, about 4 o'clock, the *San Carlos* began working her way toward the harbor entrance, and Vila's report noted that

"at this place we began to enter a kelp-field with thick patches of seaweed. When the packet had been under way for more than two knots, she stopped almost still and did not answer the helm. I sounded until we had passed it completely, hauling very close to the point in 14 and 15 fathoms."

At five o'clock, the *San Carlos* passed into the channel and discovered the packet *San Antonio* anchored at Point Guijarros, or Cobblestone Point, now known as Ballast Point, and "we broke out our colors. She broke out hers and fired one gun to call her launch which was ashore." The *San Carlos* anchored in the channel, and

"at eight o'clock at night the launch of the *San Antonio* came with her second in command and pilot, Don Miguel del Pino, who gave us an account of her voyage. She arrived at this port on the eleventh of April, with half of her crew down with scurvy, of which two men died. They had only seven men who came in the launch fit for work; of these a few felt symptoms of the disease. Capt. Juan Pérez was also in poor health, and only the two missionaries were well."

Because of tides, calms and adverse winds, it wasn't until the second day that the *San Carlos* was able to move up and drop anchor alongside the *San Antonio*. All were thankful for their reunion amid so much sickness and suffering and for the opportunity for rest and fresh water.

San Diego Bay was quite different in those days, as a map made

The Coronado Islands from the air.

106

by Vila shows. The San Diego River in periods of heavy runoff spread out over wide, marshy flatlands between Point Loma and Old Town. The main channel swept around the base of Presidio Hill and turned due south to empty into the bay. The east shore line of the bay was about where Pacific Highway is today. Costansó's narrative refers to a lagoon into which the river emptied, which must have been formed by sandbars from silt carried down by river floods. Crespí remarks on the large river that ran through the valley, describing it as six or eight *varas*, or yards, wide and about a half a *vara* in depth, "but it went on diminishing from day to day, so that in three weeks after our arrival it entirely stopped flowing and there was left only water in pools."

The first task for crew members of the two ships who were still able to walk was to find a good source of fresh water. In this, they had the cooperation of the still friendly Diegueño Indians, descendants of the same tribes who had greeted Cabrillo 257 years earlier. Costansó's descriptive and revealing narrative says:

Last page of Miguel Costansó's Narrative of the Portolá Expedition. Costansó came on the San Carlos as cartographer of the expedition, and later went with Portolá.

"The first task was to look for a watering place where a supply of good water could be obtained to fill the barrels for the use of the men. For this purpose, the officers, Don Pedro Fages, Don Miguel Costansó, and the second captain of the *San Carlos*, Don Jorge Estorace, landed on the 1st of May, with 25 of the soldiers and seamen who were best able to endure the fatigue. Skirting the western shore of the port, they observed at a short distance, a band of Indians armed with bows and arrows, to whom they made signs by means of white cloths, hailing them in order to obtain information. But the Indians, regulating their pace according to that of our men, would not, for more than half an hour, let themselves be overtaken. Nor was it possible for our men to make greater speed because they were weak, and after so long a sea voyage had, as it were, lost the use of their legs.

"The Indians stopped from time to time on some height to watch our men, showing the fear which the strangers caused them, by what they did to conceal it: they stuck one end of their bows into the ground, and holding the other end, danced and whirled around it with incredible swiftness. But the moment they saw our men at hand, they took to flight with the same agility. At last we succeeded in attracting them by sending toward them a soldier, who, upon laying his arms on the ground and making gestures and signs of peace, was allowed to approach. He made them some presents, and meanwhile the others reached the Indians, and completely reassured them by giving them more presents of ribbons, glass beads, and other trifles. When asked by signs where the watering-place was, the Indians pointed to a grove which could be seen at a considerable distance to the northeast, giving to understand that a river or creek flowed through it, and that they would lead our men to it if they would follow."

They walked for about three leagues till they came to the banks of a river lined on both sides with overspreading cottonwoods of heavy foliage. Its bed was about 20 yards wide, and it emptied into a lagoon which at high tide could accommodate the launch, and afforded a convenient place to obtain water. In the grove there was

107

a variety of shrubs and sweet-smelling plants, such as rosemary, sage, Castilian rose, and above all, an abundance of wild grape-vines, which at that time were in flower. The country was of pleasing aspect, and the land in the neighborhood of the river appeared of excellent soil capable of producing all sorts of fruits. The river came down from some very high mountains through a wide canyon (Mission Valley), which ran into the interior in an easterly and north-easterly direction.

Drawing of old Spanish type gun.

"Within a musket-shot from the river, outside the wood, they discovered a town or village of the same Indians who were guiding our men. It was composed of various shelters made of branches, and huts, pyramidal in shape, covered with earth. As soon as they saw their companions with the company which they were bringing, all the inhabitants — men, women, and children — came out to receive them, and invited the strangers to their houses. The women were modestly dressed, covered from the waist to the knee with a close-woven, thick, netted fabric. The Spaniards entered the town which was composed of from thirty to forty families. On one side of it there was observed an enclosure made of branches and trunks of trees, in which, they explained, they took refuge to defend themselves against the attacks of their enemies, as it is an impregnable fortification against such arms as are in use among them. These natives are well-built, healthy and active. They go naked without other clothing than a belt — woven like a net — of ixtle, or very fine agave thread, which they obtain from a plant called lechuguilla. Their quivers, which they stick between the belt and the body, are made of the skin of the wildcat, coyote, wolf, or deer, and their bows are two yards long. In addition to these arms, they use a sort of throwing-stick of very hard wood, similar in form to a short curved sabre which they throw edge-wise, cutting the air with great force. They throw it farther than a stone, and never go into the surrounding country without it. When they see a snake or other noxious animal, they throw the throwing-stick at it, and generally cut the animal in two."

As the Spaniards learned afterwards from their continued intercourse with the natives,

"they are of an overbearing disposition, insolent, covetous, tricky, and boastful; and although they have little courage, they boast much of their strength and consider the strongest to be the most valiant. They beg for any rag of clothing; but after different ones on successive occasions had been clothed, on the following day they again presented themselves naked . . . Fish constitutes the principal food of the Indians who inhabit the shore of this port, and they consume much shell-fish because of the greater ease they have in procuring them. They use rafts made of reeds, which they manage dexterously by means of a paddle or double-bladed oar. Their harpoons are several yards long, and the point is a very sharp bone inserted in the wood; they are so adroit in throwing this weapon that they very seldom miss their mark."

Having examined the watering-place, the Spaniards returned to their ships, but, on account of the condition of the crews, Vila reluctantly issued orders that the *San Antonio* was to remain at San Diego, instead of going on to Monterey, and that both ships should proceed into the inner harbor and anchor nearer a source of water in order to lighten the work of handling the launch and landing the sick. There they would await the arrival of the land expeditions or the arrival of the *San José*, the little supply ship that never came.

Vila's diary makes clear that the first camp of white men was established on the east shore of the bay, and not on Point Loma as has previously been believed. Its exact location wasn't stated but from evidence in the diaries of the explorers who arrived overland, the camp must have been about a league, or three miles, south of Presidio Hill and thus somewhere near Laurel Street on a hillock east of Pacific Highway.

Vila's journal is almost an epic of tragedy. His diary takes up the return to the ship of the first exploring party, and the move deeper into the bay, a physical ordeal which required four days:

"From Monday, 1, to Tuesday, May 2 — At sunset, the sky and horizon were obscured by so dense a fog that I was afraid that the launch might lose her way, and in order to help her I had to make repeated signals with gunshots and cannon, and with a lantern at the flagstaff, and to ring the ship's-bell. It was evident from the shots they fired from time to time that the men in the launch were desirous of this.

"At nine o'clock at night she hauled alongside, luckily. The laymen and the missionaries on board of her explained that they had walked about three leagues along the shore, and at that distance they had come upon an Indian village on the banks of a river of excellent water . . . At five o'clock in the morning, I weighed anchor, and with the launch of the *San Antonio* out ahead I took advantage of the rising tide to penetrate farther into the harbor. At half-past seven, I anchored in seven fathoms. Muddy black sand. The tide was already running out.

"From Tuesday, 2, to Wednesday, May 3. — At half-past twelve, the sea-breeze changed to SSW, moderate. The tide had already lost its force at flood. Accordingly I weighed anchor and, with the launch out forward and under the jib, I stood inside in order to approach the river or watering-place as nearly as possible.

"At half-past four in the afternoon, after reconnoitering and finding that the harbor extended inland toward the SE more than four leagues, and that the watering-place still lay on my port quarter with no channel to approach it on account of the keys and sand banks extending seaward, I brought out the grapnel to the SE, on account of the tide, and ordered soundings taken of the bank lying toward the watering-place, in order to see if there were any channel, but none was found. I sent the launch to the *San Antonio* with my two seamen who were well and eight soldiers that Don Pedro Fages had detailed to help along the work of raising the anchor, and of making the vessel fast near us for the sake of mutual service and help.

"From Wednesday, 3, to Thursday, May 4 — At half-past one in the afternoon, the *San Antonio* weighed, and at three o'clock, anchored. At five o'clock in the afternoon, several soldiers with Fray Fernando Parrón, Don Pedro Fages, and Don Jorge Estorace went off in the launch to bury the dead seamen ashore. At sunset, they returned aboard. At eleven o'clock in the morning, the *San Antonio* weighed anchor, and as she passed alongside, her captain shouted that she was going to tie up as near the watering-place as possible, as we had agreed. At twelve o'clock, she anchored a full gunshot from the beach. The sick showed no improvement.

The title page of the Diary of Vicente Vila, Captain of the San Carlos, in which he describes the interminable voyage of 110 days and the hardships resulting from adverse winds, lack of fresh drinking water and scurvy.

The Diary of Vicente Vila, captain of the San Carlos. Entries for May 5-7 describe the serious situation presented by the many sick men, and plans for a hospital on shore.

"*From Thursday, 4, to Friday, May 5* — At five o'clock in the afternoon, the launch came from the *San Antonio* with the two missionary fathers and Don Miguel del Pino; the latter told me on behalf of Don Juan Pérez that in the place where they had anchored there was a good anchorage, free from swells, currents, and surf. In virtue of this information I bade him tell Don Juan Pérez to send me the launch at dawn to help me weigh anchor.

"At sunrise, the launch came with one man less. He had fallen ill that night. I raised the grapnel, hove the anchor apeak, hauled out and raised the top-sails, and at half-past seven made sail. At ten o'clock in the morning, I anchored astern of the *San Antonio*, at a distance of a full cable's-length, in two fathoms of water. Sand. I furled the topsails, ran out the grapnel to the north, and, at noon, was fast, lying NW and SE. The wind continued from the south.

"*From Friday, 5, to Saturday, May 6* — After twelve o'clock I sent back the launch with orders to her men to return under arms at two o'clock in the afternoon to make a reconnaisance by sea of the river-mouths, along with Lieutenant Pedro Fages, and to prepare a few shelters on shore where we could place the sick. The wind continued at south.

"At three o'clock in the afternoon, four of the least ailing seamen, Don Pedro Fages, and several armed soldiers, embarked in the launch. The launch of the *San Antonio*, with her captain and several soldiers, went around to reconnoiter to the SE, in which direction the port extended.

"At sunset, the launches, with all the men, returned. Don Pedro Fages had found by examination of the river-mouths that at high tide the launch could enter quite easily to fill the casks. The construction of the shelters was postponed until the following morning. At six o'clock in the morning, a Philippine seaman, named Agustín Fernández de Medina, died.

"At eight o'clock in the morning, the launch of the *San Antonio* put off with Don Pedro Fages, Don Miguel Costansó, Fray Juan Vizcaíno, and the soldiers who were best able, in order to set about the construction of the shelters.

"*From Saturday, 6, to Sunday, May 7* — The day was foggy and drizzly with the wind at south. At one o'clock in the afternoon, the wind shifted to NW. At sunset, the launch returned with the missionary and the officers. They had decided to build the shelters for the sick on a hillock close to the beach and a cannon-shot from the packets. To this end they had gathered a quantity of brushwood and earth to make roofs for those who were to be placed in the shelters . . . At half-past ten in the morning, the launch went ashore with the officers and the missionary to take charge of the building of the quarters. No improvement among the sick.

"*From Sunday, 7, to Monday, May 8* — The sky continued cloudy, with the wind at south. At sunset, the launch returned alongside with those that she had taken ashore. The night passed without event, and at ten o'clock in the morning, the launch went ashore with the officers, soldiers, and seamen who were fit for work. We saw many painted Indians with bows and arrows on shore in various places to the north and south. At sunset, the launch returned alongside. The sick continue without relief.

"*From Monday, 8, to Tuesday, May 9* — The day was foggy, with unsteady catspaws between south and NW. At eight o'clock in the morning, the launch went ashore. In her there were shipped two cannon from the packet's equipment with their carriages and everything needed to handle them, two boxes of cartridges for the aforesaid cannon, a supply of muskets with a bag of bullets of all calibers for grape-shot, eight day's supply of corn, pulse, and jerked beef for the soldiers in the garrison on shore and hard-tack from the cabin to be used in soups for the sick.

"After the completion of the lodgings and shelters, the disembarking of the sick was begun and at four o'clock in the afternoon they were all ashore; I remained on board with the quartermaster, who was extremely ill, a Galician seaman, and a little cabin-boy who also had touches of the disease. I was unable to walk, and Fray Fernando Parrón also was ill. Several Indians and Indian women came to the lodgings as on the day before.

"The weather continued foggy and cool; the wind from the south and SW. No improvement among the sick.

"*From Tuesday, 9, to Wednesday, May 10* — The weather was foggy and cool; the wind from south to west.

"Today I set up the guns from the ship, pointing them from both sides of the lodgings, so that they could be used to protect the men on shore. At eight o'clock in the morning, I sent the launch ashore with the mizzen and spritsails, to construct another shelter in which to put ten sick men from the packet *San Antonio*.

"At ten o'clock, I despatched the said packet's launch with my mate, Don Jorge Estorace, and several casks to take water. Don Pedro Fages, of his own accord, sent several soldiers ashore to help this work along and to act as guard for the launch.

"This same day four soldiers fell sick, and Don Miguel Costansó told me that only eight men fit for any work were left on shore. The day was cool and chilly; the wind raw from west and NW. At two o'clock in the afternoon, a cabin-boy named Manuel Sánchez died. At one o'clock at night, the launch returned with ten casks of water. At eight o'clock in the morning, a Philippine sailor named Matheo Francisco died. At eleven o'clock in the morning, the launch again put off to go to the river in search of water. The sick without any improvement whatever.

"*From Thursday, 11, to Friday, May 12* — The wind continued cold and raw from west and NW. For this reason I determined not to order the seamen from the packet *San Antonio* who were ill to be put ashore. At two o'clock in the morning, the launch returned with ten casks of water. No improvement was found in the sick."

The two ships were lying near the present edge of the tidelands enclosed by Harbor Drive, and thus protected by North Island from the effects of sea and wind. Costansó says the camp was enclosed by a parapet of earth and brushwood, and sails and awnings were landed to make hospital tents and to provide accommodations for the officers:

"These measures, however, were not sufficient to restore their health; for medicines and fresh food, most of which had been used up during the voyage, were wanting. The surgeon, Don Pedro Prat, supplied this want as far as possible, with some herbs which he sought with much trouble in the fields and whose properties he knew. He himself needed them as much as his patients, for he was all but prostrated by the same disease as they. In the barracks the cold made itself severely felt at night, and the sun by day — extremes which caused the sick to suffer cruelly. Every day, two or three of them died and the whole expedition, which had been composed of more than ninety men, was reduced to only eight soldiers and as many sailors who were in a condition to assist in guarding the ships, handling the launches, protecting the camp, and waiting upon the sick. Nothing had been heard of the land-expedition."

Nothing had been heard, either, of the third vessel, the *San José*,

1782 map of bay on which first campsite can be located.

which was to join the other two at San Diego. She was built by order of Gálvez at San Blas, as a supply ship, and, after being loaded on the coast of Sonora with corn, beans and peas, she sailed for Loreto and took on dried meat, fish, figs, raisins, brandy, wine, cloth, vestments, and three steeple bells for the new California missions. How much these things would have meant to those at San Diego! She hoisted sail for San Diego on June 16th, but in three months was back in the port of Escondido, Oaxaca, with a broken foremast. After repairs at San Blas, she was re-cargoed at Cape San Lucas and again put out for San Diego, almost a year later, in May of 1770. Her failure to arrive was to cause continued hardships at San Diego.

CHAPTER NINE

EXPEDITIONS BY LAND

The expeditions to San Diego by land were to find their journey much easier. Capt. Rivera, after gathering animals and supplies from the missions on the route north along the trail first explored by Fr. Link, arrived at Santa María Mission, the last outpost of the existing mission system, in December, and not finding enough pasturage there made camp about forty miles northwest at Velicatá. This became an important post on what later was known as the Pacific Trail, connecting the later Dominican coastal missions. Velicatá is about 270 miles south of San Diego, but, by a road twisting over a great part of upper Baja California, it is about 360 miles.

When Fr. Crespí arrived, the expedition was ready to start. Besides Capt. Rivera and Fr. Crespí, there were Juan Cañizares, engineer, 25 leatherjackets from the presidio of Loreto, three muleteers, and between forty-four and fifty-two Indians, of whom most deserted or died on the march to San Diego. On March 24th, Good Friday, with a pack train of 180 mules, the members of the expedition turned their faces north and began the long march. Fr. Crespí noted in his diary: "The country continues like the rest of Cali-

SAN JAVIER, west of Loreto, oldest existing mission of both Californias, helped supply the new mission at San Diego.

Street scene in town of Loreto.

fornia, sterile, arid, lacking grass and water, and abounding in stones and thorns."

They slowly worked their way northward, staying fairly close to the coast, though the death of a number of Indian helpers and the gradual disappearance of many others during the night caused anxiety and increasing difficulties with the pack train. They encountered many Indian tribes and settlements, but only on one occasion were they threatened, a few arrows falling harmlessly at their feet.

Forty-six days after leaving Velicatá they descended into a deep green valley thick with Indian houses and got the first indications that their journey was drawing to an end. This was near the present village of San Miguel, just north of Ensenada. The date was May 9th. Fr. Crespí's diary noted that the moment the Indians "saw us they broke into an uproar, all coming out of their houses and running to some knolls, most of them not stopping until they reached a hill on the other side of the valley." The lure of gifts restored confidence and "the Indians told us, as we understood perfectly by signs, that they had seen two barks pass by, and that they were not far away."

The next day they arrived in sight of another valley as green and pleasant as the one they had just left, at what is now Descanso, Baja California, and found themselves surrounded by so many naked and painted Indians they were unable to count them:

"They apparently belonged to four villages, for we observed that four of them, who were doubtless captains or chiefs, made us long speeches, of which we understood nothing, although we inferred from their signs that they offered themselves and their lands to us. We understood also, the same as from the preceding village, that they had seen two barks, and that they were anchored. They also spoke of the people who had come in them, and said that there were three fathers who wore the same dress as I, pointing to me and taking hold of my habit."

Adobe reminders of Loreto's past.

On May 12th, they crossed over to the coast, near the present Tahiti Beach, halfway between Rosarito Beach and the border, where they could see the Coronado Islands, and finding a pool of fresh water named it the Pool of the Holy Martyrs. The next morning, because of cliffs on the beach, they cut back up onto the mesa west of Tijuana and soon saw

"in a long stretch the level shore that we were to follow, all the land being well covered with green grass. From a height on this plain we could see that the ocean enters far into the land. In the bay we saw the mainmasts of the two barks, which were scarcely to be made out on account of the distance we were still away from them. This sight was a great consolation and a joy for everybody, for we found ourselves at last so near the desired harbor of San Diego."

Three hours of marching brought them to a populous Indian village along which ran "a good arroyo of water," the Tia Juana River, and Fr. Crespí named the village Sancti Spiritus. There

116

they remained overnight, soaked by rain, and, departing on Sunday morning, May 14th, despite more showers, continued north over the broad plain of the South Bay area, withdrawing a little from the shore for fear that there might be marshes. Indians were everywhere. Thus they circled the southern and eastern shores of San Diego Bay, and in a march of six and a half hours drew near the camp which had been set up by those who had come on the *San Carlos* and the *San Antonio*.

"As soon as we descried the camp the soldiers discharged their guns, giving a salute, and immediately those who were in the camp, as well as those on the packets, responded with their artillery and firearms. Immediately the three fathers who had come in the barks, and also the officers who were on the land, came to meet us and gave us hearty embraces and congratulations that we were now all united in this port of San Diego."

They were the first white men to reach San Diego by land. Though they had suffered deprivations, arriving weary and emaciated, they had walked the distance with less trouble than coming by sea. Costansó tells how the weary marchers rested, and then how the camp was moved nearer the river. Thus Presidio Hill became the site of the first Royal Presidio in California and eventually the site of the first little mission.

Presidio Hill rose from a fairly wooded area and the Indian village called Cosoy actually was a collection of huts scattered among the trees. Fire pits have been excavated on Presidio Hill and mortars and pestles found on the golf course just below it.

"The whole land expedition arrived without having lost a single man or even carrying one sick person after a journey of two months, although they were on half rations, and with no more provisions than three sacks of flour, of which each man received two cakes for his entire day's ration. They rested on that day near the camp of the sick, and were supplied with food to recover their strength. The officers resolved to move the camp close to the river, which had not been done before because it was not deemed advisable to divide the small force they had for the protection at once of the vessels and of the people lodged on the shore; at the same time, the greater convenience of a shorter distance for the transportation had to be taken into consideration, in order not to tire unduly the men who were handling the launch, as the want of beasts of burden obliged them to carry on their shoulders everything that was brought on shore. All moved to the new camp which was transferred one league farther north on the right bank of the river, on a hill of moderate height (Presidio Hill) where it was possible to attend with greater care to the sick, whom the surgeon, Don Pedro Prat, did not leave for a moment and nursed with the utmost kindness. Seeing, however, that they did not improve, and that the contingency would arise in which the two packets would find it impossible to leave the port for want of seamen, they thought seriously of dispatching one of them to San Blas with letters to inform the viceroy and the inspector-general of the condition of both expeditions. Don Juan Pérez, Captain of the Príncipe (or *San Antonio*) was appointed for this purpose, Don Vicente Vila deciding to remain at San Diego till he received new orders and the re-enforcements necessary to carry out whatever his superiors might determine. The packet *San Antonio* was . . . unloaded. Part of the cargo was transferred to the camp . . . and the remainder was put on board the *San Carlos*. The ship was made ready."

"Always go forward; never turn back." This is the creed by which Fr. Serra lived. And on Tuesday, March 28th, long past his physical prime and with a painfully infected leg, he mounted a decrepit burro, and, accompanied only by a faithful servant and a soldier guard, set out on the first leg of his long journey leading to San Diego. He had been at Loreto a year, and though his needs were slight he noted in his diary that "from my mission of Loreto I took along no more provisions for so long a journey than a loaf of bread and a piece of cheese, for I was there a whole year, in economic matters, as a mere guest to receive the crumbs of the royal soldier commissioner, whose liberality at my departure did not extend beyond the aforementioned articles." What a start for so great an adventure!

Interior of Mother of Missions at Loreto.

He went first to the nearby Mission San Javier, where he met his friend Fr. Palóu, who supplied him with more provisions and the first articles for the new California missions, a silver-plated chalice, a small bronze bell, a new chasuble of cloth of gold and a used red one, and a few other necessary church goods. Seeing Fr. Serra's condition, Fr. Palóu offered to go in his place.

"When I saw the wound and swelling of his foot and leg, I could not restrain my tears, when I considered how much he would have to suffer traveling over the very rough and arduous roads known to exist up to the frontier, as well as those still unknown and later to be found, with no other physician and surgeon with him but the Divine Healer."

But his pleadings were to no avail, and Fr. Serra pushed his tired burro on the hard trail to the frontier mission of Santa María, 200 miles north, where he met Capt. Portolá on May 5th.

Capt. Portolá has been criticized for some of his actions, or lack of them, but he had more than his share of troubles. A sympathetic man, things sometimes came hard for him. In his own narrative he recalls his sadness at the stripping of the missions to supply the expedition:

Trail Serra took to San Javier.

"While I was passing, my friend, through the missions established by the Jesuits to that one on the frontier named Santa María, we experienced no hardships worth mentioning, neither I nor my companions; for, in addition to the fact that we took from the presidio vegetables and delicacies, in exchange for the lamentations of the settlers, we were fortunate enough to be able to sleep under roofs, and make the march with some comfort. In consideration of the great deserts into which I was going, and of the Russian hunger with which I foresaw we were going to contend, I was obliged to seize everything I saw as I passed through these poor missions, leaving them, to my keen regret . . . scantily provided for . . ."

Meanwhile Father Serra and Portolá moved on to Velicatá. The new Mission San Fernando was formally founded; a cross was raised and bells were hung. Here, for the first time, Serra encountered truly primitive Indians untouched by civilization. In his diary he writes of them:

May 15: "It was for me a day of great rejoicing, because just after the Masses, while I was praying, retired inside of the little brush hut, they came to tell me that the Indians were coming and were close by. I gave praise to the Lord, kissing the ground, and thanking His Majesty for the fact, that after so many years of looking forward to it, He now permitted me to be among the pagans in their own country. I came out at once, and found myself in front of twelve of them, all men and grown up, except two who were boys, one about ten years old and the other fifteen. I saw something I could not believe when I had read of it, or had been told about it. It was this: they were entirely naked, as Adam in the garden, before sin."

Serra said that even though the Indians saw that the Padres were clothed he could not notice the least sign of shame in them.

The expedition had now been completely assembled. It consisted of Sergeant José Francisco de Ortega, with ten leatherjackets, 44 Christian Indians, four muleteers, two servants, several hundred head of cattle, and a pack train.

It was time to move on, and the expedition left for San Diego on May 15th. From Fr. Palóu we learn of the trials of Fr. Serra during this long march, even though Palóu was not present:

"During the three days he remained at Velicatá our Venerable Father did not suffer any pain in the leg, for from the start the joy and distraction over the foundation (of the new mission) made him forget about his pain. But it was not so afterwards, for on the first journey of three leagues the leg and foot became so inflamed that it appeared there was a cancerous condition there. They were so painful that they gave him no rest. Nevertheless, without complaining to anyone, he traveled another day, also of three leagues' duration, until he came to a place called San Juan de Dios. There he felt so burdened with his infirmity that he could neither stand nor sit, but had to lie down in bed, suffering such pain that it was impossible for him to sleep. When the governor saw him in this condition he said to him: 'Father President, Your Reverence now sees how incapable you are of accompanying the expedition. We are only six leagues from the starting point. If Your Reverence wishes, we shall carry you to the first mission, where you can recuperate, and we shall continue on our journey.' But our Venerable Father, whose hope never waned, answered him in this way: 'Let Your Honor not speak of this, for I trust that God will give me the strength to arrive at San Diego, as He has given me to arrive this far. If this should not be the case, I conform myself to His Most Holy Will. But even though I die on the road, I will not turn back. Although I be buried there, I shall gladly remain among the pagans, if it be the Will of God.' When the governor realized the firm determination of the Venerable Father and, on the other hand, his inability either to ride horseback or to walk, he ordered a litter constructed, fashioned in the manner of a stretcher or bier for carrying the dead, and made of rods, so that he might be laid thereon and be carried by the neophyte Indians of Old California who were accompanying the expedition as scouts and for whatever chores they might be called on to perform. When the Venerable Father heard of this, he became very sad, when in his prudence and humility he considered the great labor involved in his

This old volume contains both the diaries of Frs. Serra and Crespí, and was found in the National Archives of Mexico.

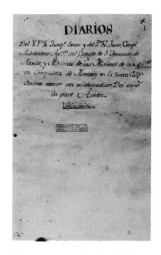

Title page of the Diary.

119

being carried by those poor Indians. With this sadness, having retired within himself, he asked God to improve his condition in order to remove the burden to be imposed on the Indians if they should have to carry him in this manner. Rekindling his faith and confidence in God, that afternoon he called the muleteer Juan Antonio Coronel and said to him: 'Son, do you know how to prepare a remedy for the wound in my foot and leg?' But the muleteer answered him: 'Father, what remedy could I know of? Do you think I am a surgeon? I'm a muleteer; I've healed only the sores of animals.' 'Well then, son, just imagine me to be an animal, and that this wound is the sore of an animal from which has developed this swelling of the leg and the great pains I experience, which permit me neither to rest nor to sleep. Make me the same remedy which you would apply to an animal.' The muleteer smiled, as did the rest who heard the answer. He replied: 'Father, I shall do so in order to please you.' He obtained a little tallow and crushed it between two stones and mixed it with herbs from the field which he found round about; and when he had fried this, he applied it to the foot and leg, and left the application of both materials on the wound in the form of a plaster. God worked in such a way (as the servant of God wrote me from San Diego) that he slept that night through till morning and that he awoke so relieved from his pain and wound that he arose to say Matins and Prime as he customarily did. And, these prayers finished, he said Mass as if he had not suffered any such trouble. The governor and the rest of the soldiers were surprised on seeing the Venerable Father well so suddenly, and relieved that in order to go on with the expedition not the least delay had to be made on his account."

Fr. Serra himself says little about it in his diary. Under the date of May 17th, and referring to a place named San Juan de Dios, he writes simply,

"I said Mass there, but I had much trouble in standing on my feet, because the left one was much inflamed. For a year now, and more, I have been suffering considerably, and by now the swelling has reached halfway up my leg, which is covered with sores. That is why for the rest of the time we stayed here, I had to lie prostrate most of the time on my bed, and I was afraid that before long I should have to follow the expedition on a stretcher."

On May 18th he notes that "our stay there continued, but I could not say Mass for the aforesaid reason."

That is all. There is no mention of the cure by the muleteer, about which Fr. Palóu learned later from members of the expedition. But, in a letter to Fr. Palóu, Serra says:

"As I crossed the frontier my leg and foot were in bad shape. But God was good to me. Every day I felt better, and kept up with the day's marches just as if nothing were wrong with me. At the present time the foot is completely well as the other; but from the ankle half way up the leg, it is like the foot was before — one large wound, but without swelling or pain except a certain amount of itching. Anyway it is a matter of little moment."

Fr. Maynard J. Geiger, O.F.M., who has written the life of Junípero Serra for the Academy of American Franciscan History, believes that Fr. Serra rode his mule the entire distance.

The expedition followed the route of Capt. Rivera and Fr. Crespí,

This page of the Diary of Father Junípero Serra describes his meeting with Gálvez, the man who planned the Portolá expedition, and the ceremonies at the sailing of the San Carlos and the San Antonio.

except for the last few leagues. The rather laconic Capt. Portolá later described to a friend the troubles en route.

"I began my march to the bay named San Diego, in company with thirty soldiers of the presidio and many Indian auxiliaries; but friend, in a few days we saw with extreme regret that our food was gone, with no source of supplies unless we should turn back. As a result, some of the Indians died, and the rest of them deserted from natural necessity. So I was left alone with the cuirassiers; without stopping the march, we went on, lamenting, now to the mountains to kill geese and rabbits, now to the beach for clams and small fish, and then in search of water, which we did not find for three or four days, the animals going twice that long without drinking, as we ourselves did sometimes. Overcoming these and other innumerable hardships, natural results of such unhappy fortune, we arrived at the port of San Diego."

The facts in the various versions of the expeditions to San Diego do not always agree, as many of the reports or narratives were written in later months or years, when details had grown dim.

The country slowly grew more green and more pleasant as they walked or rode north, and at last on June 20th, from a hill they saw the Pacific Ocean, and that night camped by the sea at what is now Ensenada, eighty miles south of San Diego. It was a welcome relief from the deserts and sharp hills they had crossed in the weeks that lay behind them. For the rest of the journey they kept as close to the coast as possible, generally following the route of the present-day highway, until finally Sgt. Ortega and a companion were sent ahead to take word to San Diego of their impending arrival. On June 27th, at Rosarito, they met an Indian dressed in blue cotton, which could only mean he had come from San Diego; he gave the joyous news that their goal was less than two days ahead and that he had met the sergeant and his companion on the road. The next morning the sound of pounding hoofs heralded the return of the sergeant with ten soldiers and fresh horses sent by Capt. Rivera. They carried letters for Fr. Serra from Crespí and Parrón.

Portolá decided to push on ahead, while Serra and the main body of the expedition followed more slowly. Serra writes:

"Early in the morning the Governor, with his servant and eight soldiers, started out ahead of us in order to reach the Port of San Diego the same day; which in fact he did . . . In the afternoon, a march of two hours and a half was made, this time with two guides from San Diego. We followed the shore all the time, our only trouble being the numerous ravines similar to those of the day before. But today they were not quite so bad. We stopped near a gentile *ranchería*, situated on a pretty piece of elevated land that has the appearance of an island. Where the ocean does not wash it, there is a ravine. The gentiles, as soon as they saw us, came to us, inviting us to stop with them near their huts. But it seemed to us more advisable to encamp on the other side of the ravine where there is another mesa of large dimensions . . . The land encircled by the ravine near the *ranchería* has a spring of good, sweet water of medium size . . . On both sides of us — where we were encamped and

Map of La Frontera, the northern part of Baja California, showing the Pacific Trail pioneered by the Portolá expedition. This was to become a much traveled road between the settlements of Lower and Upper California.

121

Smugglers gulch through which Serra made his way into San Diego County.

where the gentiles had their homes — high mountains make a complete circle; and thus the place can never be more than what it is; so I gave it the name of Cárcel de San Pedro, whose feast we celebrate today."

This was near the present Tahiti Beach, not far below the border. The next morning, with the guides knowing the direction of the port from the way in which the wind blew, they took a short cut off the traveled Indian road and dropped down into the Tia Juana River Valley, and camped that night at a place which they called San Pablo. This river site was a mile within San Diego County.

"We started early, and the first thing was to cross the ravine and climb up the opposite hillside. After a few ups and downs we saw a wondrous sight — a measureless plain stretching out before us over which our footsteps had to tread. The hills we left on our right. And over that plain we trudged that day for four hours and a half. But the ravines we had to cross were, and are, quite numerous, without any possibility of avoiding them or flanking them — they are all alike coming straight out from the mountains. And although I continued to pray and resign myself to the will of God, etc., I summoned up all my courage — because you were no sooner out of one ravine than you were into another, and each one was dangerous. At one time I asked the guides: 'Is this the last one?' 'There are plenty more to come,' was their answer. And they were right as events proved. Anyway like all things in this world, the gullies came to an end; and after little more than three hours on the way, we arrived at a gentile settlement, thickly populated. We were very tired and inclined to stop there. But we were told by the Sergeant that they were an insolent tribe . . . For this reason, and in order to arrive more fully rested at San Diego the next day, we went ahead, with the intention of reaching another hamlet some leagues farther. Here there was sufficient water, although inferior in quality to what we left to those disagreeable fellows. And now the road being all easy going and the guides knowing the direction of the port from the way in which the wind blew, we made a short cut, leaving on our right the traveled road. At the short distance of about one hour's going we found that the country was not only nice pasture land, but it had also a pleasant river of good water. There we stopped without going to the next *rancheria*. That place, which neither the Sergeant who passed by this road for the third time nor others for whom it was the fifth had ever previously seen, and which appeared to us very attractive for placing a good mission, we called San Pablo. It is a very large plain and I would judge that it is located about a league from the sea, more or less. There the animals traveled splendidly, and we went without any further anxiety . . ."

Serra trail led from Gulch across Tia Juana River Valley west of National Avenue.

The last day's journey lay ahead. It was July 1st.

The routes of Serra and Crespí into San Diego are not known precisely, but from their diaries the general course is easily established. From Sancti Spiritu, where Crespí camped on the Tia Juana River one and a third miles from where it empties into the Pacific, the route was probably northeast across the valley, crossing today's railroad line at about Palm Avenue and skirting northeast to Palm Avenue hill. It is evident that Serra entered San Diego County from Mexico through a sloping vale now known as Smugglers' Gulch, about two and a half miles from the seacoast. Serra crossed the broad Tia Juana River valley to camp on the north side, which put him nearer the foot of the bay, one-third to one-half a mile south of Coronado Avenue. Serra crossed the Otay River at some point east of National Avenue and west of Third Avenue in Otay. Here the river bed is a wide, dry wash. Then he went north and gradually northwest, skirting the hills, yet keeping back from the shore to avoid sloughs and marshes. He crossed the Sweetwater River probably in the vicinity of Fourth Avenue in Chula Vista, usually a dry bed. Going through the present National City he reached San Diego approximately on the line of Main Street, ever drawing closer to the bay as the hills drew in. The shore was reached near Market Street, and so along the bay to the camp near the vicinity of Laurel Street.

Serra's diary reads:

"We started early in the morning on our last day's journey. Already the beginnings of the port we were seeking are partly visible, and already our guides explained to us its entrance and limits, and thus the labor of the road which is quite flat was made much more supportable to us than usual. On the road we encountered three encampments of gentiles . . . The road in its last half winds considerably in order to avoid the many sloughs which more or less penetrate the land from the sea, a reason why the journey, which it seems ought to take three hours at most, cost us something more than five, at the end of which we found ourselves on the bank of the port area — not far from its mouth — where the two packet-boats *San Carlos* and *San Antonio* were at anchor. From the first of these, being the newest, they came off with the launch to bid us welcome, although we stayed a very short time. Having been informed that to arrive at the place where the land expedition was encamped . . . we would need to go nearly a league, we therefore continued on and finally arrived at said camp . . . a little before noon of the above-mentioned day."

All expeditions, at last, were united at the Port of San Diego. "Thanks be to God, I arrived here the day before yesterday, July 1st, at this Port of San Diego," Serra wrote Palóu. "It is beautiful to behold, and does not belie its reputation. Here I met all who had set out before me whether by sea or by land; but not the dead." Indeed, Capt. Portolá and Fr. Serra found a grim situation, one that was to call on their courage and their resourcefulness. When Fr. Crespí had arrived on May 14th, he had found the crews of both ships ill with scurvy, and 21 sailors and a few soldiers already dead. By the time Fr. Serra arrived, all of the sailors of the *San Carlos*, except one and the cook, had succumbed, and all those of the *San Antonio* were ill. Perhaps sixty of the 159 persons who reached San Diego had succumbed to scurvy.

Fr. Serra, along with many others of the time, believed that scurvy was contagious. He wrote that "nearly all the people [were] ill, many having died and every day others continuing to die from the

Near here, south of Leon St. in Nestor area, Serra made his first camp.

Sweetwater river bed at Fourth Avenue, Chula Vista, near where Serra crossed

This Market St. Monument also marks area where Serra reached bay.

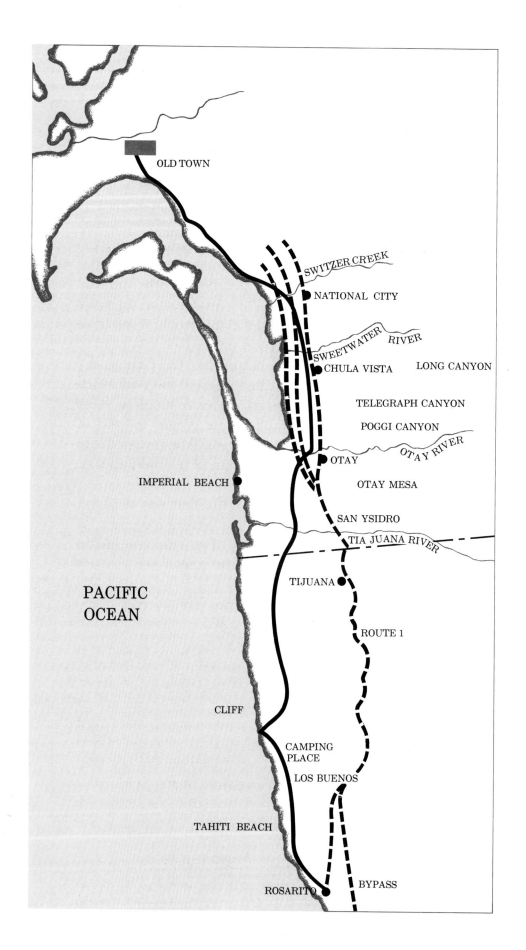

sickness of Loanda, or scurvy." According to Fr. Geiger, this type of scurvy was named after a particularly virulent variety often afflicting sailors who visited the coasts of Loanda, the Portuguese colony of Angola.

The little camp on Presidio Hill was nothing more than a hospital, and the dead must have been buried nearby. It seems strange that none of the bodies has ever been turned up by flood or excavation.

Despite the troubles, Fr. Serra found San Diego to be all that he had hoped and all that had been described by the early explorers. To him, it was a truly beautiful land and justly famous. There were many willows, poplar and sycamore trees along the river banks, wild grapes grew in profusion, there were plenty of acorns and wild asparagus, and game seemed abundant. "There are so many vines grown by nature and without human help that it would mean little expense to follow the example of our good father Noe (Noah) . . . In short it is a good country—distinctly better than Old California."

The humble but zealous friar at last had reached the goal which he had set for himself when he first arrived in Mexico nineteen years before. He was in a virgin land surrounded by pagans in need of conversion and "a harvest of souls that might easily be gathered into the bosom of our Holy Mother, the Church, and it would appear, with very little trouble."

A new life was opening up before him — a life that was to play a rich part in the history of California. He had come a long way for this moment, 5,000 miles from the sanctuary of an academic life on the peaceful island of Mallorca in the Mediterranean Sea.

MAP SHOWING THE LAST SECTION of the probable route of the Portolá Expedition of 1769, from Rosarito Beach in Baja California to the first camp on San Diego Bay. The route is arrived at from evidence in the diaries of Fathers Crespi and Serra in describing the terrain over which they crossed.

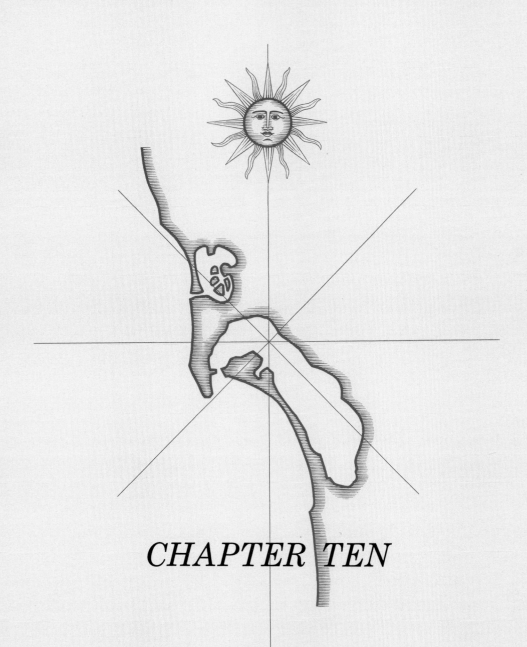

CHAPTER TEN

PORTOLA GOES NORTH

There was much to be done; the expedition must not fail and the king must not be disappointed. The *San Antonio*, under Captain Juan Pérez, was prepared to sail — not for Monterey but back to San Blas — with letters to inform the Viceroy and Inspector-General of the conditions at San Diego. Vicente Vila was to remain at San Diego until he received further orders and reinforcements. But Portolá, anxious to carry out the original instructions, offered to give Vila sixteen men from his own command to continue the voyage to Monterey.

A dispute arose, and Costansó reports that "as there was not one sailor among them, Vila could not accept the offer, especially because he had lost all his sea officers — boatswain, quartermaster, and coxswain — without having anybody to replace them. The governor was of the opinion that the unforeseen misfortune of the ships did not excuse him from continuing his journey to Monterey by land, in view of the fact that all his soldiers and the rest of his men

PORTOLÁ WENT NORTH to find Monterey Bay, after seeing the tiny colony established and first prayers said on Presidio Hill. Failing to recognize it, he continued on until he and his men emerged on the shores of San Francisco Bay, 600 miles from San Diego.

were in good health, and that he had in his division 163 mules laden with provisions."

Portolá, counting on the arrival of the *San José*, decided to push ahead, regardless, "without waiting till the season had too far advanced, so as to avoid the risk of the snows blocking passage across the mountains that might be encountered on the way. For it was known already, from the experience of that year, that it snowed much, even at San Diego where the hills were seen to be covered with snow by the men who had arrived by sea in April...."

An agreement was reached. Portolá would push on to Monterey by land, with the two army officers Fages and Costansó, Rivera and six surviving Catalán volunteers, Sergeant Ortega and twenty-six soldiers, Frs. Crespí and Gómez, seven muleteers, fifteen Baja California Indians, and two servants. The *San Antonio* was to sail for San Blas with reports for the Viceroy and Gálvez. She left on July 9th, with a crew of only eight men. Six of them died on the way.

Left behind on the *San Carlos* were Vila; the second pilot, José de Cañizares, who later was to be the first white man to sail through the Golden Gate; a few convalescing sailors, and two soldiers.

On shore were the Frs. Serra, Juan Vizcaíno and Fernando Parrón, Dr. Prat, a handful of soldiers to guard the camp, a corporal, a blacksmith, a carpenter, one servant, eight Indians, and a number of sick men still lodged in the crude hospital.

On July 14th, after High Mass in a brushwood shack, Portolá's party of sixty-three, weakened and hungry, started for Monterey. Portolá looked at his feeble little army and remarked that they were nothing but skeletons.

The soldiers were protected against possible Indian attack and against the rough country through which they were to ride. From their equipment originated that of the Western cowboys and the California lancers of the romantic Mexican period. As described by Costansó, each wore a leather jacket shaped like a coat without sleeves and made of six or seven plies of white tanned deerskin, proof against arrows except at very close range. The shield was made of two plies of raw bull's hide and was carried on the left arm to turn aside spears and arrows, the rider being able to defend his horse as well as himself. In addition each wore a sort of a leather apron, which the Spanish called "*armas*" or "*defensas*," fastened to the pommel of the saddle and hanging down on both sides to protect the thighs and legs in thickets and woods.

Costansó records:

"Their offensive arms are the lance—which they handle adroitly on horseback—the broadsword, and the short musket which they carry securely

Sword worn by the Conquistadores.

130

fastened in its case. They are men of great fortitude and patience . . . and we do not hesitate to say that they are the best horsemen in the world . . ."

There was always the threat of the loss of their pack animals — which frequently stampeded at the unexpected appearance of animal life — the necessity of reconnoitering the country ahead from day to day to regulate the day's march according to the distance between watering places, and the need of occasional periods of rest . . . "In the course of time there were many whose strength gave way under the continuous fatigue, and the excessive heat and intense cold." It took them eight days to cross the country, and they marked their progress in leagues. Their league was about 2.6 miles in length. In general they followed age-old Indian trails, which they called roads; these became the thread of El Camino Real. Much of the route over which they passed, from San Diego to San Luis Rey, is designated on older maps as El Camino Real, and sections of roads along it were still posted as such in 1960. They chose the low valleys just behind the first row of coastal hills, when they could do so, to avoid unnecessary climbing.

Leaving late in the afternoon, after the animals had been watered, they crossed the bed of the San Diego River, marched north along the east shore of Mission Bay and past a large Indian village situated at its northeast corner (at the present site of a drive-in theater), and then turned into Rose Canyon. The Spaniards called it the Canyon of San Diego. They camped the first night where it widens out just above the Convair warehouse and brick plant of today, after a march of only about five miles. Many years ago there was a railroad station near here identifying the area as Ladrillo, meaning brick, where tiles were made for olden San Diego. Fr. Crespí's diary tells us the most about this first journey of white men across northern San Diego County. It reads:

"We set out from this port of San Diego on this day of the seraphic doctor, San Buenaventura, about four in the afternoon. We went northwest, over level land well covered with grass on account of the proximity of the estuaries, which have good salt deposits. Afterwards we came upon the beach of the second harbor that San Diego has, although it is closed so that it cannot be entered. On some parts of the road there are rosemary and other small bushes not known to us, and on the right hand we have a mountain range, moderately high, bare of trees, of pure earth well covered with grass. We saw many hares and rabbits, for this port abounds in them. At about two leagues we came to a very large village of heathen who are in the valley formed by this second harbor where there are some small springs of water. We called this spot the Village of the Springs of Rinconada de San Diego. As soon as the heathen saw us approaching they all came out into the road, men, women and children, as though they came to welcome us, with signs of great pleasure. We gave them such presents as we could. Here we left the shore, and entered a valley between hills but on the same road. It has many willows and some

Spanish spur, bit found in Mission area.

Rose Canyon where Portolá pitched first camp on march north.

Diario del Viage que haze por tierra D.n Gaspar de Sorrolá Capitan de Dragones del Regim.to de España Governador de Californias á los Puertos de San Diego y Monterrey situados en 33 y 37 grados haviendo sido nombrado Comandante en Gefe de esta expedicion por el Ill.mo Señor D.n Joseph de Galbez en virtud de las facultades Vice-Regias que le há concedido su Excel.a Dicha expedicion se componia de 37 Soldados de Cuera con su Capitan D.n Fernando de Rivera deviendo este adelantarse con Veinte y siete Soldados, y el Governador con diez, y un Sargento

Horas	
	El dia 11 de Mayo salí de Sancta Maria ultima mision del Norte, escoltado de quatro Soldados en compañia del Padre Junipero Serra Presidente de las Misiones, y el R. P. Fr.
6	Miguel Campa: en este dia se handuvo como quatro horas con poquissima agua para las Bestias, nada de pasto, por lo que obligó á marchar por la tarde para lograrlo aunque sin agua.
5	En él handuvimos por buen camino cinco horas paramos en el paraje que llaman la Losa de agua dulce sin pasto.

alders and live oaks, and we understood from the heathen of the preceding village that in this valley there were some pools of good water, and we believed it to be so because it was so green. Although the valley is not very broad it is well covered with grass, and on all sides of it there are knolls, ridges, and hills, all of good land. We found small pools which contained water enough for the people but the horses had nothing to drink. After traveling two hours and three-fourths, in which we must have covered two and a half leagues, we stopped and made camp near the little ponds which we called the Pools of the Valley of San Diego. As soon as we arrived at this place, it being already dark, the heathen came. They brought some very large sardines, and one of them made a long speech, after which the governor and the captain accepted the sardines, reciprocating with beads and some clothing, with which they left in great good humor."

Portolá's description of their first day's march is terse, to say the least. He wrote in his diary: "We marched for three hours. Much pasture, but no water for man or beast."

The next morning they broke camp and followed Rose Canyon as it turns east. The route selected by Portolá's advance scouts is the same one that was selected by the Santa Fe Railroad. Near the head of Rose Canyon, about four miles inland, they climbed a low hill and crossed the wide, flat Miramar Mesa, as does the railroad track, and then dropped down along one of the sloping hillsides into the south end of the wide Soledad Valley, sometimes known as Sorrento Valley, which they named the Valley of Santa Isabel, Queen of Portugal. At the north end they entered the gently rising meadow which runs well back of Del Mar and opens up into San Dieguito Valley. Their route from Sorrento to San Dieguito generally is followed by a road still marked as El Camino Real. San Dieguito was named San Jacome de la Marca by Crespí, though the soldiers named it La Poza de Ozuna. It was a day's journey of about ten miles. Crespí's diary reads:

"About half-past eight in the morning we left the place, following the same direction to the northwest. We ascended a large grassy hill, all of pure earth, and then found ourselves on some very broad mesas of good soft ground, all covered with grass, not having encountered a stone since leaving San Diego nor any other trees than those spoken of in the preceding valley, except that here and there we saw some very small oaks and chaparral. We saw seven antelopes running together on this mesa and at every moment hares and rabbits came running out. After about one and a half leagues of travel, we came to a very beautiful valley, which, when we saw it, seemed to us to be nothing less than a cultivated cornfield or farm, on account of its mass of verdure. On a small eminence in this valley we saw a village of heathen, with six little straw houses. Upon seeing us, all of them came out into the road, in great

El Camino Real follows old route of Portolá in Soledad Valley.

TITLE PAGE and first entries of the Diary of Gaspar de Portolá, leader of the Spanish expedition of 1769 to find and settle Monterey. Ever mindful of the welfare of his men, his entries are terse, practical, and contain little description of the country.

Old well site marks water hole noted by Fr. Crespí in Soledad.

Through this vale Portolá marched into San Dieguito Valley.

good humor and making demonstrations of joy. We descended to this valley and saw that its verdure consisted of very leafy wild calabashes, and many Castilian roses. These heathen have near their village a pool of water in an arroyo. This valley runs from southeast to northwest, and is about one league long and some 400 *varas* wide, all of good pasture, with some live oaks and alders. We called it the Valley of Santa Isabel, Queen of Portugal.

"We stopped a little while so that the commander might distribute some beads among the heathen of this village, and then continued on our way to the north side of the valley, with a heathen of the village who voluntarily offered to accompany us to the camping place. In about half a league's travel, at the end of the valley we came to a medium-sized pool of fresh water, in which we saw two pots of baked clay, very well made. Here we turned into a valley which lies to the north and traveled through it, over level land well covered with grass, from which we saw another valley better than the preceding, and went down to it. We pitched camp near a large pool of good, fresh water, which the soldiers called the Well of Ozuna, and which we called the valley of San Jacome de la Marca, asking that saint to intercede with the Most High for the conversion of its heathen natives, and that a mission might be formed here, with him as its patron, since the site is apparently very suitable and invites it. The march this day covered three and a half leagues. The valley must measure about one league from north to south and about half a league from east to west; all the land is level, very verdant, with much pasture, many wild grapes, and other herbs. To the south of this valley there are three large pools, and to the north, according to the story of the explorers, there is a very verdant arroyo, and some other very large pools. Near the southern pools, on a slope, there is a large village of heathen and many well built houses with grass roofs. As soon as we arrived about eighteen heathen came to visit us, with their women and children, all very affable and not at all noisy. It seems that this place is near the sea, judging by our view of it as we came down the valley. The hills that surround this valley are not very high, and all are of pure earth, covered with pasture, the only thing lacking to the site being trees. Many scorpions have been seen, but no one has been bitten by them."

The portion of the San Dieguito Valley in which they camped runs in a northeasterly and southwesterly direction. Looking inland it seems to be partially cut off by the hills from the rest of the valley formed by the San Dieguito River. They came into the valley just west of El Camino Real and camped near some pools of water. On the third day of marching, they crossed the valley and turned up the sloping canyon along the present Camino Viejo, which runs north from Via de la Valle, took a route through Rancho Santa Fe generally followed today by Paseo del Prado, El Puente, and La Noria, then on to La Bajada to the San Marcos Road and west to S 11, or El Camino Real, which runs north through Green Valley. However, they did not know about Green Valley and pushed on over the hills. They went down to Escondido Creek, which empties into San Elijo Lagoon near Cardiff and named it the Valley of the Triumph of the Holy Cross. Climbing and dropping again they came to Encinitas Creek and they named the valley as the Spring of the Valley of Los Encinos, or oaks. From there they crossed to San Marcos

Creek and camped near where it flows into Batiquitos Lagoon, at the north end of Green Valley. They named it San Alejo.

"At half-past two in the afternoon we set out north and northwest traversing the entire plain; then we climbed a bare hill which followed soon afterwards, with a small wood of little trees unknown to us, and some chaparral. Passing over it, we came out upon some broad grassy mesas, and in about 2½ leagues we descended to a very green valley, with good level land covered with alders. In this valley we came across a village of heathen who, as soon as they saw us, all came running to us, in great good humor. They showed us a little pool of water that was there for their use, and we understood that they were asking us to remain; but, as this was not the spot the explorers had picked out for the camping place, we stopped only a little while. The commander gave some beads to the chiefs, and in passing, we called this place the Valley of the Triumph of the Holy Cross, to which we prayed.

"We proceeded on our way, accompanied by all the heathen, who told us that farther on there was another small watering place. In about half a league we came to another little valley with many live oaks, where we found a small stream of water, which ran a short way in the midst of some blackberry bushes, where we found another village which had only six women. We saw that they had some pots and jugs of baked clay, well made. We called this place the Spring of the Valley of Los Encinos. Then followed extensive hills, with good land and pasture. After about one more league of travel we descended to another very green valley, with good black soil, and from this we entered still another, very green and with good land well covered with grass. In the last valley we made camp near a hill which has two springs of water, one on one side of the hill which had about a limón [sic] of water, and one on the other side with about one finger of running water, from which, by digging it out a little, the animals could drink. Both springs are surrounded by Castilian roses, of which I gathered a branch with six roses open and twelve about to open. Right after this valley comes another, with a village of heathen. As soon as they saw the camp made, the whole village, which was composed of eight men, three women, and four children, came down. Their chief made us a harangue, and when it was concluded they sat down as though they had always known us. One of the heathen came smoking a pipe of black clay, well made. We called this place San Alejo."

Batiquitos Lagoon, looking west toward the ocean.

The trail then led by way of Agua Hedionda Creek, which they named San Simón Lipnica, still along the old El Camino Real. The valley is not far from shore, with an estuary at the end of it. After about two and a half miles of hills and mesas they descended into a small green valley with a narrow plain fifty yards wide, and camped on the west slope. There were several springs forming pools and marshes of reeds and grass. This is Buena Vista Creek, just north of Carlsbad, which they named Santa Sinforosa. They covered only about five miles altogether.

Buena Vista Lagoon, looking to east toward Portolá camp.

"At three in the afternoon we left the camp, following the valley in a northerly direction. In a little while we climbed a very grassy hill without rocks, in open country, then traveled over mesas that are in part covered with grass and in part by a grove of young oaks, rosemary, and other shrubs not known to us. Aside from this all the land is well covered with grass and is

135

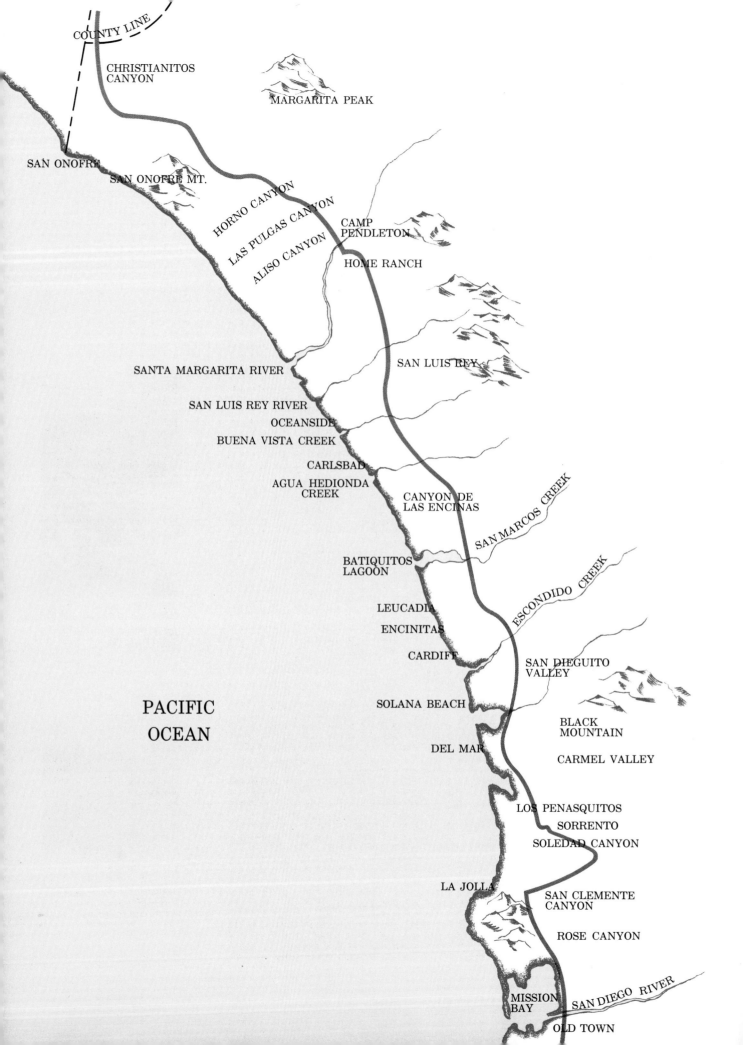

mellow. After traveling about a league we descended to a valley full of alders, in which we saw a village, but without people. In passing we named this valley San Simón Lipnica. It is not very far from the shore, and at the end of it we saw an estuary although the sea was not visible. We continued on our way in the same northerly direction, over hills and broad mesas supplied with good pasture, and after about one more league's travel we descended to a small very green valley, which has a narrow plain some fifty *varas* wide. We pitched camp on the slope of the valley on the west side. The water is collected in pools, and we noticed that it flowed out of several springs, forming about it marshes, or stagnant pools, covered with rushes and grass. We named this place Santa Sinforosa."

The next day's march was only about five miles, and they came to a beautiful watering place previously located by the scouts. It was San Luis Rey Valley, to which they gave the name San Juan Capistrano. The San Luis Rey Mission was founded near the campsite several years later. This marks the end of the old El Camino Real in San Diego County.

On their way into the valley they left the country of the Diegueño Indians, who belonged to the Yuman tribes, and entered the territory of the Luiseños, who were of Shoshonean linguistic stock.

Strange Indian stone gargoyle at Mission San Luis Rey.

"A little after three in the afternoon we set out to the north. We climbed a hill of good soil, all covered with grass, and then went on over hills of the same kind of land and pasture. We must have traveled about two short leagues, when we descended to a large and beautiful valley, so green that it seemed to us that it had been planted. We crossed it straight to the north and pitched camp near a large pool of water, one of several in the plain. At the extremities or ends of the plain there are two large villages . . . This valley must be two leagues long from northeast to southwest, and about half a league wide in the narrowest place. To the southwest it ends on the beach, which must be half a league distant from the camp, although there is a hill which prevents us from seeing the ocean. We found no running water, although we saw three arroyos which are dry and apparently run only when it rains. There are, indeed, pools of good water, with tules on the banks. The valley is all green with good grass, and has many wild grapes, and one sees some spots that resemble vineyards. I gave this valley the name of San Juan Capistrano, for a mission, so that this glorious saint, who in life converted so many souls, may pray God in heaven for the conversion of these poor heathen."

Crespí took a little time here to seek out the Indians. He showed them the image of Christ and tried to make them understand about the crucifixion and about heaven and hell. "They showed they understood some of it, and looked remorseful and sighed." But the Indians refused to kiss the images, to the father's disappointment.

MAP SHOWING THE ROUTE OF THE PORTOLÁ expedition from San Diego Bay to the Orange County Line. Contrary to popular belief, Portolá did not follow the present Route 101, but of necessity kept inland to get around the marshes and to find fresh water and pasturage for their animals.

137

The Indian men were naked and painted, the women modestly covered, wearing a woven apron in front and a deerskin behind, with their breasts capped with little capes made of hare and rabbit skins. Crespí rather indignantly noted that "most of the women are clothed in this manner, but all the men go as naked as Adam in Paradise before he sinned, and they did not feel the least shame in presenting themselves before us, nor did they make any movement to cover themselves, just as though the clothing given them by nature were some fine garment."

They noted large pools of water in Santa Margarita Valley.

On Thursday, July 20th, they followed the valley north for a short time and then cut over the hills and mesas to reach the location of the old Home ranch on the Santa Margarita River near the present headquarters of Camp Pendleton. The site can be reached by following the highway from San Luis Rey and into the camp on Vandergrift Blvd. Camp Pendleton was once known as Santa Margarita y Las Flores Rancho. Crespí describes the route and the camp:

"We set out about seven in the morning, which dawned cloudy, and, taking the road straight to the north, we traveled by a valley road about one league long, with good land, grassy, and full of alders. This passed, we ascended a little hill and entered upon some mesas covered with dry grass, in parts burned by the heathen for the purpose of hunting hares and rabbits, which live there in abundance. In some places there are clumps of wild prickly pear and some rosemary. One league and a half from the camping place we saw another beautiful green valley, well grown with alders and other smaller trees. On going down to it we saw a lagoon which the explorers said was salt water. We pitched camp in this valley near a pool of fresh water; the reason for stopping, although the march has only covered one league and a half, is because, since the departure from San Diego, we have had on the right a very high mountain range, and we are now apparently going to meet it, and it is necessary to explore it before crossing it for it seems as though it is going to end on the beach. The pool of water, which I just saw, is more than a hundred *varas* in length, and its water is very clear and good. Besides this one the explorers say that lower down in the arroyo from the north, there are some more pools, and that a good stream of water runs from them, and they have good lands on which crops might be raised by irrigation. According to this, the place is better suited for a town than the preceding. Because we arrived at this place on the day of Santa Margarita, we christened it with the name of this holy virgin and martyr."

The wild pink castilian rose reminded them of Spain.

After traveling only two hours the next day along a route marked today by Basilone Road, they camped along Pulgas Creek in the heart of Camp Pendleton. On July 22nd, they kept along the Basilone Road route to where it turns west to San Onofre. Here, keeping north, they reached Christianitos Canyon just this side of the Orange County line. There is a historical monument at this point, at a spring in the canyon, which records the first baptisms in California. The Spanish called it the "Valley of Los Bautismos." Crespí tells the story:

"This day dawned cloudy for us. About seven o'clock we set out west and climbed a grassy hill. In a little while we entered a valley which turned to the north-northwest, and which communicates with that of Los Rosales. We traveled in the mountains, for they are not rough but open, with hills and extensive mesas, covered with a great deal of grass and grown with live oaks and alders, especially in the little valleys and arroyos, with an abundance of Castilian roses. Three mesas covered with large live oaks were encountered. About eleven o'clock we came to a pool of water, after having traveled some four leagues from the preceding place. This pool of fresh water is in a dry arroyo, which is grown with many alders. We made camp near the pool, and immediately about fourteen heathen, and as many women, with boys and girls, came and showed themselves to be very friendly; we entertained them and made them gifts. The explorers (scouts) informed us that on the preceding day they saw in the village two sick little girls. After asking the commander for some soldiers to go with us to visit them we went, and found one which the mother had at her breast apparently dying. We asked for it, saying that we wished to see it, but it was impossible to get it from its mother. So we said to her by signs that we would not do it any harm, but wished to sprinkle its head so that if it died it might go to heaven. She consented to this, and my companion, Fray Francisco Gómez, baptized it, giving it the name of María Magdalena. We went to the other, also small, who had been burned and was apparently about to die. In the same way I baptized it, giving it the name of Margarita. We did not doubt that both would die and go to heaven. With this, the only success that we have obtained, we fathers consider well worth while the long journey and the hardships that are being suffered in it and that are still awaiting us. May it all be for the greater glory of God and the salvation of souls. For this reason this place is known to the soldiers as Los Christianos; I named it San Apolinario; others called it Valley of Los Bautismos."

The valley is little disturbed from the time of Portolá. The Castilian rose still blooms there, as it did in the time of the first baptisms. This little rose, which they found all along their road to Monterey, and which grows from Baja California to Oregon, is not the true Rose of Castile, imported later from Spain but *rosa californica*, the little wild rose, pale-pink and sweet smelling. The explorers mentioned it many times, calling it the Rose of Castile because it reminded them of home.

Portolá's expedition was finding the journey easy and pleasant going. Now they walked, for a time, out of the history of San Diego County, to find hardships and disappointments. But back on Presidio Hill, an important chapter was being written, with only a handful of witnesses.

Cross overlooks Christianitos Canyon at county's edge.

Little wellhouse and plaque mark baptismal site.

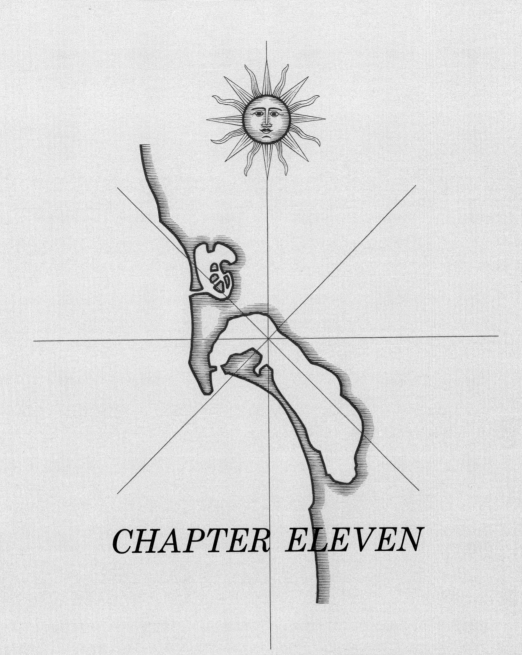

CHAPTER ELEVEN

THE CROSS IS RAISED

Early in the morning of July 16, 1769, two days after the departure of the expedition to Monterey, a little band of men gathered half-way up the sloping side of Presidio Hill in Old Town. Below them was the quiet, sheltering bay of San Diego. Beyond that was the vast ocean that had proved to be such a cruel and tyrannical master. Behind them stretched a seemingly endless, rising flow of green hills and blue mountains, of which they knew nothing. Watching them from various points of vantage were suspicious and increasingly resentful Indians who were beginning to dimly realize that their world was coming to an end.

A crude cross was raised on the site chosen for the first mission in California, and Serra sang High Mass and preached a sermon in honor of the occasion. His words have not come down to us, as he was too harassed in those trying days to keep up with his diary, but he certainly asked for courage and strength to meet the trials ahead and expressed thanks for the opportunity of offering their lives in the service of God.

THE PRESIDIO AT SAN DIEGO lived because at the moment of lost hope, help arrived by ship for near-starving padres and soldiers.

143

The first chapel was built of wooden stakes, with tule reeds for roofing. It was named Mission San Diego de Alcalá, after St. Didacus of Alcalá, whose name was first given to San Diego by the explorer Sebastián Vizcaíno in 1602. St. Didacus was a Franciscan friar who was sainted by Pope Sixtus V in 1588.

Serra knew, however, that others would follow and that some day there would be missions stretching all the way up New California, which the missionaries had wanted to christianize for more than a hundred years. "Above all," he wrote, "let those who are to come here as missionaries not imagine that they are coming for any other purpose but to endure hardships for the love of God and for the salvation of souls, for in far-off places such as these, where there is no way for the old missions to help the new ones because of the great distance between them, the presence of pagans, and the lack of communication by sea, it will be necessary in the beginning to suffer many real privations. However, all things are sweet to a lover."

Trouble was not long in coming. The Indians were treated with kindness and given gifts, but with their original curiosity satisfied, they began to press in on the white invaders. They became insolent, pestering the sick at night, craftily watching the burials of those who died of scurvy, and mimicking the sounds of guns. They stole anything they could find, being especially fond of cloth, and on one occasion went out to the *San Carlos* on rafts and tried to steal the sails. Guards had to be placed on the ship and two others always accompanied the fathers when they went aboard to say Mass.

As the Spaniards died one by one from the effects of the lingering scurvy, the Indians became emboldened by the diminishing strength of the garrison, and it soon became evident that an attack of some kind was imminent. The hour of peril that came on August 15th is described by Serra.

"When these natives, with whom the soldiers from the very beginning showed much familiarity, noticed how small our numbers were, and that we were continually burying a great number, and that many besides were prostrate in bed, on the Assumption Day of Our Blessed Lady, they imagined they could kill us all very easily. The more so when out of our very limited number they saw four going to the beach to change escort and bring back Father Fernando. He had gone on the preceding Saturday to say Mass for those on the boat. They broke in all of a sudden; and the only four soldiers present, seeing their ugly mood, immediately snatched up their arms. The fight was on. There were wounded both on our side and theirs. The one worst hurt was a young Spanish lad from the diocese of Guadalajara. He came to me in Loreto to be my servant on the road, and to be with me wherever I should be established. At the first shot he darted into my hut, spouting so much blood at the mouth and from his temples, that I had hardly time to absolve him and help him to meet his end. This came in less than a quarter of an hour. He expired on the ground before me bathed in his own blood. And so I was quite a while with him there dead, and my little apartment a pool of blood. Still the exchange of shots — bullets and arrows — went on. There were only four on our side against more than twenty on theirs. And there I was with the dead man, thinking it most probable I would soon have to follow him, but at the same time praying to God that the victory would be for our Catholic Faith without losing a single soul. And so it turned out, thank God, for seeing many of their companions covered with blood, they all fled."

The boy who died was José María Vergerano, an arrow piercing his throat. Three Indians were killed and a number were wounded, two later dying. This fact either was kept from Serra or else he chose to ignore it, as in his correspondence he mentioned he did not believe any Indians had been killed. Serra came to convert, not to kill. Death was not important.

STICKS AND REEDS were used to build a stockade and the first crude California mission on Presidio Hill.

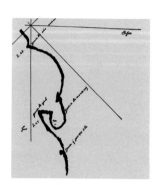

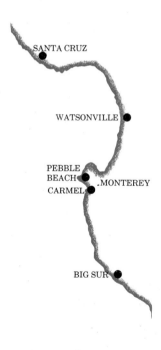

This is Monterey Bay as Vizcaíno mapped it, and below is how it actually looks.

Fr. Vizcaíno, a blacksmith named Chacón, and a Christian Indian who came with them from San Ignacio Mission were wounded, although not seriously. An arrow went through a carpet which had been hung up and struck Vizcaíno in the hand, splinters piercing two fingers. The soldiers also may have been hurt, but the records are not clear and reports of the incident, mostly written afterward, vary. One version is that the fight started when Indians tried to snatch sheets from the beds of the sick.

After the battle, the Spanish soldiers built a stockade of poles around the mission building and forbade the Indians to enter. The latter quieted down for a time but would not yield to conversion, to Serra's great disappointment. Seemingly, almost in desperation, he took a child and attempted to baptize it, but the parents snatched it back amid the jeers and laughter of the Indians.

The three fathers, however, largely were occupied with the problems of the sick and with bare survival. Eight more Catalán volunteers, four more soldiers, one servant and six more faithful Baja California Indians died of scurvy and were buried. The *San José* was given up for lost.

Meanwhile, the courageous and unhappy Portolá was struggling northward in California toward the port of Monterey, which Sebastián Vizcaíno had described with such exaggeration, seeing nothing on the way, he reported, except rocks, brushwood and rugged mountains covered with snow. Portolá reached the area of the bay in thirty-eight days, but, as it did not come up to Vizcaíno's description, he went on. With a sinking feeling, the Spaniards on October 31st sighted Port Reyes and the Farallon Islands off San Francisco, landmarks easily recognizable from earlier maps. They knew they had gone past the port of Monterey. Before turning back, a band of hunters went into the hills and from the top of one caught sight of an arm of the sea running inland to the southeast. The next day a scouting expedition under Sgt. Ortega came to the shore of San Francisco Bay, which Crespí noted was large enough to hold all the ships in Europe. None of the early explorers had reported such a harbor, and Portolá failed to appreciate the significance of his discovery. To him it was only another barrier in his search for Monterey. "In this confusion and distress, friend, not under compulsion from the Russians but from keen hunger which was wearing us out," Portolá notes, "we decided to return to San Diego." They speculated that perhaps the bay had filled with sand.

They began the long trek back:

"In order that we might not die meanwhile, I ordered that at the end of each day's march, one of the weak old mules which carried our baggage and ourselves should be killed. The flesh we roasted or half-fried in a fire made in a hole in the ground. The mule thus being prepared without a grain of salt or seasoning — for we had none — we shut our eyes and fell to on that skinny mule (what misery!) like hungry lions."

Costansó tells that as they approached San Diego they began to wonder about the conditions they would find at the new settlement they had left six months before.

"Each one discussed the meeting according to his temperament and the mood affecting him. Some, seeing things in a favorable light, expected to find them there in every comfort and help, others grieved, considering its weak state and the few resources we had left them. In truth, all of us were returning with a misgiving lest, through the continued force of the maladies and mortality among the people, the settlement had become a place of solitude. On the other hand, there was every reason to fear the evil disposition of the natives of San Diego, whose greediness to rob can only be restrained by superior power and authority, and we feared lest they dared to commit some outrage against the mission and its small garrison."

The sixty-four man expedition emerged from Rose Canyon on January 24, 1770. They found the three missionary fathers well and those who had survived recovering from injuries and scurvy. When Portolá said he couldn't find Monterey, Serra rebuked him with a remark, "You come from Rome without having seen the Pope." Serra and Vila realized from Portolá's descriptions that he actually had reached Monterey but had failed to recognize it. There was more distress, too, for Serra. He learned that Crespí and Gómez had baptized two Indian girls at Christianitos Canyon, the first baptismal ceremony in California. Serra was to recall with unhappiness to his dying day that he had not been the one to perform it.

The shortage of food was more critical than ever. For several more months they waited, subsisting on geese, fish, and other food brought by the Indians in exchange for clothing. Portolá complained that some of the soldiers were left with hardly enough to cover their backs. Though they planted a small quantity of corn which grew well, the birds ate most of it.

Portolá decided to send Captain Rivera down the peninsula for more cattle and a pack train of supplies. Rivera departed on February 10th with some of the soldiers, thereby partially alleviating the drain on the scanty food supply. There are conflicting reports of Portolá's attitude on San Diego. Costansó says that Rivera went because Portolá was determined to hold the port lest he incur discredit by abandoning it. Palóu says that Portolá was in favor of giving it up but was restrained by the pleas of Serra. Serra himself notes: "There is even talk of abandonment and suppression of my poor little mission in San Diego. May God avert such a tragedy."

However, in conversation with Serra, Portolá set a deadline, resolving that, if on the day of St. Joseph, March 19th, a bark did not arrive with help, the expedition should leave the next day because "there were not enough provisions to wait longer and the men had not come to perish from hunger."

Palóu says that "from the very first moment when the governor made public the fact that the expedition would return to Old California in the event that no ship had arrived by March 19th, hardly any other topic of conversation but that of the return trip was heard in San Diego . . . All these conversations and preparations were as so many arrows that pierced the fervent heart of our venerable Father President."

Serra felt that if the port were to be abandoned, centuries might pass before it could be settled again, and this brought forth his own resolution to remain in California, even if the rest of the expedition should return. To this end, he invited his former pupil, Crespí, to remain with him. The latter gratefully complied. Vila also confided to Serra his intention to keep the *San Carlos* in San Diego harbor, as he thought the port could be held.

It was now well into March, and they had no way of knowing whether help was actually on the way or whether they had been abandoned by those for whom they had endured so much. The *San Antonio*, of course, was on her way back up the coast.

But what had happened to the *San José*? Reloaded at San Blas and San Lucas, she had swung around the cape for the run to San Diego. In a month she was back once more, this time for more water. She sailed again in May of 1770 and vanished. Moreover, the *San Antonio* had instructions to by-pass San Diego and proceed directly to Monterey, on the assumption that Portolá and Serra already had established a colony and mission there as planned.

Serra proposed to Portolá that all should make a novena, a nineday devotion, in honor of St. Joseph, who was the patron saint of the expedition, and it was begun in time to have the closing on this feast day, March 19th. But it seemed that all was to no avail. The morning of the feast brought no sighting of a ship. Portolá and his men completed their preparations to leave for Velicatá. At three o'clock in the afternoon, the sails of a ship were discernible on the distant horizon. The ship went right past the entrance to the bay, but somehow all felt that their troubles were over. Portolá postponed his departure. Four days later, the *San Antonia* entered the

THIS MAP OF SAN DIEGO BAY, made in 1782 by the pilot Juan Pantoja, gives the water depths and makes it possible to locate approximately the first camp of the Portolá expedition. It was near the edge of the shoals, at about the present intersection of Laurel St. and Pacific Highway. The camp then was moved to Presidio Hill, to be nearer the river and fresh water. It became the Presidio of San Diego.

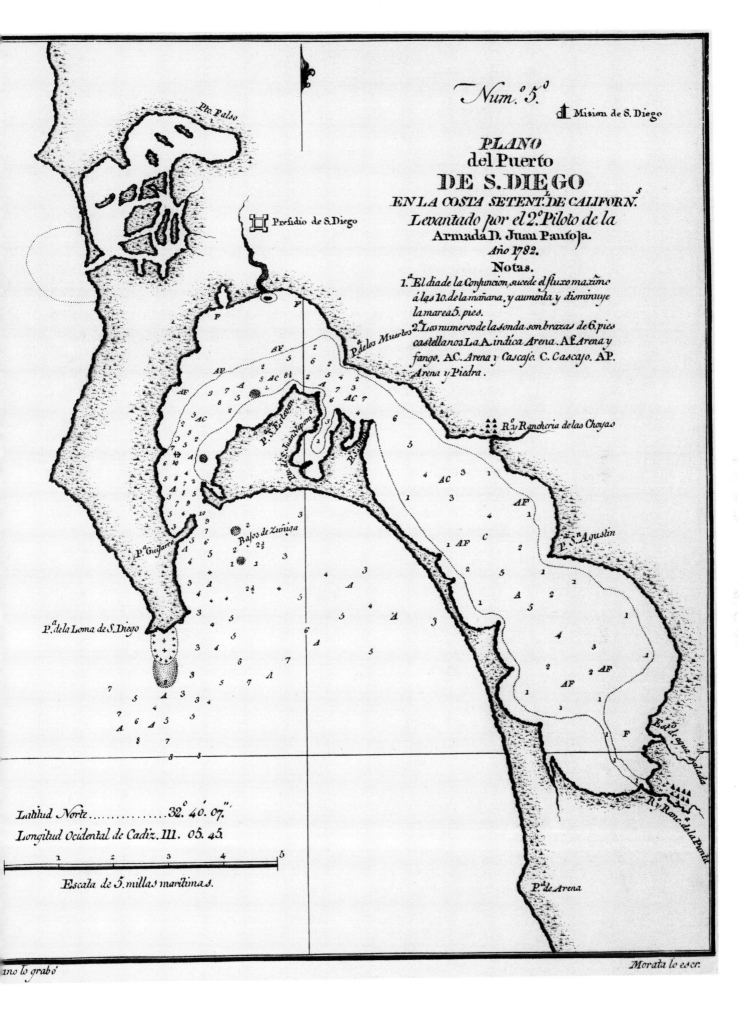

Num.º 5.º ⚓ Mision de S. Diego

PLANO
del Puerto
DE S. DIEGO
EN LA COSTA SETENT. DE CALIFORN.ˢ
Levantado por el 2.º Piloto de la
Armada D. Juan Pantoja.
Año 1782.
Notas.
1.ª El dia de la Conpuncion, sucede el fluxo maxĩmo
á las 10. de la mañana, y aumenta y disminuye
la marea 5. pies.
2.ª Los numeros de la sonda son brazas de 6. pies
castellanos La A. indica Arena. Aℓ. Arena y
fango. AC. Arena y Cascajo. C. Cascajo. AP.
Arena y Piedra.

Pto. Falso

☗ Presidio de S. Diego

P. de los Muertos

▲ Rº y Ranchería de las Choyas

P.ᵗ S.ᵗ Estevan

Ba. de S.ᵗ Juan Nepom.

P. Guijarro

P. S.ⁿ Agustin

Bajos de Zúñiga

P.ᵃ de la Loma de S. Diego

P.ᵗ de Arena

Eʳ.º de la gua Salada

Rº y Ranchª de la Punta

Latitud Norte............. 32.º 40. 07."
Longitud Ocidental de Cadiz. 111. 05. 45.

Escala de 5. millas maritimas.

...ano lo grabó

Morata lo escr.

harbor of San Diego. On her way to Monterey she had lost an anchor near Point Conception, and crewmen going ashore for fresh water learned from friendly Indians that the expedition which had gone north had long since turned back for San Diego. Pérez decided to go directly to San Diego to obtain an anchor from the *San Carlos*, which he knew was still in the bay. Although the *San Antonio* again had lost most of her crew from scurvy, she brought the corn, flour and rice which meant salvation for the presidio and city of San Diego. The cost had been terrible, but it was small in comparison to the great things that lay ahead.

All of the principal participants testify in their reports, diaries and correspondence to the events on Presidio Hill preceding the arrival of the *San Antonio*. Crespí writes: "Nine days before the feast of the most holy patron of both expeditions of sea and land, the glorious patriarch St. Joseph, all began to participate in a novena imploring the intercession of divine aid, and on the very day of the feast, March 19th, on which a high mass had been sung, a sermon preached, and at which many confessions were heard, and communions received, at about three o'clock in the afternoon, we saw outside of our desired port a ship that was coming supplied with every kind of provision." Forever after, Serra celebrated a high mass on the 19th of every month, in honor of the saving of San Diego and the first mission in California.

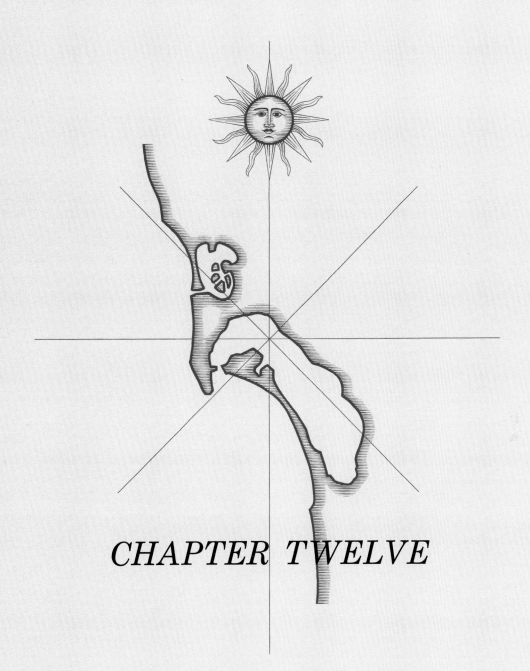

CHAPTER TWELVE

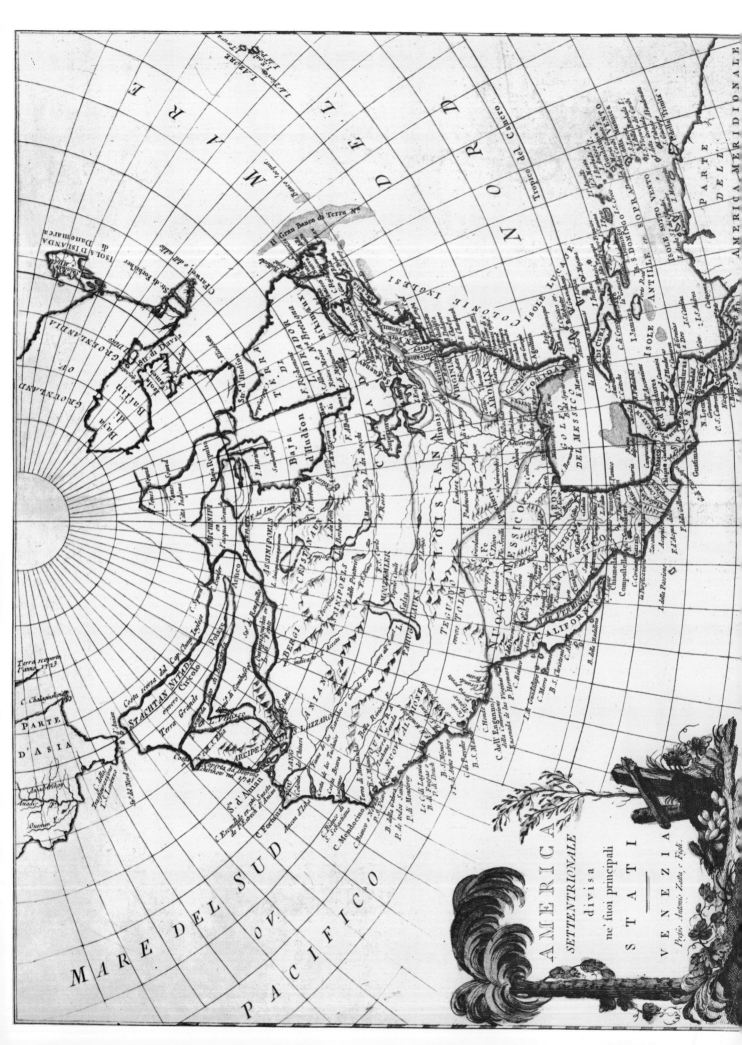

ANZA FINDS THE WAY

The next three years were difficult ones for those who remained at the San Diego Mission on Presidio Hill. Serra went with Portolá on his second expedition to find Monterey and to carry out the king's orders to build a settlement there. A mission was founded east of what is now Los Angeles at San Gabriel, the second in southern California. Then Serra was forced to return to Mexico to see what he could do to help in solving the continual problem of obtaining supplies. Twice the San Diego Mission had been nearly starved out. The sea route from La Paz or west coast mainland ports was long and dangerous, as had been proved, and the arrival of the faithful supply ships, the *San Carlos* and the *San Antonio*, was never certain. Most of the provisions and manufactured goods had to come from Baja California — which also was in a state of impoverishment — or from Mexico. Supplies often were transported up through Mexico, then shipped by boat across the Gulf to Baja California and packed by mule train up the peninsula to San Diego. There was a great need for more soldiers, laborers and colonists,

THIS MAP OF NORTH AMERICA, made in 1785 by an Italian, is of interest because it still shows the Strait of Anián, actually the Northwest Passage; and San Miguel Bay (misplaced), Cabrillo's name for San Diego Bay.

153

Mission near Tubac where trek began.

but the little ships hardly had room for more than a minimum of supplies and their own crews. It was obvious another answer had to be found, or California still might be lost. The man who thought he had found the answer was Don Juan Bautista de Anza.

Anza, a frontiersman by birth, was captain of the presidio at Tubac, a settlement in the wedge Spain had driven into the Apache country of Arizona. Tubac today is a village north of Nogales, Arizona, on the highway to Tucson. Anza's father and grandfather also had been in military service along the northern frontier. His father, once a temporary governor of Sonora, was killed by the Apaches and the son grew up as an Indian fighter in the town of Frontera in Sonora, just south of Douglas, Arizona. He volunteered for military duty at eighteen, became a lieutenant in 1755 and a captain five years later, and in 1763 married the sister of José Manuel Díaz del Carpio, chaplain of Tubac. The historic events in which he was destined to take part were to prove him a man of unusual ability and character. He was heavily bearded to the ears, with a strong and large nose and arched eyebrows. Rugged, as one had to be to dominate a wild and uncertain frontier, at the same time he was dignified in bearing and considerate of those in his command. That he was a thoughtful man was also of importance to the history of California.

The idea that a land route could be opened from Mexico to the new colonies in Alta California came to Anza in conversations with the Pima Indians in the area of Tubac. From them he learned that the Yuma Indians in the vicinity of the Colorado River had reported hearing of white men ranging up and down the coast. If the news of the Portolá expeditions had been passed from one Indian tribe to another across mountains and deserts, as it obviously had, it must mean that there was a direct land route from Sonora to San Diego and Monterey. The fever of exploration began burning in Anza, as it had in so many before him.

Anza received support from a missionary, Fr. Francisco Garcés, a Franciscan of Mission San Xavier del Bac in Arizona, north of Tubac, an intrepid and insatiable explorer, who knew the Pima language and probably some of the Yuman. Traveling alone, on one of his many expeditions, he had gone down the Gila River to its junction with the Colorado and made friends with the Yuman chief, Salvador Palma. Then he had crossed the river, followed it downstream almost to the head of the Gulf, and returned in a northwesterly direction across the Baja California desert to a place called San Jacome near the base of the Cocopa Mountains, from which he sighted Cierro Prieto, or Black Mountain, thirty miles southeast of today's Mexicali. He followed the interior desert valley north and

154

crossed into what is now Imperial Valley, north of Laguna Salada, and, from a place near Santa Rosa or Yuha Wells, his eyes followed the high blue coastal range in San Diego County far into the distance where he could see a gap in the San Jacinto Mountains, which to him meant that there was a pass and so a possible land route to Monterey. This gap, of course, was San Carlos Pass leading north out of Borrego Valley between the San Ysidro and Santa Rosa Mountains. It was an incredible journey for a lone man, made in the intense heat of the summer. Often he was without water but managed to live off the land through his ability to make friends with the Indians.

On his return, Garcés told Anza what he had seen; his report crystalized Anza's resolve to try and open an overland route to the new missions. Anza at first met indifference, but the appointment of a new viceroy of Mexico, Don Antonio María Bucareli y Ursúa, was to bring action. On May 2, 1772, Anza wrote a letter to the viceroy in which he outlined his plan for opening communication between the port of Monterey and Sonora.

The letter reads, in part:

"The fervent desire which at all times moves me to serve his Majesty and advance his conquests, impels me to beg of your Excellency, in case you learn that it is to be granted to anyone, permission to make the necessary efforts to see if we can open communication between the port of Monte Rey and the province of Sonora . . . In 1769, the same year in which the expedition was made to find the Monte Rey mentioned, I learned through the heathen Pima tribe, which maintains communication with us and lives fifty leagues from this presidio, and the same distance or a little more from the junction of this river with the Colorado, that the vast tribes which live there had told them that on the other side of the Colorado, at some distance, white men were passing, a thing which they had never seen before. Having been assigned to the expedition which was then being made against the Pima and the Seris, I reported this news to the governor of the provinces, to my Colonel, Don Domingo Elizondo, commander of the expedition, and to officials who reside in that capital, and, finally, to the Señor Visitor-General, Don Joseph de Gálvez, at the time of his coming to this province that year. In the same year this tribe repeated the story to the very reverend father Fray Francisco Garcés, missionary *de propaganda fide*, who went to visit it, and who is now engaged in his ministry in the pueblo of San Xavier del Bac, distant from here fifteen leagues. And on another occasion the same tribe has recently repeated the same thing to me, which it never had done before. To all this it is to be added that this zealous missionary, with the aim of preparing the heathen situated in the northwest and west to receive the Holy Evangel, went in to them alone and with inexpressible hardships in the month of August of last year. Having been at the junction of the Colorado and Gila Rivers, he remained on these streams many days, conversing with the tribes who live there, by whom he was well received because of their natural docility. And through the Yuma tribe, which embraces a large part of the Colorado, he learned, without asking, that at no great distance from them there were white people. Those who had chanced to see them begged him by signs, which was the common language, that he should show them the compass, the

Antonio M. Bucareli, viceroy of Mexico, who brought about the Anza expeditions to new land.

glass for making fire, and other instruments which we use but which the father did not have, and which, if they had not seen them in that country, they could not have known about, for from this region no one has gone into their land, nor do they come out to ours, on account of the many enemies who keep the way closed to them. Likewise, they gave this father to understand that to the north and east of them there were also people of our own kind, distinct from those whom they indicated to the west, and that some of their relatives maintained communication with the Indians ... who live in New Mexico, for otherwise, it would seem, they must be strangers.

"From the same Colorado River this father discovered a great mountain chain of blue color, and although he did not cross it he thinks that it may be the one which our troops skirted when they went to Monte Rey. And if it is on the other side of the river, as is believed, the lack of water on the way will presumably be much less than has been stated hitherto, because everybody has thought it to be through level country. Indeed, up to now, at least in these parts, we have had no notice of this sierra, and I believe that this is because those who have gone to the Colorado have always inclined toward the coast, and since they did not go up to the north they could not see it. In view of all these considerations, this reverend father and I are convinced that the distance from here to Monte Rey cannot be so great as formerly has been estimated, and that it will not be impossible to overcome any obstacles encountered on the way. Therefore, if all this should merit the approval of your Excellency, I hope that you will charge the president of these missions to grant the father mentioned permission to accompany me, for I am in accord with him to sacrifice myself to this purpose and to whatever may redound to the service of his Majesty and the glory of your Excellency ...

"May God our Lord spare the important life of your Excellency the many years which I beg of him. Presidio of Tubac, May 2, 1772. Most excellent Sir,

Juan Bapta. de Anza"

Anza's letter was referred to Costansó, now in Mexico, the engineer who had been with the Portolá expedition and wrote so much descriptive detail about San Diego and California. He confirmed the belief that a land route was possible. By his calculations the distance between old Tubac and San Diego ought to be about 180 common leagues, or 540 miles, while from Loreto to San Diego over a difficult terrain it was about 300 leagues, or 900 miles. He also noted the fact there was direct communication between the many Indian peoples.

"This I know from experience, for I saw in the hands of Indians of the Channel of Santa Barbara certain articles which came from the Spaniards in New Mexico, such as pieces of wrought silver, knives, pieces of broadsword, and of manufactured iron, and blankets and fabrics of wool, for they told me they had obtained them from the east where lived some men dressed and armed like ourselves."

As the territory had been explored as far as the Colorado River, to Costansó there remained only one difficulty, that of "seeking a way to the mountains which intervene between the Colorado and the coast of the South Sea. These, indeed, are wide and rough, in so far as I was able to judge from what I saw during my journey;

but, on the other hand, some openings were seen, and since the Indians cross them easily, our people will be able to do likewise . . ."

In Mexico City, Serra also expressed his interest in favor of a land route for supply, though he suggested a different route, one from Santa Fe, New Mexico, directly to Monterey. Bucareli cast the decision for an expedition from Sonora by way of the junction of the Gila and Colorado Rivers, with Anza as organizer and leader.

The good news was brought to Anza by Juan Bautista Valdés, who also originally had been with Portolá and now rode the 1500 miles from Mexico City to Tubac with Bucareli's orders. Loneliness and distance were nothing to him, and after the expedition reached its first goal, the mission at San Gabriel, he rode all the way back to Mexico City with Anza's diary telling of the discovery of the land route to Alta California, news which the delighted Bucareli forwarded immediately to King Carlos III. California could be saved from the Russians.

Thus Anza became the first of the great land explorers who were to open up the American west; the two pioneering treks which he led from Mexico up into California, with the loss of only one person, compare favorably with any in history. His first trek in 1774 broke 600 miles of new trail. The second, made in 1775-1776 with the first colonists for the new settlements in California, covered 1600 miles from its starting point, Culiacán, Sinaloa, to Monterey. Three children were born en route.

Accompanying Anza on the first expedition were two missionaries, the eager Garcés and Fr. Juan Díaz, also a Franciscan, both of whom were fated to be martyred in an Indian massacre at Yuma in 1781; and an Indian named Sebastián Tarabal. Sebastián had been over much of the land to the north. A Baja California Indian, he had been sent to New California to help the mission fathers, but after a short time had run away from San Gabriel with his wife and a relative, and crossing the San Jacinto Mountains had struggled through the Borrego Desert, and among the sand dunes near the Colorado River, where his wife and relative lost their lives, before reaching Yuma. From there Sebastián went to Tubac, arriving just in time to serve as a guide.

One other white man had ventured into the forbidding desert. This was Pedro Fages, whom we remember from the Portolá expedition. In 1772, in pursuit of deserters from the San Diego Presidio, he crossed the high Cuyamaca Mountains and penetrated deep into Imperial Valley, thus establishing a direct route to San Diego, which, however, would not be used for another decade.

There were 34 persons altogether in Anza's expedition, including

Valdés, who knew the road from San Diego to Monterey; 35 pack loads of provisions, equipment, tobacco, carpenters' tools, and other necessities; 65 cattle and 140 saddle animals. Unfortunately, 130 of the horses were stolen in an Indian raid before the expedition left, and this loss, plus fear of the Apaches in southwestern Arizona, caused them to take a considerable detour.

The royal flag of Spain fluttered in the breeze as the expedition began its march from Tubac on January 8th — its hoped-for goal, Monterey, a thousand miles away. They dropped down into the narrow strip of Mexico which runs along the southwestern border of Arizona to reach Caborca in the Altar Valley, a distance of about

MAP SHOWING ANZA'S ROUTES in 1774 and 1775, from Tubac in Arizona to Los Angeles in California. After crossing the Colorado River at Yuma, by skirting the Colorado Desert and keeping near the base of the Sierra, Anza found enough water to get his people through Borrego Valley in San Diego County, and up over the San Carlos Pass. Dotted line shows variation in the second expedition route when accompanied by women and children.

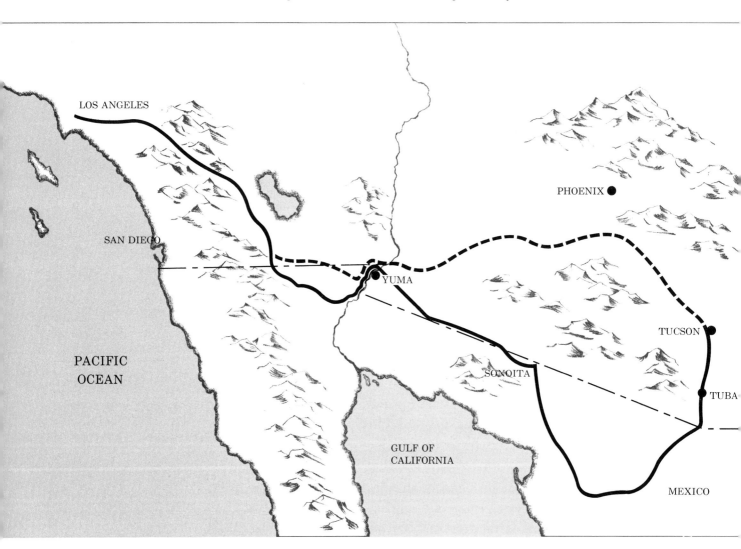

150 miles, where they hoped to replace the mounts stolen by the Apaches. But drought and more Indian raids had depleted the available stock, and Anza obtained only a few mules which he described as mere "stacks of bones." This was home for Fr. Díaz, as he had left the mission here to join the expedition. It was a country alive with memories of Spain's diminishing greatness. Nearby was Mission Dolores, founded by Fr. Kino, and Magdalena Mission, where he had been buried sixty years before. The missions were old, many of them in ruins. Time already was dealing Spain out of the New World, but nobody fully realized it yet. A new adventure was still ahead. It was 600 miles from Caborca to New California. The trail from here led north 125 miles to the Sonoita River over a country first explored by Kino and Salvatierra, and traveled more recently by Garcés, Tarabal and Anza himself.

Then began the worst part of the journey, to the Colorado River over Camino del Diablo, the Road of the Devil, which had held so many terrors for Spanish explorers for 200 years and which was to take the lives of scores of persons during the Gold Rush to California 75 years later. Water holes were a matter of life and death in the 100 miles between El Carrizal on the Sonoita River and Yuma. Many times in the rugged mountains they were saved from death by finding water in potholes or rock tanks, some of which hold thousands of gallons of water.

Upon reaching Yuma and the junction of the rivers, they were welcomed by Garcés' old friend, the Yuman chief Palma; 600 Indians — men, women and children, mostly naked — joined in the task of helping them cross the Colorado River. Any hope of a straight crossing of the desert to the west toward the distant mountains had to be given up, in the face of the seemingly impassable barrier of the great sand dunes of the Imperial Valley. The expedition followed the river south to a place called Santa Olaya, a few miles west of the Colorado, where there was pasturage and fresh water. Here Anza decided to leave the river and strike west to the Cocopa range and then follow it north to the main sierra. But it was at this point that Garcés' memory of landmarks became confused, and an Indian guide, fearful of entering enemy territory, left them. But before doing so, he pointed to a mountain peak rising out of the flat desert far to the north. That, he said, should be their guiding beacon, and near there water could be found. This was Signal Mountain, west of Mexicali.

Signal Mountain became a beacon, which, however, seemed to keep receding as the weary pioneers fought to find a way through new masses of drifting sand dunes. The Spanish dubbed Signal

Signal Mountain, explorers' beacon.

Santa Rosa campsite in Yuha Desert.

Mountain Cerro del Imposible, or the Impossible Hill. Ten days were lost in hopeless wandering and finally they were forced to return to Santa Olaya. It was decided that many of the supplies would have to be left behind, and enough men and mules were released to carry them back to Yuma. A stripped-down expedition pushed still farther south to get around the dunes and then followed the base of the small Cocopa mountain range in northeast Baja California. Signal Mountain slowly began to loom larger on the horizon. Before reaching it, they sighted a gap in the Cocopas, now known as the Lower Pass, and through this they dropped down to the shore of a vast salt lake, Laguna Salada, and made camp near a marsh at its dry north end, which they called San Eusebio. On the banks of the lake they found stranded sea fish, indicating that the lake was filled and emptied by tidal action from the surging waters of the Gulf of California.

The next camp was at Santo Tomás in the Pinto Canyon along the road between Mexicali and Tijuana, and from there they crossed today's International Line. Before them stretched the vast bed of a dead sea. Crushed bits of sea shells were everywhere, and old shore lines rippled across the dirty wastes of sand. It was a strange, upside down world sunk below the level of the oceans. The sand was on top and the water underneath. The ocean itself long since had retreated, and even at this time there was no trace left of the fresh water lake that once filled a large part of the desert in wetter ages. The Salton Sea had not yet been formed by a rampant Colorado River. But ahead, on the far hazy horizon, they could see the pass they had been seeking in weeks of walking and riding. Where distant mountain groups came together to the north of Borrego Valley there was a giant cleft or rift which indicated a passable canyon. This was the same pass which Garcés had sighted two and a half years before. Their first camp in California was made just over the border from a place where scouts captured some Indians and learned of nearby wells. The wells, in a wash in Imperial Valley about four miles north of the border and about seven miles south of Plaster City in the vicinity of the present Yuha Springs, were named Santa Rosa of the Flat Rocks. A motorist can almost see the spot from Highway 98, which cuts off from Highway 80 at In-KoPah Gorge and runs to Calexico and Mexicali.

Anza's detailed diaries, now in the National Archives of Mexico, under the date of March 8th, tell of this event:

"At seven o'clock in the morning we took up the march over good country towards the northeast, and having gone about a league and a quarter we reached the wells mentioned, and when they were opened they poured forth an abundance of the finest water. We called them Santa Rosa de las Lajas.

Because there was some pasturage in this place and our riding animals had become badly worn out, I decided to stop here for the day. These wells are in such a location that in two convenient journeys we might have come to them from the Laguna de Santa Olaya. Indeed, the two places cannot be more than eighteen leagues apart, but traveling through unknown country inevitably involves these detours. Notwithstanding the one which we have made, we celebrated our arrival at this place, because from it the California Indian has recognized that he is now near a place where he formerly was, and therefore we now promise ourselves that our expedition will not fail."

Sebastián had struggled through here on his way to the Colorado River. Though the Anza and Borrego Deserts still lay ahead, they knew the worst was over. Anza writes that they had traveled 197 leagues, or 591 miles, in the two months since leaving Tubac.

White men were to cross into San Diego County, from northeast of the desert country, for the first time, and there Anza was to demonstrate his skill as a diplomat in establishing peace between warring Indian tribes.

They left the pleasant wells Wednesday afternoon and camped that night in a thin pasturage about four or five miles north of to-day's Plaster City. Thursday was a big day. Leaving at dawn, they kept the high mountain chain to their left, passing the volcanic Superstition Mountain and the mudstone and sandstone of Super-stition Hills on their right, and, punching through more sand dunes, they reached a watering place which Anza named San Sebastián, alias del Peregrino, in honor of the wanderings of the Indian Se-bastián. It was a large marsh with a small lake and a well of fresh water on San Felipe Creek near its junction with Carrizo Creek, and near a spot now identified as Harper's Well, lying more than 160 feet below sea level. It is directly west of Highway 99, about three miles from Kane Spring and south of Highway 78 running from Highway 99 to Borrego Valley, from which it can be seen.

"At daybreak we took the same direction, toward the north, and at seven o'clock we began to cross some little points of sand dunes which extend for about half a league. At the beginning of them most of the soldiers dismounted, agreeing among themselves to make most of the following journeys on foot, in order that they might not lack mounts on which to carry their saddles and other necessary things. Having traveled seven leagues, at one o'clock in the afternoon we reached the watering place . . . This place is a very large marsh with many waters and much pasturage, but both are very salty, except for one spring where we are, which is fair sized and running. Here we found a small village of mountain Indians who took flight, abandoning all their little possessions, which I did not permit anyone to touch. I had the native of California, our guide from here forward, go to overtake someone. He went after them and brought a woman to my presence, and I gave her beads and tobacco, telling her that she could call her friends, with assurance that no harm would be done them and that it would be good for them to accept our gifts. She did so, and at three o'clock in the afternoon seven men came, al-though with much perturbation, and I gave them the usual presents . . . After

This is the catalogue of the journal and letters of Capt. de Anza on his trail-breaking, and recommendation for his promotion.

They noted large pools of water in Santa Margarita Valley.

161

Precidio de tubac que es el de mi cargo

En el encargue al Reverendo Padre Frai Juan Diaz, q.e ha sido, quien a hecho las Obcervaciones, de nuestro
trancito, expresase, en un Mapa, el q.e hemos efectuado, p.ª
darte una idea, al Exmo s.r Virrey, delos Rumbos, Mar-
chenias, y demas particurinidades, q.e hemos Notado.

A las doce d el. llego al mencionado Precidio el resto
dela expedicion, q.e deje atras, en lo q.e se ha verificado, la
totaloconclucion, de ella, con las felicidades, y ventajas q.e
quedan, expresadas, en lo descripto anterior, p.r lo q.e sea
el S.r de los Exercitos, Vendito y Alavado

Di trece de Noviembre de mil setecientos setenta y quatro
años, saqué esta copia, p.ª entregar en el mismo dia, al
Exmo S.r Virrey, Governador, y capitan General, en esta Ciudad de Mexico, en cuias manos, igualm.te tengo
entregado, el Mapa, q.e antecedente m.te se cita ———

a 27
s.ñ.z

Del consue Rey al
Precidio de tubac
291- leg

Juan B.ta de Anza

En 24 de Noviembre de
74 se saca la comunid
por principal Veste
Mad.o para Vax cu.
enva a S. M.

nightfall many more of these heathen assembled, and I made them embrace two Yumas who voluntarily have come with me. They have been continually at war, but I gave them to understand that war was ceasing from this day, as the nations farther back had been informed. This news caused them great rejoicing, and they celebrated it by breaking the few arrows which they were carrying. At the same time they promised that they would comply with my precept, never more going to the Colorado River for war, but only to visit, since now the two Yumas were their friends. Before this, however, they informed me by signs, that solely on seeing tracks of the Yumas they were going to cut off their heads, although they were in our company. They were now so completely relieved of their terror that this night they camped with their rivals, and regaled each other with such miserable possessions as these people customarily have."

Garcés was moved emotionally by the numbers of the Indians who obviously needed instruction and conversion:

"Oh, what a vast heathendom! Oh, what lands so suitable for missions! Oh! What a heathendom so docile! How fine it would be if the wise and pious Don Carlos III might see these lands! And oh, if at least we might bring it about that one who so worthily governs these kingdoms might see these provinces . . ."

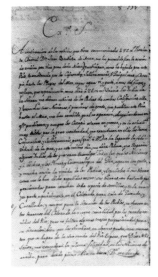

Fr. Garcés' report on desert trek.

Little progress was made the next day, because of a late start, and they camped still in the same marshes in the area of San Sebastián, where the pasturage proved so salty that the animals were made sick. Too, the pasturage was so soggy some of the animals became mired and almost were lost. Here they received the first definite word of the port of San Diego. In answer to questions, Indians indicated to Anza that "the sea must be distant three days' journey, and from the direction in which they pointed we inferred that it was the Philippine Ocean. They also gave me to understand that in five or six days' journey some relatives of theirs who lived near them came to some people like ourselves. We are convinced that they must be those who live at the port of San Diego." From their answers, however, Anza erroneously concluded that San Diego must be somewhere near the mouth of the Colorado River where it empties into the Gulf of California.

Saturday took them into Borrego Valley, where the territories of a number of Indian tribes came together. The Spanish first met two Yuman speaking groups, the Kamia and the Northern Diegueño, in the San Felipe Creek area. At that time the Kamia held the territory near where the creek emptied into the Salton Sea and the Northern Diegueños held the rest. The Cahuillas, who were Shoshoneans, occupied the northern part of Borrego Valley. The Desert Cahuillas were settled around the northern shore of the

WITH A FLOURISH, Capt. Juan Bautista de Anza signed his name to the journal of one of history's greatest marches.

present Salton Sea and extended west into Borrego Park and around Travertine Wash. The Mountain Cahuilla were in the western section, in the drainage area of Coyote Canyon and Clark Valley.

To enter Borrego the Spaniards cut north from the present route of Highway 78, where it crosses San Felipe Creek four miles east of Ocotillo, and following the creek they rounded Borrego Mountain and camped near the alkali sink to the west of it just below the grim, uninviting Borrego badlands. A small monument today marks the spot, but it is considerably off the traveled road. The spring that Anza found has long since dried up. The Indians living there were found to be exceptionally timid. Among them the Indian Sebastián found some who spoke the San Diego idiom, "which seems to confirm the opinion which has been formed that this port is not very far away."

The land was lifting now, and so were their spirits. Anza wrote:

The area of the original Borrego Springs, which Anza named San Gregorio. It is now dry.

"An hour before dawn we set forth west-northwest, toward a large valley formed by another sierra and the one which we have had on our left since leaving Santo Tomás. Having traveled over good terrain about six leagues, we arrived at a little water which was running slightly and of good quality, with better pasturage than any which has been seen since we left the Pimería. This place I named San Gregorio. When we arrived we discovered more than sixty heathen who were hunting. I made an effort to have some of them come to where we were encamped, sending the Californian to bring them, but just as he arrived with them near to where I was, our pack mules and relay saddle animals also arrived. Scenting the water they began to bray according to their custom, whereupon our much-sought heathen made precipitate flight. While among them the Californian observed that they spoke the language of San Diego. Our animals reached this place in the most deplorable state that can be imagined, because of the bad pasturage of San Sebastián, as has been said, and for this reason I decided not to travel tomorrow."

Garcés' diary notes that the Indians seemed to "eat a great quantity of wild onions, which abound in these parts."

Sunday was a day of rest. From the little watering hole 500 feet above sea level they could look west across the flat valley to the bleak, sharp but beautiful San Ysidro mountains, which rise so abruptly from the valley floor. Pink by day and somber velvet by night, they seem an impenetrable barrier between the harshness of the desert and the greenness of the sloping hills and valleys. To the northeast were the Santa Rosa Mountains. Between the two ranges was Coyote Canyon. Green fields now spread across the open wastes of yesterday. In the fitful shadows of tropical nights, with the gentle

San Gregorio Monument on Anza trail.

MAP SHOWING ANZA'S ROUTE *through Imperial, San Diego, and Riverside counties in 1774, when he pioneered the trail, and in 1775, when he led a large group of settlers from Mexico safely to San Gabriel Mission at Los Angeles.*

164

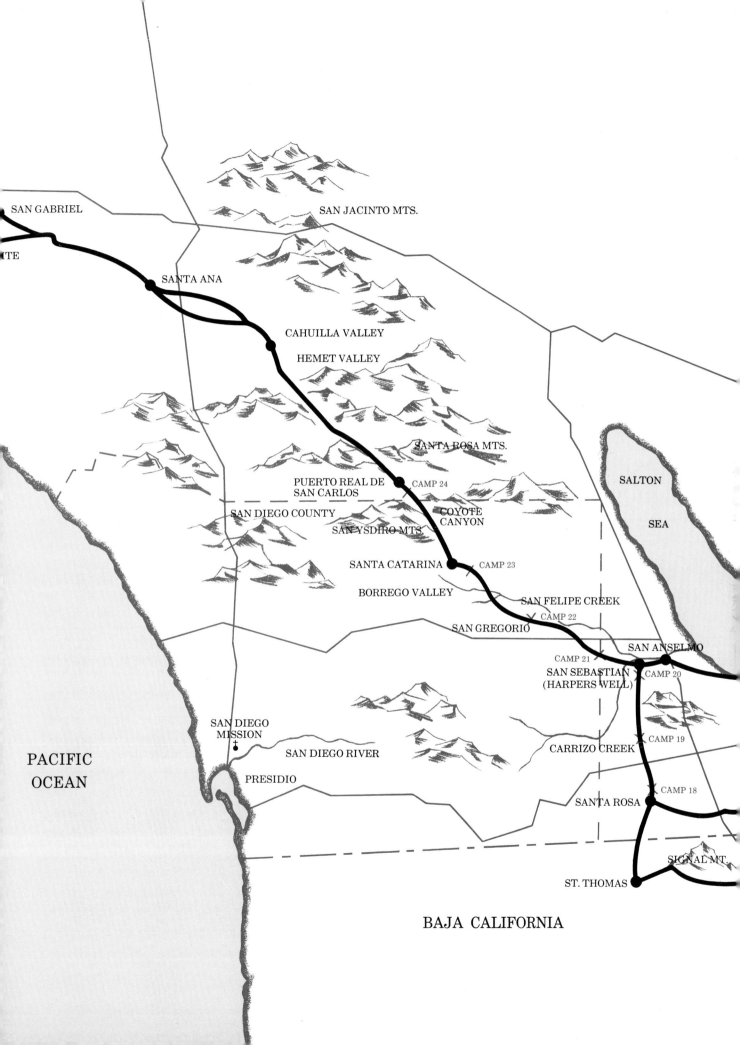

wind stirring the palms and citrus trees, one can almost see the ghosts of Anza's men as they ride the old trails of generations of people long since passed from the scene.

After their day of rest, they again set forth toward the north, crossing the area of the present airport, grape fields and orchards, and turning into Coyote Canyon, the pass which held so much hope.

This is the scene at the entrance of Coyote Canyon through which Anza passed to north.

"A little before daybreak we set forth toward the north, and having traveled about six leagues through various valleys with reasonable footing, we arrived at a spring or fountain of the finest water, which runs for about two leagues, having many willows most of the way. At its head, we halted for the night, and to the place I gave the name of Santa Catarina. Here we found much grass and other green plants, as well as wild vines and trees, which announce an improvement in the country from here forward."

The springs, almost tropical in richness, can be found on the maps as Santa Catarina Springs, or Lower Willows, at the entrance to Collins Valley in Coyote Canyon. The wise Anza saw the bubbling water, and, suspecting perhaps the deep reservoir that lay below the entire land, suggested in his diary the possibility of irrigation and "judging from the humidity in the land here, some seasonal crops might be planted." They found the Indians in the canyon more degenerate and cowardly than heretofore, without arms, and fleeing in panic at the whinnying of a horse. The Yuma tribes called these Indians the "sandal wearers." The idiom which they used suggested close ties with the Indians of the San Diego and San Gabriel Missions.

Coyote Canyon and route up through pass.

The next morning the expedition set forth up the arroyo,
"which runs north-northwest, dividing the large mountain chain through which it flows. The floor of the valley is very even and of considerable width for four leagues, where in various places running water is found. Two more leagues were traveled where the valley is narrower, and then, leaving it at the left, we climbed a ridge which did not cause the animals the greatest fatigue, and at whose crest we camped for the night in a place of good pasturage and water. Right here there is a pass which I named the Royal Pass of San Carlos. From it are seen the most beautiful green and flower-strewn prairies, and snow-covered mountains with pines, oaks, and other trees which grow in cold countries. Likewise here the waters divide, some flowing this way toward the Gulf and others toward the Philippine Ocean. It is now proved that the sierra in which we are traveling connects with the sierras of Lower California. In the course of the journey made today we have seen an improvement in the country in every way, and have concluded from its moisture that it may be suitable for seasonal crops and the planting of fruit trees, and that there are pastures sufficient for maintaining cattle."

San Carlos Pass is at an elevation of 1880 feet and well inside the Riverside county line. The Indians in this region appeared to be scrawny and excitable, more given to stealing than those in the lower deserts, and to delivering long harangues with violent movements of their hands and feet. Anza dubbed them The Dancers, but later a cynical padre described them as jumping around like wild goats. Rain and snow slowed their progress so that they were unable to get under way until the afternoon of the next day, when they climbed some small hills where a fair-sized vein of silver ore was found, reached the summit of the divide, and descended a slope into Valle del Príncipe to camp on the shores of a lake. This is now called Dry Lake in Terwilliger Valley, a part of Cahuilla Valley in southern Riverside County.

In one week they had crossed over sections of Imperial and San Diego counties, rising from the heat of deserts lying below sea level, to the moist climate of mountain passes. Three days of rain and snow slowed their progress across the San Jacinto Mountains. Then they dropped down into San Jacinto Valley, passed through areas now named Moreno, Riverside, Ontario and San Dimas, and finally swerved westward to San Gabriel Mission, arriving on March 22nd.

The geographical isolation of far-off California had been broken, or at least so they all thought. Though Fr. Paterna was happy to see the arrival of the expedition, the poor mission at San Gabriel did not have enough food to resupply Anza and enable him to push right on to Monterey. Word was received that a supply ship with Fr. Serra aboard had arrived at San Diego from Mexico, and it was decided to send Garcés and a pack train to the port. When Garcés returned to San Gabriel Mission, Anza was disappointed to find that the provisions they had brought from San Diego were inadequate, and that there were no replacements for their saddle animals. Anza and four soldiers, with two men from the mission to show the way, went on to Monterey while the others returned to Yuma. Garcés made the journey to Santa Olaya in eleven days by a new and shorter route. Anza, on his return trip from Monterey, followed Garcés' trail by notes left here and there on the route, and at Yuma followed the Gila River, cutting across Gila Bend to Casa Grande, then turning south to Tubac. This proved to be a shorter and much better route than the deadly road to Sonoita.

Anza arrived back at Tubac on May 26th, after an absence of four and a half months and a ride of approximately 2,200 miles. There was a great rejoicing in Mexico City. Bucareli was convinced of the practicality of the route. He promoted Anza to the rank of lieutenant colonel of cavalry and gave bonuses to the seventeen soldiers who had accompanied him. Bucareli wrote that "his presence, good judgment and talents, which I have now seen close at hand, have confirmed me in the opinion which I have had of him ever since the time when he proposed the exploration." The Franciscans were delighted.

CHAPTER THIRTEEN

SETTLEMENT AT LAST

With a land route to California now open, Viceroy Bucareli in Mexico City was anxious to send settlers to San Francisco, an area which Capt. Rivera, now at Monterey, had been instructed to explore. Again, Anza was assigned to do the job; his orders were to conduct the colonists, hand them over to Capt. Rivera upon arrival, do some more exploring of the San Francisco area, and return with ten veteran soldiers. A new expedition was put together at Culiacán, with colonists drawn from the impoverished settlers of the state of Sinaloa. Before they left, a considerable number of horses again were stolen in another Apache raid, and some of the colonists had to walk all the way to Monterey. More settlers joined up at Tubac.

Of all the treks across the wilderness areas of North America, none was more strange nor more fortunate than this one. Altogether there were 240 persons, including the 30 soldiers — of whom 29 had wives — four other families of colonists, and 115 children. Three more children were to be born en route, one in California. Only one person died on the march of more than 1600 weary miles. In addition,

JUAN BAUTISTA DE ANZA rides at the head of a column of settlers, accompanied by fathers and soldiers, as they journey to far-off California in the winter of 1775-1776.

171

there were herders, interpreters, muleteers, servants, and twenty army recruits; 140 pack mules carrying food and, among other things, women's clothing and four casks of brandy; 450 saddle horses and riding mules, and 355 cattle. Fr. Pedro Font was chosen to be the diarist and observer, and Frs. Garcés and Eixarch were to accompany him as far as Yuma and remain there to work among the Indians whose cooperation was so necessary.

What Anza had learned on his return trip from the first expedition now stood him in good stead. This time the expedition moved north from Culiacán to Tubac, where Font said final Mass on October 23, 1775. Then it moved north by way of Tucson and followed the Gila River west to its junction with the Colorado at the old Yuma crossing. There, a woman died in childbirth, but her son survived to reach California. At the Colorado they searched for a new fording place, as the old one was too deep at that time of year, and once over they went south over the former route to Santa Olaya in Baja California. The winter proved to be a hard one; there was a great deal of suffering ahead for all of them.

At Santa Olaya, Anza decided to split up the expedition into three sections, each starting on a different day in order to allow water holes to fill up between arrivals. Anza led the first one with Font, twelve soldiers and families, a pack train and some loose mules and horses; the second and third divisions were to be led by Sergeant Grijalva and Lt. Moraga respectively. The cattle were to be driven directly from El Carrizal to San Sebastián near Harper's Well, in Imperial Valley, accompanied by the herders and the rest of the soldiers carrying water bags. Anza went by the old route to the wells of Santa Rosa of the Flat Rocks, but all were finally reunited at San Sebastián. Winter was closing in fast, the desert was freezing at night and wet often, and snow was piling up in the mountain valleys through which they knew they must pass. Relations between Anza and Font were beginning to grow strained, Font being ill much of the time and critical of Anza's giving liquor to his men after strenuous marches.

Just as it did in 1774, the trail led from San Sebastián to Borrego Valley and San Gregorio in San Felipe Wash, and then up Coyote Canyon. As they neared Borrego Valley, they saw their first sunshine in six days, though the mountains, except those directly on

MAP MADE BY FATHER PEDRO FONT, who accompanied Anza on the second expedition as astrologer and cartographer. His map shows the route from the Yuma Crossing of the Colorado River, and the California coast from south of San Diego Bay to San Francisco Bay, with settlements and trails.

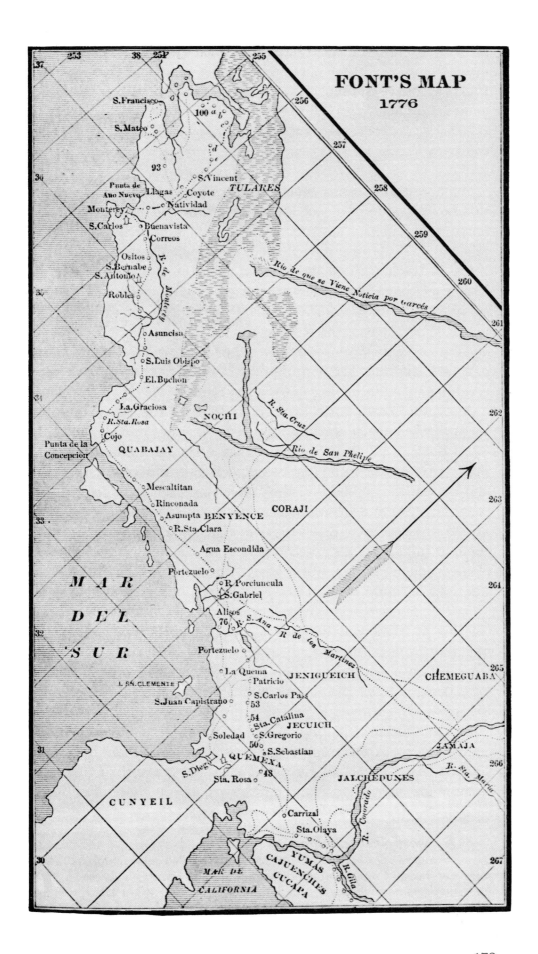

FONT'S MAP
1776

S.Francisco

100 *a b*

S.Mateo

d

e

93

S.Vincent

Punta de

Ano Nuevo   Llagas   Coyote   TULARES

Monterey   Natividad

S.Carlos   Buenavista

Correos

Ositos

S.Bernabe

S.Antonio

Robles

Asuncion

Rio de que se Viene Noticia por Garcés

S.Luis Obispo

El Buchon

La Graciosa

NOCHI

R. Sta. Cruz

R.Sta.Rosa

Cojo

Punta de la

Concepcion   QUABAJAY

Rio de San Phelipe

Mescaltitan

Rinconada

Asumpta BENYENCE   CORAJI

R.Sta.Clara

Agua Escondida

Portezuelo

M A R

R. Porciuncula

S.Gabriel

Alisos

D E L   76   R. S. Ana   R de los Martinez

Portezuelo

S U R

JENIGUEICH   CHEMEGUABA

La Quema

I. SN. CLEMENTE   Patricio

S.Carlos Pass

S.Juan Capistrano   53

54   Sta.Catalina   JECUICH

Soledad   S.Gregorio

50   S.Sebastian   JAMAJA

31   QUEMEXA   R. Sta. Maria

S.Diego   48

Sta. Rosa   JALCHEDUNES

CUNYEIL

Carrizal

Sta.Olaya

MAR DE   YUMAS

CAJUENCHES   R. Gila

CALIFORNIA   CUCAPA

37 253   38 254   255   256   257   258   259   260   261   262   263   264   265   266   267

36   35   34   33   32   31   30

their line of march, were covered with snow. The cold was taking its toll of the cattle, seven being lost in 24 hours. It was at this time that Anza let the sorry company relax, amid some drinking, and Font was most unhappy at the result. He took particular offense at a widow's ribald singing. His diary records the following:

"I said Mass and in it spoke a few words about the fandango of last night, censuring the performance, saying that instead of thanking God for having arrived with their lives, and not having died from such hardship, as the animals did, it appeared that they were making such festivities in honor of the Devil. I do not think that the commander liked this very well, for he did not speak to me during the whole morning. I suppose he was offended at me a good many times, for I spent most of the journey in this way; because, since he has a sensitive and proud spirit, he took offense at every little thing, appearing very much hurt and bearing an air of great seriousness. Sometimes he even went two or three more days without speaking to me, or passing very few remarks with me, and sometimes he spoke somewhat gruffly without listening to what I said, even though he might have asked me a question. This, together with the illness which I suffered from flux, and which kept me very much prostrated, served me as quite a sufficient cross, thank God."

At San Gregorio, in the entrance to the valley, the springs that had flowed so well two years before were dry before half of the cattle were watered. More stock was left dead in the cold desert. For the first time, Anza mentions in his diary that there seemed to be openings in the sierra, not only ahead but farther south, through which they could pass directly to the Mission of San Diego. On the morning of December 20th, after a night in which few slept because of the intense cold, they found that three saddle animals and five cattle had frozen to death, and others had stampeded in the darkness back toward the water of San Sebastián. They pushed on across the valley floor to begin the crossing of the range, camping to rest for a few days at a place Anza named El Vado (The Ford) along Coyote Creek at the entrance to Coyote Canyon. The loss of stock continued, and then came the greatest blow of all. They learned that at least fifty cattle in a train behind them had been found dead in the mire of the San Sebastián marsh. That night, Friday, December 22nd, it began to rain, and they could see the snow falling in the mountains. They spent the night at Santa Catarina, in Coyote Canyon. Most of the expedition welcomed the sight of some trees and fresh water, but to Font it was just another dreary stop on an unhappy journey. He describes the upper part of Coyote Canyon as follows:

"The canyon is formed by various high and very rocky hills, or better, by great mountains of rocks, boulders, and smaller stones which look as if they had been brought and piled up there, like the sweepings of the world. Consequently it is arid, fruitless, and without trees or any green thing. Of grass in this place there is none, and on the way there are only a few small willows

A monument marks the ford, El Vado, where the Anza expeditions began climbing.

on the banks of the arroyo. The road in places is somewhat broken and grown with shrubs or brush and a little hediondilla, for since this is a shrub of evil augury, it is not lacking in these salty and worthless lands. We saw several Indians on the tops of the hills, hiding among the rocks, totally naked, and so wild that they appeared like fauns."

They also caught glimpses of big horn mountain sheep.

Sunday, December 24th, they drove on despite the rain. After going seven or eight miles up the canyon they halted for one of the important occurrences in California's pioneer history, just over the San Diego county line near a place called the Upper Willows. Anza's diary tells the story.

"Although it continued to rain until nearly daylight and the signs of rain continued, I decided to leave this place and did so at half past nine, continuing along the valley to the northwest with some turns to the west-northwest, through the stoniest country. Having traveled in this direction three leagues in as many hours, we halted at the villages of the people who on our last journey we called Los Danzantes (The Dancers), the stop being made necessary because a woman was taken with childbirth pains. Although from seven o'clock in the morning until two in the afternoon it had been cloudy, with a fog so dense that one could hardly see anything twelve yards away, several heathen as timid as the foregoing allowed themselves to be seen by us on the march . . . At a quarter to eleven in the night our patient was successfully delivered of a boy."

Font consoled the mother but rebuked Anza for the celebration that he permitted to take place in observance of Christmas Eve. His diary records the exchanges he had with Anza as a result of that evening's events:

"I learned at night that because it was Christmas Eve refreshments would be given to the soldiers; and in order if possible to prevent a drunken carousal, after dinner I said to the commander:

" 'Sir, although my opinion is of no value and I do not cut any figure here, I can do no less than to tell you that I have learned that there is drinking today.'

" 'Yes, there is,' he replied.

" 'Well, Sir,' I continued, 'I wish to say that it does not seem to me right that we should celebrate the birth of the Infant Jesus with drunkenness.'

" 'Father,' he said, 'I do not give it to them in order that they may get drunk.'

" 'Clearly this would be the case,' I said to him, 'because then the sin would be even greater, but if you know that they are sure to get drunk you should not give it to them.'

"He said to me then, 'The king sends it for me and they deliver it to me in order that I may give it to the soldiers.'

" 'This would be all right at the proper time,' I replied. 'But I understand that to be in case of necessity.'

" 'Well, Father,' he said, 'It is better that they should get drunk than to do some other things.'

" 'But, Sir,' I replied, 'drunkenness is a sin, and one who cooperates also sins, and so if you know that a person will get drunk on so much you should give him less, or none at all.'

Rock cave home of Coyote Canyon Indians.

Santa Catarina Springs, which meant food and water after a long desert march to mountains.

175

"He did not say any more, and I went to my tent without being able to prevent this disorder, because the commander had already made up his mind to distribute the liquor. And so he immediately gave it to the people, a pint to each one, saying in a loud voice:

" 'Be careful that you don't get drunk, because if anyone is found drunk outside of his tent, I'll punish him.'

"With this he satisfied his conscience, and the people that night were very noisy, singing and dancing from the effects of the liquor, not caring that we were in so bad a mountain in the rain, and so delayed with the saddle animals and the tired and dead cattle. Such is the rule of these absolute lords, in evidence of which I have related this incident.

"In the afternoon they called to me to confess the wife of a soldier who since yesterday had been suffering childbirth pains, the one of the delicacy which I mentioned on November 24. She was very fearful of dying, but having consoled her and encouraged her as best I could I returned to my tent and at half past eleven at night she very happily and quickly gave birth to a boy."

On Monday, Christmas Day, the expedition remained at rest, because the mother was unable to continue the march. Font had an opportunity to say three Masses, and after them he baptized the baby boy, naming him Salvador Ygnacio.

Anza's diary continues:

Near the top of Coyote Canyon and just ahead lies San Carlos pass in Riverside County.

"Tuesday, December 26. Today having dawned fair, at the regular hour the sun came out bright. For this reason and because the mother was better and had the pluck to march, we prepared to break camp, and at a quarter to nine set forth, ascending the valley which has been mentioned, going west-northwest. Having traveled along the valley for about three-quarters of a league, at a place where it narrowed greatly we left it at our left and immediately climbed a small ridge. This was followed by two other smaller ones, by which we arrived at the pass or opening of San Carlos . . . Here we halted for the night because it has been raining ever since nine o'clock, although very lightly, since this rain, if it should become harder, might injure the woman who was delivered night before last, and since the march although short has been for the most part up and down. With this march the sierra or cordillera which runs to and ends at Baja California is now overcome or passed. Rain continued until half past four in the afternoon. After it began to get dark, a heavy, distant thunder was heard, and this was followed by an earthquake which lasted four minutes."

Continuing generally over the route set out on the previous expedition, they entered Cahuilla Valley, and though he evidently hoped at this point to be able to by-pass the San Gabriel Mission and go on directly to Monterey, Anza knew this could not be done because of the poor condition of the stock, and the unhappiness of so many of his people. He wrote:

"All the sierras which we have seen today in the direction of the South Sea, which in the main are independent of the cordillera of Baja California, are so snow-covered that scarcely any trees can be seen on the summits. This sight has been terrifying to most of the people of our expedition, who, since they were born in Tierra Caliente (hot country), have never seen such a thing before. As a result they have become so melancholy that some of the women had to weep. Through their tears they managed to say, 'If so many animals died of cold and the people nearly died in places where there was less snow, how will it be in the place where we see so much of it?' I checked these complaints by various counsels, telling them that the cold would be moderated when we got to the seacoast and its missions, as had already been experienced. And so, since the coast where they were born is hot, they have concluded that it will be the same here, and that in the missions there will be a remedy for troubles which may arise."

There were many difficulties for Anza to face at San Gabriel, and these, along with a revolt of Indians at the San Diego Mission, delayed his departure for San Francisco until February 21st. Anza and a little band of some of the colonists finally arrived at Monterey on March 10th in a pouring rain. After he recovered from a brief illness, he and a few of the soldiers went on to San Francisco to locate sites for a presidio and mission. When it was time for Anza to say farewell to Monterey and return to Mexico, he wrote graphically of the hour:

"This day has been the saddest one experienced by this presidio since its founding. When I mounted my horse in the plaza, the people whom I have led from their fatherlands, to which I am returning, remembering the good or bad treatment which they have experienced at my hands while they have been under my orders, most of them, especially of the female sex, came to me sobbing with tears, which they declared they were shedding more because of my departure than of their exile, filling me with compassion. They showered me with embraces, best wishes, and praises which I do not merit. But in remembrance of them, and of the gratitude which I feel to all, and the affection which I have had for them ever since I recruited them, and in eulogy of their faithfulness, for up to now I have not seen a single sign of desertion in anyone of those whom I brought to remain in this exile, I may be permitted to record this praise of people who, as time goes on, will be very useful to the monarchy in whose service they have voluntarily left their relatives and their fatherland, which is all they have to lose."

On his return to Mexico, Anza received the honors which were due to his great leadership. He eventually became governor of New Mexico, serving with dignity and distinction, and winning more fame as an administrator and Indian fighter. He died in 1788 at the age of 51.

From Cabrillo's discovery of California to the arrival of Anza's first colonists, it had been 234 years. A finger of Old Spain in the form of a thin chain of little missions was extended from San Diego to San Francisco. It was still a lonely and isolated land. Far away on the eastern seaboard the Battles of Lexington and Concord were being fought, and the Declaration of Independence adopted. But Spain's great explorations were over, and her day in the Americas was drawing to a close. Six years after Anza's second expedition, Chief Palma, his old friend, led an Indian uprising which saw the massacre of fifty persons, including Frs. Garcés and Díaz, at the Yuma crossing. The myth of the invincibility of Spanish arms was shattered, and the land route to California was all but closed. Then Spain forgot. But the names of Cabrillo, Vizcaíno, Serra and Anza are written forever in the history books of California, on its buildings and monuments, and in its culture and even its language. The old paths of the explorers can be retraced, and the raising of Point Loma never ceases to be a thrill to those, who, as did Cabrillo, approach from the sea. The past never dies.

ADOBE AND TILE RUINS on Presidio Hill mark where the padres closed the Age of The Explorers and opened the Age of Settlement.

TRANSLATIONS

Historiae Verdadera of Bernal Díaz del Castillo* (page 39)

"Then Cortés sent to Villa Rica for much of the iron and the bolts of the ships which we had destroyed, and for anchors, sails and rigging and for cables and tow and all the other materials for building ships, and he ordered all the blacksmiths to come, and one Hernando de Aguilar who was half a blacksmith and helped in the forging. Cortés sent a certain Santa Cruz as Captain to Villa Rica with orders to bring all the material I have mentioned. He brought everything, even to the cauldrons for melting the pitch, and all the things that they had taken out of the ships, and transported them with the help of more than a thousand Indians, for all the towns of those provinces were enemies of the Mexicans, and at once gave men to carry the loads. Then as we had no pitch with which to caulk the launches, and the Indians did not know how to extract it, Cortés ordered four sailors who understood the work to go and make pitch in some fine pine woods near Huexotzingo."

*Translated by A. P. Maudslay, *The Discovery and Conquest of Mexico* of Bernal Diaz del Castillo, 337.

"I remember that Juan Rodriguez Cabrillo went in charge of these as captain. He was a good soldier in the war of Mexico, and afterward as a citizen of Guatemala and very much honored. He was captain and *Almirante* of thirteen ships for Pedro de Alvarado. He served his Majesty very well in everything that offered and died in royal service."

Translated by Don Joaquin Pardo, Director of the Archivo General de la Nación, Guatemala.

Relation of the Voyage of Cabrillo *
(page 49)

Having departed from Cabo de la Cruz, because of head-winds they found themselves on the following Saturday two leagues from the same cape on a coast running from north-northwest to south-southeast. At the shore they saw Indians in some very small canoes. The land is very high, bare, and dry. All the land from California to here is sandy near the shore, but here begins land of another sort, the soil being reddish and of better appearance.

On Sunday, the 17th of the said month, they sailed on in continuation of their voyage, and

181

about six leagues from Cabo de Cruz they found a good and closed port. To reach it they passed a small island which is near the mainland. In this port they took on water from a small lake of rain-water. There are groves of trees like silk-cotton trees, excepting that they are of hard wood. They found thick and tall trees which the sea brings. This port is called San Mateo. The land appears to be good; there are large savannahs, and the grass is like that of Spain. The land is high and broken. They saw some herds of animals like cattle, which went in droves of a hundred or more, and which, from their appearance, from their gait, and the long wool, looked like Peruvian sheep. They have small horns, a span in length and as thick as the thumb. The tail is broad and round and a palm long. This place is in thirty-three and one-third degrees. They took possession here. They remained in this port until the following Saturday.

On Saturday, the 23rd of said month, they left said port of San Mateo and sailed along the coast until the Monday following, when they must have gone about eighteen leagues. They saw very beautiful valleys and groves, and country both level and rough, but no Indians were seen.

On the following Tuesday and Wednesday they sailed along the coast about eight leagues, passing by some three islands completely denuded of soil. One of them is larger than the others. It is about two leagues in circumference and affords shelter from the west winds. They are three leagues from the mainland, and are in thirty-four degrees. They called them Islas Desiertas. This day great smokes were seen on the land. The country appears to be good and has large valleys, and in the interior there are high mountains.

On the following Thursday they went about six leagues along a coast running north-northwest and discovered a port, closed and very good, which they named San Miguel. It is in thirty-four and one-third degrees. Having cast anchor in it, they went ashore where there were people. Three of them waited, but all the rest fled. To these three they gave some presents and they said by signs that in the interior men like the Spaniards had passed. They gave signs of great fear. On the night of this day they went ashore from the ships to fish with a net, and it appears that here there were some Indians, and that they began to shoot at them with arrows and wounded three men.

Next day in the morning they went with the boat farther into the port, which is large, and brought two boys, who understood nothing by signs. They gave them both shirts and sent them away immediately.

Next day in the morning three adult Indians came to the ships and said by signs that in the interior men like us were travelling about, bearded, clothed, and armed like those of the ships. They made signs that they carried crossbows and swords; and they made gestures with the right arm as if they were throwing lances, and ran around as if they were on horse-back. They made signs that they were killing many native Indians, and that for this reason they were afraid.

*Translated by Herbert Eugene Bolton in *Spanish Exploration in the Southwest,* 21-23, published by Barnes & Noble.

Relation of the Voyage of Cabrillo* (page 50)

They examined the coast at a point which projects into the sea and forms a cape. The point is covered with timber, and is in forty degrees.

On Wednesday, the 15th of said month, they sighted the consort, whereupon they heartily thanked God, for they had thought her lost. They made toward her, and in the afternoon they joined company. Those on the other ship had experienced greater labor and risk than those of the captain's ship, since it was a small vessel and had no deck. This country where they were sailing is apparently very good, but they saw no Indians or smokes. There are large mountains covered with snow, and there is heavy timber. At night they lowered sails and lay-to.

On the following Thursday, the 16th of the said month of November, they found themselves at daybreak in a great bay, which came at a turn, and which appeared to have a port and a river. They held on, beating about that day and night and on the following Friday, until they saw that there was neither river nor shelter. In order to take possession they cast anchor in forty-five fathoms, but they did not dare go ashore because of the high sea. This bay is in thirty-nine degrees, full, and its entire shore is covered with pines clear to the sea. They named it Bay of Los Pinos. That night they lay-to until the following day.

The following Saturday they ran along the coast, and at night found themselves off Cape San Martin. All the coast run this day is very bold; the sea has a heavy swell, and the coast is very high. There are mountains which reach the sky, and the sea beats upon them. When sailing along near the land, it seems as if the mountains would fall upon the ships. They are covered with snow to the summit, and they named them the Sierras Nevadas. At the beginning of them a cape is formed which projects into the sea, and which they named Cape Nieve. The coast runs from north-northwest to south-southwest. It does not appear that Indians live on this coast. This Cape Nieve is in thirty-eight and two-thirds degrees. Whenever the wind blew from the northwest the weather was clear and fair.

On Thursday, the 23rd of the month, they arrived, on the return, in the islands of San Lucas, at one of them called La Posesión. They had run the entire coast, point by point, from Cape Pinos to the islands, and had found no shelter whatever, wherefore they were forced to return to said island because during these past days there was a strong wind from the west-northwest, and the swell of the sea was heavy. From Cape Martin to Cape Pinos we did not see a single Indian, the reason being that the coast is bold, rugged, and without shelter. But southeast of Cape Martin for fifteen leagues they found the land inhabited, and with many smokes, because the country is good. But from Cape Martin up to forty degrees we saw no sign of Indians. Cape Martin is in thirty-seven and one-half degrees.

Passing the winter on the island of La Posesión, on the 3rd of the month of January, 1543, Juan Rodriguez Cabrillo, captain of the said ships, departed from this life, as the result of a fall which he suffered on said island when they were there before, from which he broke an arm near the shoulder. He left as captain the chief pilot, who was one Bartolome Ferrelo, a native of the Levant. At the time of his death he emphatically charged them not to leave off exploring as much as possible of all that coast. They named the island [the Island of Juan Rodriguez].

*Translated by Herbert Eugene Bolton in *Spanish Exploration in the Southwest*, 31-33, published by Barnes & Noble.

Informacion of 1560 (page 52)

In the City of Santiago de Guatemala, on 9 February 1560.

Being in session the President and the Judges of His Majesty's Audiencia and Royal Chancery, who reside in the aforesaid city, the following petition was presented before me, Luis Sanchez, their secretary, by Juan de Arguijo, procurator: Very Powerful Sir,

On behalf of Juan Rodríguez Cabrillo, resident of this city, I state that my party desires to make an affadavit in order to prove to your Royal

Person and to the Royal Council of the Indies, the merits, works, and services which, in these parts, his father, Juan Rodríguez Cabrillo, has rendered Your Highness and, likewise, to prove what my party has sustained and served in order to request that he be favored by some land grants or that he be given some appointments which may be beneficial to him.

I request and pray Your Highness that the witnesses presented be ordered to be examined on the questions that will be read to them concerning what I ask and implore justice from the Royal Office.

Juan de Arguijo.

Let all who may see this letter know that I, Juan Rodríguez Cabrillo, resident of this city of Santiago de Guatemala where the Audencia and Royal Chancery of the Confines is and resides, revoking as I revoke every power of attorney and all powers of attorney whatever which I have given or granted to every person or to any persons whatever....

Translated by Brig. Gen. Maurice G. Holmes, USMC, Ret.

Title page of Father Ascensión's *Account* * (page 66)

An account of the expedition for the discovery of the Californias which *General* Sebastian Vizcaino carried into effect in the year 1602 by order of His Excellency the Señor Conde de Monterey, the viceroy of New Spain, written by the reverend father, Fray Antonio de la Ascension of the Barefoot Order of Nuestra Señora del Carmen, one of the three friars who went on the journey.

*Translated by Henry R. Wagner in *Spanish Voyages to the Northwest Coast in the Sixteenth Century*, Calif. Historical Society *Quarterly*, Vol. III — 295.

Father Ascensión's Account of the Voyage of Sebastián Vizcaíno * (page 67)

[These the Indians made, as if calling to the ships] to come close to their country, which showed indications of being good, fertile and level and was of pleasing aspect. Following the land they reached four small islands, two shaped like sugar loaves and the other two somewhat larger. These were named the "Cuatro Coronados." To the north of them in the mainland there is a large extended *enseñada*, all surrounded by hills which form a very fine port. This was named "San Diego." In this the fleet entered November 10, on the eve of San Martín's day, at seven o'clock at night.

The following morning the *General* ordered some men to go and look over a little hill which protected the port from the northwest wind. Captains Alarcón [and Peguero and Father Antonio went etc.].

*Translated by Henry R. Wagner, in *Spanish Voyages to the Northwest Coast in the 16th Century*, California Historical Society Quarterly, Vol. VII, 345-346.

Diary of Sebastián Vizcaíno* (page 68)

Until the next day, when we set sail, they [Indians] remained on the beach shouting. This port was given the name of San Diego.

"Departure from the Port of San Diego and Arrival at the Island of Santa Catalina"

We left the port of San Diego, as has been said, on a Wednesday, the 20th of the said month, and the same day the general ordered Ensign Sebastian Melendes to go ahead with the frigate to examine a bay which was to windward some four leagues, and directed that the pilot should sound it, map it, and find out what was there. He did so, and the next day ordered the return to the captain's ship. He reported to the general that he had entered the said bay, that it was a good port, although it had at its entrance a bar of little more than two fathoms depth, and that there was a very large grove at an estuary which extended into the land, and many Indians: and that he had not gone ashore. Thereupon we continued our voyage, skirting along the coast until the 24th of the month, which was the eve of the feast of the glorious Santa Catalina, when we discovered three large islands. We approached them with difficulty because of a head-wind, and arrived at the middle one, which is more than twenty-five leagues around.

On the 27th of the month, and before casting anchor in a very good cove which was found, a multitude of Indians came out in canoes of cedar and pine, made of planks very well joined and calked, each one with eight oars and with fourteen or fifteen Indians, who looked like galley-slaves. They came alongside without the least fear and came on board our ships, mooring their own. They showed great pleasure at seeing us, telling us by signs that we must land, and guiding us like pilots to the anchorage. The general received them kindly and gave them some presents, especially to the boys. We anchored, and the admiral, Ensign Alarcon, Father Fray Antonio, and Captain Peguero, with some soldiers, went ashore. Many Indians were on the beach, and the women treated us to roasted sardines and a small fruit like sweet potatoes.

*Translated by Herbert Eugene Bolton in *Spanish Exploration in the Southwest*, 82-83, published by Barnes & Noble.

Palóu's *Historical Memoirs of New California** (page 99)

JESUS, MARY, AND JOSEPH

This is a collection of memoirs of Old California, for the time when its missions were administered by the missionaries of the Regular Observance of Our Seraphic Father of San Fernando de Mexico; and of the missions which these missionaries founded in the new establishments of San Diego and Monterey.

It was written by the least, because the most unworthy, of these missionaries, one who, having been in Old California from the time when it was taken charge of by that College until it was delivered to the reverend fathers of the Sacred Order of Our Cherubic Father Santo Domingo, afterward went up to the missions of Monterey with other missionaries of the same College of San Fernando. This material labor, which follows the trails marked out for me by the apostolic ministry, has no other purpose than to note down whatever has happened and may happen while God may give me life and health to labor [in this new vineyard of the Lord etc.].

*Translated by Herbert Eugene Bolton in *Historical Memoirs of New California* by Fray Francisco Palóu, O.F.M., XCV.

Costansó's *Narrative of the Portolá Expedition** (page 107)

. . . for those of the new missions which are to be founded, and that they will grow under the protection and patronage of his Excellency the Marquis de Croix, viceroy, governor, and captain-general of this vast empire, under whose mild rule, which is extolled by the people, the inhabitants live gratefully. But this enterprise, desired for so many years and attempted many times with great preparations and costs, will doubtless be very acceptable to the august monarch who wears the crown of Spain. His generous heart Heaven rewards by arousing in his glorious reign great and illustrious men of all estates — ecclesiastical, military, and political — who vie with one another and are equally zealous in the discharge of the high responsibilities confided to their eminent capabilities and talents, which are never employed more worthily than in furthering the extension of the gospel and the public welfare of his loyal and devoted subjects.

Mexico, October 24, 1770.

D. Miguel Costansó

*Translated by Adolph Van Hemmert-Engert & Frederick J. Teggart in *Publications of the Academy of Pacific Coast History,* Vol. I, 69.

Title Page Diary of Vicente Vila* (page 109)

Log-Book of H.M. Packet *San Carlos,* or *Toyson,* Don Vicente Vila, Sailing-Master of the First Class, Commander, on the voyage from the port of La Paz in Southern California, in latitude 24° 20′ north and longitude 266° 5′ of the meridian of Teneriffe, to the port of San Diego on the west coast of California, situated in latitude 32° 45′ north and in longitude 258° 4′ of the same meridian — carrying troops and missionaries, and with a cargo of stores and supplies — in order to take possession of the country in the name of the Crown of Spain; to set up in that port a presidio and a mission; and to effect the conversion of the native heathen to the Holy Catholic Faith.

*Translated by Robert Selden Rose in *Publications of the Academy of Pacific Coast History,* Vol. II, 5.

Diary of Vicente Vila* (page 110)

The construction of the shelters was postponed until the following morning.

At six o'clock in the morning, a Philippine seaman, named Agustin Fernandez de Medina died.

At eight o'clock in the morning, the launch of the *San Antonio* put off with Don Pedro Fages, Don Miguel Costansó, Fray Juan Vizcaíno, and the soldiers who were best able, in order to set about the construction of the shelters.

From Saturday, 6, to Sunday, May 7. — The day was foggy and drizzly, with the wind at south.

At one o'clock in the afternoon, the wind shifted to northwest.

At sunset, the launch returned with the missionary and the officers. They had decided to build the shelters for the sick on a hillock close to the beach and a cannon-shot from the packets. To this end they had gathered a quantity of brushwood and earth to make roofs for those who were to be placed in the shelters.

Between eight and nine o'clock in the morning, seven or eight Indians came alongside on their rafts, and, in exchange for a few trinkets . . .

*Translated by Robert Selden Rose in *Publications of the Academy of Pacific Coast History,* Vol. II, 101.

Diary of Junípero Serra, Loreto to San Diego, March 28-July 1, 1769* (page 120)

Diary

Of the expedition to the Ports of San Diego and Monterey by land, which for God's greater glory and the conversion of the infidels to our Holy Catholic Faith, I began, on March 28, the third day after the feast of the Resurrection, in the year 1769, starting from my Mission and the Royal Presidio of Loreto, in California, after a visitation of the southern missions, where I met and had long conversations about this expedition with the Most Illustrious Lord Don Joseph de Gálvez, of his Majesty's State and Privy Council, Inspector General of this New Spain and chief director of these conquests.

First Note

January 6, of this same year, finding myself at the Port of La Paz, with the Most Illustrious Lord Inspector, I blessed the packet boat named the *San Carlos.* I went aboard to sing the Mass and bless the flags. The litany was sung and other prayers in honor of Our Lady. And the Most Illustrious Lord made an eloquent speech which greatly encouraged those who were to sail on the boat for the said Ports of San Diego and Monterey. January 9, at night, they embarked; and January 10, set sail, under the command of Don Vicente Vila, appointed Commandant for the sea expedition and a celebrated sailor in European waters. The engineer was Don Miguel Costansó; the commander of the troop Don Pedro Fages, lieutenant of the company of Catalonian volunteers. I appointed Father Fray Fernando Parrón, my former companion at Loreto since we came to California, as chaplain of the expedition and later as missionary to the pagans. All of them started out in high spirits on January 10.

Second Note

February 15, after returning to Loreto, the same celebrations were held at Cape San Lucas, with the blessing of boat and flags, of the second packet boat, the *San Antonio,* also called *El Príncipe.* It sailed immediately for the said ports. There were on board, for the same purpose, the Fathers Preachers Fray Juan Gonzáles Vizcaíno, and Fray Francisco Gómez. The first had just arrived from Mexico, and the second had been minister in the mission of La Pasión, suppressed by order of the Most Illustrious Lord, the Indians having been transferred to the Mission of Todos los Santos. And in this manner the sea or naval expedition set forth.

*Translation by Antonine Tibesar, O.F.M., in *Writings of Junípero Serra,* Vol. I, 39-41.

Diary of Don Gaspar de Portolá* (page 132)

Diary of the journey that Don Gaspar de Portolá, captain of dragoons in the España Regiment, Governor of the Californias, made by land to the ports of San Diego and Monterey, situated in 33° and 37° [N. Latitude], having been appointed commander-in-chief of this expedition by the Most Illustrious Don Joseph de Gálvez, in virtue of the viceregal powers which had been granted to him by His Excellency [The Viceroy]. The expedition was composed of 37 soldiers in leather jackets with their captain, Don Fernando de Rivera; this officer was sent in advance with twenty-seven soldiers and the Governor [followed] with ten men and a sergeant.

The 11th day of May, [1769], I set out from Santa María, the last mission to the north, escorted by four soldiers, in company with Father Junípero Serra, president of the missions, and Father Miguel Campa. This day we proceeded for about four hours with very little water for the animals and without any pasture, which obliged us to go on farther in the afternoon to find some. There was, however, no water.

The 12th, we proceeded over a good road for five hours and halted at a place called La Poza de Agua Dulce. No pasture.

*Translated by Donald Eugene Smith and Frederick J. Teggart in *Publications of the Academy of Pacific Coast History,* Vol. I, 39.

De Anza Diary (page 162)

. . . at sunset I arrived at the Presidio of Tubac, which is the one in my charge. Here I requested Reverend Fray Juan Díaz, the one who has made the observations in our transit, to show on a map what we have done, in order to give an idea to his Excellency, the Viceroy, of the routes, villages, and other particulars which we have noted.

Friday, May 27, at twelve o'clock today, the rest of the caravan, which I left behind, arrived at this presidio. Herewith the expedition has come completely to an end, with the successes and advantages which are set forth in the foregoing document, wherefore may the Lord of Hosts be blessed and praised – From Monte Rey to the presidio of Tubac, 294 leagues.

Today, the 13th of November, 1774, I made this copy to deliver on the same day to his Excellency, the Viceroy, Governor, and Captain-General in this City of Mexico, into whose hands likewise I have delivered the map which has been mentioned.

Juan Bautista de Anza

On the 24th day of December, 1774, a certified copy was made from the original of this diary with which to make a report to his Majesty.

Translated by Brig. Gen. Maurice G. Holmes, USMC, Ret.

Father Garcés' Diary (page 163)

Most Excellent Sir

In continuation of the reports which Lieutenant Colonel Don Juan Bautista de Anza has sent you, it has occurred to me (improving the occasion of sending for wine in order to say Mass) to inform you how I have come down this river passing through the tribes, Cajuenches, Tallicuamais or Quiguimas, and Cucarpa. I came to the ocean where I observed and tasted the water besides noting the flood and ebb of the tides as I told you in my diary.

The Indians of the sierra gave me accounts of the priests in both Californias, Upper and Lower. The three nations or groups of people who inhabit this river line down to the sea have received me as I had not expected, showing me all the courtesies they possibly could, although the Cucapa [sic] were at war and very sad on account of their great losses. These had been inflicted upon them by the Yumas, Cajuenches, and Tallicuamais but, thank God, the joy of peace has been attained. This very day, Palma tells me that some Indians will come in here who formerly were enemies.

All the four nations aforesaid, and the Pimas and the Cocomaricopas from the Gila River, are awaiting with pleasure and great eagerness the coming of the priests and the Spaniards to their country, as they have told me repeatedly. Their land is well-suited to the production of every sort of grain. In the greater portion, especially along the Colorado, it is adapted to raising cattle and horses. Although with respect to the location of towns, this Colorado terrain does not offer the greatest advantages due to widespread overflowing of the river, yet, some tablelands adaptable for town locations are not lacking. So it is, that in some areas, plantings will have to be made on the other side of the stream.

I hope that God our Lord may grant me the same felicity among the nations upstream to which, God willing, I intend to start out soon.

Translated by Brig. Gen. Maurice G. Holmes, USMC, Ret.

Record of Voyage by Francisco de Ulloa (page 23)

MEXICO
YEAR OF 1540   MARQUES DEL VALLE

In the great city of Temuxtitán, Mexico, in this New Spain, on 29 May, year of the birth of our Savior Jesus Christ 1540, Francisco Sánchez de Toledo, on behalf of the Marquis del Valle, appeared in person before the very noble Juan de Burgos, regular alcalde for Their Majesties in this said city of Mexico, and before me, Alonso Díaz de Gibraleón, Their Majesties' scribe and public scribe, one of those on the numbered list in this city of Mexico, and presented a written petition of the following tenor:

Very Noble Sir, I, Francisco Sánchez de Toledo, major-domo of the very illustrious Marquis del Valle, and on behalf of the said Marquis, appear before Your Grace and state that I need certain certified transcripts of particular writings which Captain Francisco de Ulloa is sending to the aforesaid party of mine from the new country and exploration, where my party had sent him. As I fear that they will be torn or lost or wet or burned, I accordingly ask and supplicate that you order them to be copied clearly so they may be faithful. Please indicate in each one of them your authority and judicial order as much as in justice is proper, and order them delivered to me so that I may present them where suitable to the rights of my party.

And thus was presented the said written petition, in the manner aforesaid, and the said alcalde took into his hands a written report and seven acts of possession, and noted that they were not torn nor cancelled nor in any part at all suspicious, and said he was ordering and did order me the said (The remainder of this is missing.)

Translated by Brig. Gen. Maurice G. Holmes, USMC, Ret.

CHRONOLOGY

1492 Columbus discovers the New World and establishes colony at Hispaniola (Haiti).

1497 John Cabot discovers coast of North America, probably at Cape Breton Island, under patent from Henry VII of England.

1497 Amérigo Vespucci, Italian navigator living in Seville, explores the mouth of the Amazon and the northeast coast of South America.

1513 Ponce de León discovers Florida and lands near St. Augustine.

1513 Vasco Núñez de Balboa is the first to "gaze on the Pacific."

1518 Juan de Grijalva explores the Mexican coast from Yucatán to near Veracruz and is the first to hear of Moctezuma and his empire.

1519 Cortés reaches Tenochtitlan (Mexico City) and interviews Moctezuma.

1520 Cortés returns to the coast and defeats Narváez at Cempoala.

1521 The fall of Tenochtitlan.

1523- Pedro de Alvarado conquers Guatemala
1524 and becomes its Captain General.

1532 Francisco Pizarro completes the conquest of Peru.

1533 Fortún Jiménez lands at La Paz, the first white man in Lower California.

1535 Cortés lands at La Paz and establishes temporary colony.

1539 De Soto lands near Tampa Bay and explores the Mississippi and west to Oklahoma.

1539 Fr. Marcos de Niza expedition goes north to New Mexico to find seven cities of Cibola.

1539 Francisco de Ulloa, sent by Cortés, explores up the Gulf of California, lands at La Paz, and sails up the west coast at least as far as Cedros Island.

1540 Hernando Alarcón ascends the Colorado River in small boats.

1540 Melchior Díaz reaches the Colorado River overland.

1540- Coronado leads a land expedition to New
1542 Mexico and Arizona.

1542 Sent by the Viceroy Mendoza, Juan Rodríguez Cabrillo sets sail from Navidad and discovers California. (Sept. 28).

1565 Urdaneta sails from the Philippines to Acapulco on first eastern voyage of a galleon. Arellano sights Cape Mendocino.

1579 Drake sails up the California coast to 42° or 43°.

1586 Tomas Cavendish loots the *Santa Ana* off tip of Baja California.

1595 Sebastián Rodríguez Cermeno, sailing from Philippines to Acapulco, explores the California coast from Eureka to San Martin Island looking for ports.

1596 Sebastián Vizcaíno lands at La Paz, seeking pearls.

1602- Vizcaíno surveys the coast from Cape San
1603 Lucas to Cape Blanco and back.

1607 The establishment of the Jamestown Colony on Chesapeake Bay.

1620 The Pilgrims land at Plymouth, Massachusetts.

1682 William Penn establishes Pennsylvania.

1697 Fr. Juan María Salvatierra establishes a colony and mission at Loreto, the first permanent settlement in the Californias.

1701- Father Kino, at Yuma, proves that Cali-
1702 fornia is not an island.

1697- The Jesuits found 23 missions in Lower
1767 California, of which about 15 are permanent.

1767 Capt. Gaspar de Portolá becomes Governor of the Californias, with headquarters at the capital, Loreto.

1768 The Jesuits are banished from New Spain.

1768 The Franciscans, led by Fr. Junípero Serra, arrive at La Paz to take over the missions.

1769 The ships *San Carlos* and *San Antonio* arrive at San Diego. (April 11 and 29).

1769 Capt. Rivera y Moncada and his overland party arrive at San Diego, accompanied by Fr. Juan Crespí. (May 14).

1769 Capt. Portolá and the main party arrive at San Diego. (June 29).

1769 Fr. Junípero Serra arrives at San Diego. (July 1).

1769 Founding of the Mission of San Diego. (July 16).

1774 Juan Bautista de Anza opens land route from Mexico to California.

BIBLIOGRAPHY

Andrews, C. L.

   The Story of Alaska (Caldwell, Idaho, The Caxton Printers, 1938).

Baegert, Johann Jakob, S. J.

   Observations in Lower California trans. by M. M. Brandenburg and Carl L. Baumann (Berkeley and Los Angeles, University of California Press, 1952).

Bancroft, Hubert Howe

   History of Arizona and New Mexico (San Francisco, The History Company, Publishers, 1889).

   History of California Vol. I. (San Francisco, The History Company, Publishers, 1886).

   History of Central America Vols. I and II. (San Francisco, The History Company, Publishers, 1886).

   History of Mexico Vols. I and II. (San Francisco, The History Company, Publishers, 1886).

Bolton, Herbert Eugene

   Coronado, Knight of Pueblos and Plains (New York, Whittlesey House; and Albuquerque, University of New Mexico Press, 1949).

An Outpost of Empire (New York, Alfred A. Knopf, 1931).

The Padre on Horseback (San Francisco, Sonora Press, 1932).

Rim of Christendom: A Biography of Eusebio Francisco Kino, Pacific Coast Pioneer (New York, The Macmillan Company, 1936).

The Spanish Borderlands (New Haven, Yale University Press, 1921).

Wider Horizons of American History (New York, D. Appleton - Century Company, 1939).

Bolton, Herbert Eugene ed.

   Anza's California Expeditions Vols. II-V. (Berkeley, University of California Press, 1930).

   Spanish Explorations in the Southwest, 1542-1706 (New York, Barnes and Noble, 1959).

Bolton, Herbert Eugene, and
Marshall, Thomas Maitland

   The Colonization of North America, 1492-1783 (New York, The Macmillan Company, 1920).

Brady, Gerard K.

Saint Dominic (New York, P. J. Kenedy and Sons, 1957).

Chapman, Charles E.

"Catalogue of Materials in the Archivo General de Indias" etc. in University of California Publications in History, VIII (1919) complete.
A History of California: The Spanish Period (New York, The Macmillan Company, 1921).

Cleland, Robert Glass

California Pageant: The Story of Four Centuries (New York, Alfred A. Knopf, 1955).
From Wilderness to Empire: A History of California, 1542-1900 (New York, Alfred A. Knopf, 1944).
Pathfinders (Los Angeles, Powell Publishing Company, 1929).

Cortés, Hernan

Letters of Cortés ed. by Francis Augustus MacNutt (New York, G. P. Putnam's Sons, 1908).

Costansó, Miguel

"Diary of Miguel Costansó" ed. by Frederick J. Teggart in Publications of the Academy of Pacific Coast History, Vol. II (1911) 161-327.
"Narrative of the Portolá Expedition of 1769-1700" ed. by Adolph Van Hemmert-Engert and Frederick J. Teggart in Publications of the Academy of Pacific Coast History, Vol. I (1910) 91-159.

Cowan, Robert Ernest and
Cowan, Robert Grannis

Bibliography of the History of California, 1510-1930 3 vols., (San Francisco, John Henry Nash, 1933).

Culver, Henry B. and Grant, Gordan

Book of Old Ships (Garden City, New York, The Garden City Publishing Company Inc., 1935).

Curtis, Edward S.

"The Diegueños" in The North American Indian (1926) XV, 39-52.

Dana, Richard Henry

Two Years Before the Mast (New York, Random House, Modern Library, 1936).

Daniel, Hawthorne

Ships of the Seven Seas (New York, Dodd, Mead and Company, 1930).

Davidson, George

"An Examination of Some of the Early Voyages of Discovery and Exploration on the Northwest Coast of America from 1539-1603" in Report of the Superintendent, Appendix no. 7, 155-253, United States Coast and Geodetic Survey, 1887.

Davidson, Winifred

Where California Began (San Diego, McIntyre Publishing Company, 1929).

DeVoto, Bernard

Course of Empire (Boston, Houghton Mifflin Company, 1952).

Díaz de Castillo, Bernal

The Discovery and Conquest of Mexico, 1517-1521 ed. by Genaro García, trans. by A. P. Maudslay, introd. to American edition by Irving A. Leonard. (Farrar, Straus, and Cudahy, 1956).

Dubois, Constance Goddard

"Religion of the Luiseño Indians of Southern California" in University of California Publications In American Archaeology and Ethnology, Vol. VIII (1908) 69-186.

Dunne, Peter Masten

Black Robes in Lower California (Berkeley and Los Angeles, University of California Press, 1952).
Pioneer Black Robes on the West Coast (Berkeley and Los Angeles, University of California Press, 1940).
Pioneer Jesuits in Northern Mexico (Berkeley and Los Angeles, University of California Press, 1944).

Duryea, Nina Larrey

Mallorca The Magnificent (New York, The Century Company, 1927).

Eldredge, Zoeth Skinner, ed.

History of California Vol. I (New York, Century History Company, ca. 1915).

Engelhardt, Fr. Zephyrin, O.F.M.

Missions and Missionaries of California Vol. I (Santa Barbara, Mission Santa Barbara, 1929).

San Diego Mission (San Francisco, James H. Barry Company, 1920).

Federal Writers' Project

Story of the Indians of San Diego County (Bound for the Serra Museum, San Diego, by Citywide Public Library Extension Project Works Administration No. 8184, 1938).

Frossard, André

The Salt of the Earth trans. by Marjorie Villiers (New York, P. J. Kenedy and Sons, 1954).

Gardiner, C. Harvey

Naval Power in the Conquest of Mexico (Austin, University of Texas Press, 1956).

Geiger, Maynard J., O.F.M.

"The Franciscan Mission to San Fernando College" in *The Americas*, Vol. V (1948) 48-60.
"The Internal Organization and Activities of San Fernando College, Mexico City, 1734-1858" in *The Americas*, Vol. VI (1949) 3-31.
"Junípero Serra, O.F.M., in the Light of Chronology and Geography" in *The Americas*, Vol. IV (1950) 291-333.
The Life and Times of Fray Junípero Serra or The Man Who Never Turned Back, 1713-1784 2 vols. (Washington, D.C., Academy of American Franciscan History, 1959).
"The Mallorcan Contribution to Franciscan California" in *The Americas*, Vol. IV (1947) 141-150.

Gerhard, Peter and Gulick, Howard E.

Lower California Guidebook (Glendale, California, The Arthur Clark Company, 1958).

Gleason, Duncan

Islands and Ports of California (New York, The Devin-Adair Company, 1958).

Griffin, Paul F. and Young, Robert N.

California, The New Empire State: A Regional Geography (San Francisco, Fearon Publishers, 1957).

Hanna, Philip Townsend

"Hail to Alarcón, Unsung Discoverer of California" in *Westways*, August, 1960.

Harney, Martin, S.J.

The Jesuits in History: The Society of Jesus Through Four Centuries (New York, The America Press, 1941).

Heilbron, Carl H., ed.-in-chief

History of San Diego County (San Diego, San Diego Press Club, 1936).

Heizer, R. F. and Whipple, M. A., comps. and eds.

The California Indians: A Source Book (Berkeley and Los Angeles, University of California Press, 1951).

Herring, Hubert

History of Latin America From the Beginnings to the Present (New York, Alfred A. Knopf, 1955).

Hertlein, Leo George and Grant, U. S. IV

"The Geology and Paleontology of the Marine Pliocene of San Diego, California" Part I. in *Memoirs of the San Diego Society of Natural History*, Vol. II (1944) 9-72.

Hill, Joseph J.

History of Warner's Ranch and Its Environs (Los Angeles, privately printed, 1927).

Hillinger, Charles

The California Islands (Los Angeles, Academy Publishers, 1958).

Hodge, Frederick W. ed.

"The Narrative of the Expedition of Coronado" by Pedro de Castañeda in *Spanish Explorers in the Southern United States*, 281-387. (New York, Barnes and Noble Inc., 1946).

Holder, Charles Frederick

The Channel Islands of California (Chicago, A. C. McClure and Company, 1910).

Hollis, Christopher

Saint Ignatius (New York, Sheed and Ward, 1945).

Holmes, Brig. Gen. Maurice G., USMC, ret.

"Spanish Nautical Explorations Along the Coast of the Californias." Thesis for Ph.D., University of Southern California, 1959.

Hubbs, Carl L.

Recent Climatic History in California. Paper presented at Irrigation Districts Association of California, Santa Barbara, December 11, 1958.

Jaeger, Edmund

North American Deserts (Stanford University Press, 1957).

King, Kenneth M.

Mission to Paradise: The Story of Junípero Serra and the Missions of California (London, Burns and Oates, 1956).

Kroeber, A. L.

Handbook of the Indians of California (Berkeley, California Book Company Ltd., 1953).

Lagoa, Visconde de

João Rodrigues Cabrilho: A Biographical Sketch A Summary of the Portuguese Original, English version by M. Freire de Andrade (Lisboa, Agencia Geral Do Ultramar, 1957).

Latourette, Kenneth Scott

A History of Christianity (New York, Harper and Brothers, 1953).

Lee, Melicent Humanson

"The Ancient House of the San Diegueño Indian" in *Art and Archaeology*, Vol. XXV (1928) 100-105.

MacNutt, Francis Augustus

Fernando Cortés and the Conquest of Mexico, 1485-1547 (New York, G. P. Putnam's Sons, 1909).

Mardariaga, Salvador de

The Fall of the Spanish American Empire (New York, The Macmillan Company, 1948).
Hernán Cortés: The Conqueror of Mexico (New York, The Macmillan Company, 1941).
The Rise of the Spanish American Empire (New York, The Macmillan Company, 1949).

Martin, Douglas D.

Yuma Crossing (Albuquerque, University of New Mexico Press).

Maynard, Theodore

The Long Road of Father Serra (New York, Appleton-Century-Crofts Inc., 1954).
Richest of the Poor: The Life of St. Francis of Assisi (Garden City, Doubleday and Company, Inc., 1948).

Saint Ignatius and the Jesuits (New York, P. J. Kenedy and Sons, 1956).

Meigs, Peveril III.

The Dominican Mission Frontier of Lower California (Berkeley, University of California Press, 1935).

Mills, James

"Point Loma's Controversial Oaks" in *The San Diego Historical Society Quarterly*, Vol. IV (1958) 29-32.
"A Spanish Wall" in *The San Diego Historical Society Quarterly*, Vol. II (1956) 41.

Morison, Samuel Eliot

Admiral of the Ocean Sea: A Life of Columbus (Boston, Little Brown and Company, 1942).

Mosk, Sanford A.

"The Cardena Company and the Pearl Fisheries of Lower California" in *Pacific Historical Review*, Vol. III (1934) 50-61.

Nelson, Edward N.

"Lower California and Its Natural Resources" Memoirs of the National Academy of Sciences, Vol. XVI. (Washington, Government Printing Office, 1921).

Palou, Fray Francisco, O.F.M.

Historical Memoirs of New California 4 vols. ed. by Herbert Eugene Bolton (Berkeley, University of California Press, 1926).
Life of Fray Junípero Serra ed. by Maynard J. Geiger, O.F.M. (Washington, D.C., Academy of American Franciscan History, 1955).

Parker, Horace

Anza-Borrego Desert Guide Book (Palm Desert, California, Desert Magazine Press, 1957).

Parkes, Henry Bamford

A History of Mexico (Boston, Houghton Mifflin Company, 1950).

Peck, Anne Merriman

Pageant of Middle American History (New York, Longmans Green and Company, 1947).

Portolá, Gaspar de

"Diary of Gaspar de Portolá During the California Expedition of 1769-1770" ed. by Donald Eugene Smith and Frederick J. Teg-

gert in *Publications of the Academy of Pacific Coast History*, Vol. III (1909) 31-89.

Prescott, W. H.

> *The Conquest of Mexico* 2 vols. (London, J. M. Dent and Sons Ltd., 1948).

Priestley, Herbert Ingram

> *The Coming of the White Man* (New York, The Macmillan Company, 1929).

Reid, Joseph L., Jr.; Roden, Gunnar I.; and Wyllie, John G.

> *"Studies of the California Current System"* in *Contributions from The Scripps Institution of Oceanography*, New Series, No. 998, 29-57.

Roden, Gunnar I.

> *"Oceanographic and Meteorological Aspects of the Gulf of California"* in *Pacific Science*, Vol. XII (1958) 21-45.

Rush, Philip S.

> *History of the Californias* (San Diego, Philip S. Rush, 1958).

Schurz, William Lytle

> *The Manila Galleon* (New York, E. P. Dutton and Company Inc., 1959).

Serra, Junípero, O.F.M.

> *Writings of Junípero Serra* ed. by Antonine Tibesar, O.F.M. Vol. I. (Washington, D.C., Academy of American Franciscan History, 1955).

Smythe, William E.

> *History of San Diego, 1542-1908* (San Diego, The History Company, 1908).

Spier, Leslie

> *"South Diegueño Customs"* in *University of California Publications in American Archaeology and Ethnology*, Vol. XX (1923) 297-358.

Stephens, H. Morse, and Bolton, Herbert E., eds.

> *The Pacific Ocean in History* (New York, The Macmillan Company, 1917).

Sykes, Godfry

> *The Colorado Delta* Special Publication No. 19 of The American Geographical Society (Published jointly by The Carnegie Institute of Washington, and the American Geographical Society of New York, 1937).

Vila, Vicente

> *"The Portolá Expedition of 1769-1770: Diary of Vicente Vila"* ed. by Robert Selden Rose, in *Publications of the Academy of Pacific Coast History*, Vol. II (1911) 1-119.

Vizcaíno, Fr. Juan

> *Sea Diary of Fr. Juan Vizcaíno to Alta California, 1769* ed. by Arthur Woodward (Los Angeles, Glen Dawson, 1959).

von Hagen, Victor W.

> *The Aztec: Man and Tribe* (New York, New American Library of World Literature Inc., 1958).

Wagner, Henry Raup

> *"The Discovery of California"* in *The California Historical Society Quarterly*, Vol. I (1922) 36-56.
> *"Francisco de Ulloa Returned"* in *The California Historical Society Quarterly*, Vol. XIX (1940) 240-244.
> *Juan Rodríguez Cabrillo: Discoverer of the Coast of California* (San Francisco, California Historical Society, Special Publications No. 17, 1941).
> *Sir Francis Drake's Voyage Around the World* (San Francisco, John Howell, 1926).
> *The Spanish Southwest, 1542-1794: An Annotated Bibliography* 2 vols. (Albuquerque, The Quivira Society, 1937).
> *"Spanish Voyages to the Northwest Coast in the Sixteenth Century"* in *The California Historical Society Quarterly*, Vols. II (1923) 40-160; III (1924) 3-24, 307-397; VI (1927) 292-331; VII (1928) 132-193, 228-276, 295-394; VIII (1929) 2670.

Walker, Franklin

> *Literary History of Southern California* (Berkeley and Los Angeles, University of California Press, 1950).

Waters, Frank

> *The Colorado* Rivers of America Series (New York, Rinehart and Company, 1946).

Watson, Douglas S. ed.

> *The Spanish Occupation of California* (San Francisco, The Grabhorn Press, 1934).

Wheat, Carl

> *Mapping of the Transmississippi West, 1540-1861* Vol. I. (San Francisco, Institute of Historical Cartography, 1957).

Williamson, James A.

> *The Age of Drake* (London, Adam and Charles Black, 1938).

Wolf, Eric R.

> *Sons of the Shaking Earth* (Chicago, University of Chicago Press, 1959).

Wycherley, George

> *Buccaneers of the Pacific* (Indianapolis, Bobbs-Merrill Company, 1928).

PERMISSION CREDITS

Quotations from Díaz del Castillo. From THE DIS-COVERY AND CONQUEST OF MEXICO by Bernal Díaz del Castillo, copyright 1956 by Farrar, Strauss and Cudahy, Inc. Used by permission of the publisher, Farrar, Straus and Cudahy.

Excerpts re Kino and Salvatierra. From RIM OF CHRISTENDOM by H. F. Bolton. Used by permission of the publisher, The Macmillan Company.

Excerpts from translation of Conde de Monterey on Vizcaíno and Portolá. From A HISTORY OF CALI-FORNIA – THE SPANISH PERIOD, by Charles E. Chapman. Used by permission of the publisher, The Macmillan Company.

Excerpts from Narrative of Ulloa, excerpts about Ulloa, excerpts from Ascensions Account, excerpts quoting Díaz and Vargas. Used by permission of the publisher, the California Historical Society.

Excerpts re Careri and re Duro. From THE MANILA GALLEON by William Lytle. Used by permission of the publisher, E. P. Dutton & Company and Dutton Every-man Paperbacks.

Excerpt re Ulloa. From FROM WILDERNESS TO EMPIRE, by Robert Glass Cleland. Used by permission of the publisher Alfred A. Knopf Inc.

Excerpts quoting Motolinia, Montesinos and Zumárraga regarding Spanish treatment of native in Cuba and New Spain. From HISTORY OF LATIN AMERICA by Hubert Herring. Used by permission of the publisher Alfred A. Knopf, Inc.

Excerpts quoting Serra. Portolá, and Clavigero. Used by permission of the publisher, Academy of American Fran-ciscan History.

Excerpts re Baja Indians, Portolá, Bucareli, Anza Gar-cés, Costanso, Font, San Carlos, Crespí, Ugarte, San Diego. Used by permission of the publisher, University of California Press.

Excerpts re Alarcón. From CORONADO, KNIGHT OF PUEBLOS AND PLAINS, by Herbert E. Bolton, Uni-versity of New Mexico Press.

Excerpt from the second letter to the king of Spain. From LETTERS OF CORTES, edited by Francis Au-gustus Macnutt, G. P. Putnam's Sons.

Excerpts re Vizcaíno and Ascensión. From SPANISH EXPLORATIONS IN THE SOUTHWEST by Herbert Eugene Bolton, Barnes & Noble, Inc.

ARTWORK SOURCES

Map of Native Indian sites. Bureau of American Eth-nology of the Smithsonian Institution, Washington, D. C.

Paintings by Frances of Portolá and Anza, title page of Portolá's Diary. The Bancroft Library, University of California.

Diary of Father Ascensión. From the Ayer Collection, Newberry Library, Chicago.

Dourado Map, Consag's Map, Pantoja Map, Brigg's Map of 1625. Reproduced by permission of The Hunting-ton Library, San Marino, California.

Pictures of the Caravel and Galleon. From THE BOOK OF OLD SHIPS by Henry B. Culvar and Gordon Frant. Copyright 1936 by Doubleday & Company, Inc. Re-printed by permission of the publisher.

Photograph of painting of Father Serra. Angeleno Photo Service.

Map of Indian reservations. U. S. Bureau of Indian Affairs.

Photographs of Coronado Islands and Coyote Canyon. Union Title and Trust Co.

Indian artifacts, old Spanish weapons and equipment. From Serra Museum, San Diego, and Museum of Man, San Diego.

Photograph of Antigua Ruins. Pan American Airways.

Photograph of the mission at Tumacacori. National Park Service.

Vizcaíno and Vila map of San Diego Bay, Cortés map of Baja California, Ulloa documents. From Archivo Gene-ral de Indias in Seville, Spain.

Photographs of ancient Guatemalan city, photograph of home of Bernal Díaz del Castillo, Iztapa, record book of founding of Guatemalan city. From the Guatemala Tourist Bureau, Guatemala.

Photographs of Serra's home on Mallorca. From Estudio Salvat, Palma de Mallorca, Spain.

Photographs of documents on Serra, Crespí, Garcés Díaz, Vila, and Costanso. From the Archivo General de la Nación, Mexico City.

Documents on Cabrillo. From Archivo General de Indias in Seville, Spain and Archivo General de la Nación, Guatemala City, Guatemala.

Paintings of Cabrillo stepping ashore on Point Loma, sighting of the San Antonio and of the Diegueño Indian village by Darrel Millsap.

Paintings of Cabrillo's ships entering San Diego Bay, and sketch of first mission on Presido Hill by Robert Marcotte.

Color photographs of San Javier Mission and photo-graphs of Loreto Mission by Stanley Griffin; photographs of ruins on Presido Hill and the Serra-Portolá route by Ed Neil.

195

INDEX